De/Anti-Colonial African Education Futurities

Studies in Criticality

Shirley R. Steinberg
Series Editor

Vol. 560

New York - Berlin - Bruxelles - Chennai - Lausanne - Oxford

De/Anti-Colonial African Education Futurities

Challenges Possibilities and Responsibilities

Edited by
George Jerry Sefa Dei, Wambui Karanja,
Avea E. Nsoh, and Daniel Yelkpieri

New York - Berlin - Bruxelles - Chennai - Lausanne - Oxford

Library of Congress Cataloging-in-Publication Data

Names: Dei, George J. Sefa (George Jerry Sefa), editor. | Wambui Wa Karanja editor. | Nsoh, E. Avea (Ephraim Avea) editor. | Yelkpieri, Daniel, editor.
Title: De/anti-colonial African education futurities : challenges possibilities and responsibilities / Edited by George Jerry Sefa Dei, Wambui Karanja, Avea Nsoh, Daniel Yelkpieri.
Description: New York : Peter Lang, [2025] | Series: Counterpoints, 1058-1634 ; Volume 560 | Includes bibliographical references.
Identifiers: LCCN 2024043995 (print) | LCCN 2024043996 (ebook) | ISBN 9781636676630 (paperback) | ISBN 9781636676647 (pdf) | ISBN 9781636676654 (epub)
Subjects: LCSH: Education—Curricula—Africa. | Decolonization—Study and teaching—Africa. | Curriculum evaluation—Africa. | Culturally relevant pedagogy—Africa.
Classification: LCC LB1564.A43 D43 2025 (print) | LCC LB1564.A43 (ebook) | DDC 375/.001096—dc23/eng/20241018
LC record available at https://lccn.loc.gov/2024043995
LC ebook record available at https://lccn.loc.gov/2024043996
DOI 10.3726/b22383

Bibliographic information published by the Deutsche Nationalbibliothek.
The German National Library lists this publication in the German National Bibliography; detailed bibliographic data is available on the Internet at http://dnb.d-nb.de.

Cover design by Peter Lang Group AG

ISSN 1058-1634 (print)
ISBN 9781636676630 (paperback)
ISBN 9781636676647 (ebook)
ISBN 9781636676654 (epub)
DOI 10.3726/b22383

© 2025 Peter Lang Group AG, Lausanne
Published by Peter Lang Publishing Inc., New York, USA
info@peterlang.com—www.peterlang.com

All rights reserved.
All parts of this publication are protected by copyright.
Any utilization outside the strict limits of the copyright law, without the permission of the publisher, is forbidden and liable to prosecution.

This applies in particular to reproductions, translations, microfilming, and storage and processing in electronic retrieval systems.

This publication has been peer reviewed.

ACKNOWLEDGMENT

The Editors would like to thank all the contributors to this Manuscript for sharing their knowledge on decolonial African futurities in education. They would like to extend a special thank you to Dr. Danica Vidotto for her assistance in the edits on the complete manuscript. The Editors also acknowledge and thank all educators and knowledge holders engaged in de/anticolonization of educational policies, curriculum, pedagogy and spaces to challenge, resist and dismantle colonial education in all its forms, and to offer counter pathways to education, steeped in Indigenous African epistemes, ontological and spiritual pedagogies to educational content and delivery. Lastly but not least, the Editors would like to thank our Elders, our knowledge keepers for their guidance, custodianship, stewardship and teachings of our Indigenous cultural knowledges and heritage.

Dedication

This anthology is dedicated to our Ancestors, Eternal Spirit and to the Land for the gift of our Indigenous Knowledges.
and to
Elmarie Constandius (In Memoriam)

CONTENTS

Chapter 1: Introduction 1
George Jerry Sefa Dei, Wambui Karanja,
Ephraim Avea Nsoh, and Daniel Yelkpieri

Chapter 2: The Potentialities of African Indigeneity in East Africa's
Harmonized Curriculum Structure and Framework 17
Bathseba Opini and Ali A. Abdi

Chapter 3: Creating Space for African Indigenous Knowledges and
Indigeneity in Teaching through Counting Songs in Early
Childhood Education 43
Maureen K. Kanchebele-Sinyangwe and Ann E. Lopez

Chapter 4: Integrating Indigenous Knowledge into Sub-Saharan
African Schools: Curriculum Transformation for Socio-
Economic Freedom and Maintenance of African Identities 59
Kofi Poku Quan-Baffour

Chapter 5:	Mwalimu Julius Nyerere: The Philosophy of Self-Reliance from an Afrocentric Perspective *Njoki Nathani Wane, Sein A. Kipusi, and Rachael Kalaba*	75
Chapter 6:	Contextualization of the School Curriculum: Reflections of the Ghanaian Situation *Daniel Yelkpieri*	101
Chapter 7:	Making Endogenous Science in and for Everyday Life: A Conceptual Connection for Endogenous Science in Low-Income Everyday Life—A Kenyan Exploration of Makerspace *Wanja Gitari*	121
Chapter 8:	Linguistic Social Injustice in the Upper East Region of Ghana *Ephraim Avea Nsoh and Helen Atipoka Adongo*	163
Chapter 9:	Embodied Cognition and Anti-Colonial Education in Higher Education *Elmarie Costandius and Shelley Pryde*	191
Chapter 10:	Some Concluding Thoughts: Possibilities for Imagining New Decolonial Educational Futurities *George Jerry Sefa Dei, Wambui Karanja, Ephraim Avea Nsoh, and Daniel Yelkpieri*	215
	Notes on Contributors	237

· 1 ·

INTRODUCTION

George Jerry Sefa Dei, Wambui Karanja,
Ephraim Avea Nsoh, and Daniel Yelkpieri

This collection of essays addresses the challenges, possibilities, and responsibilities for de/anti-colonial African educational futurities. Decolonization has become a buzzword of late so we must use with some trepidation. But what this book is getting at is the approach to dismantle colonial educational systems in Africa and to re-envision African education. This should be duly informed by our local cultural resource knowing, what we know ourselves from the grounded everyday practice of African educators. In other words, to learn from what educators know and are doing for the lessons in envisioning schooling and education in Africa. While we seek lessons and partnerships with others, African educators are urged to think through solutions to our own problems and challenges and meet the call of our times to provide education to young learners that not only empower these souls, but so they are able to design their own futures. So how do we do decolonial education from the standpoint of African educators and learners everyday schooling practice and knowledge? We believe a careful embrace of our African Indigenous and cultural knowings has a lot to do with our success in answering this question. We also engage both the decolonial and the anti-colonial with a reading that the "decolonial" (as many have pointed out, see Parry, 1994) is a process, in other words, the path toward an end, which is the goal of the "anti-colonial" (see also Dei, 2022).

Arguably, the search for new educational futures for Africa has become more pressing than ever before. This is in part due to emerging global educational challenges that demand that education responds to the needs of local specificities and global conditionalities simultaneously. There is an urgent need for a genuinely African-centered education that utilizes context-based knowledge and cultural resource material for local contexts to think through educational futures for Africa. This collection of essays is from scholars and educational practitioners who share their research ideas and findings of the theory and practice of anti-colonial education in African and African Diasporic contexts. The focus is on anti-colonizing African education (broadly defined) using the curriculum, pedagogy and classroom instruction as significant entry points. Among the questions posed are: How do we conceptualize decolonization in the context of African education? How do we link questions of Indigeneity, curriculum, pedagogy and instructional development? How can African scholars on the continent and counterparts in the Diaspora work together to bring professional and intellectual skills for pedagogic, instructional and curricular initiatives toward de/anti-colonial African education? What does it entail to address these educational challenges in contemporary times? How do we address questions of identity, setting target goals, incentivizing and promoting effective strategies for educational success through decolonized education? How do African and Black Diaspora scholars articulate relevance and debt to community?

The book is particularly framed within an anti-colonial interrogation of collective educational leadership, responsibility and accountability to address the invisibilization and marginalization of African Indigenous knowledges systems and to examine the critical role these knowledges can play in the decolonization of African education (see also Emeagwali & Dei, 2014; Emeagwali & Shizha, 2016). We acknowledge there are many paths to decolonization (Ndlovu-Gathsheni, 2015; Smith, 2012), and it is particularly important for educators to begin by grounding our de/anti-colonial projects in Black and Indigenous ontologies and epistemologies (see also Dei & Cacciavillani (2022); Dei & Lloyd-Henry, 2024). To reframe a decolonial education is to ask questions about omissions, negations, absences in school curriculum and classroom pedagogues, and how we provide critical comprehensive knowledge that accounts for the diversity of the human experiences, histories and ways of knowing. Decolonization, as many have noted, begins by asking new questions grounded in non-Western epistemes and Indigenous philosophies (see Dei, 2024a; Parry 1994). It should be a "subversive educational approach, not a superficial add-on, and requires actions to dismantle and rebuild" (see also Mihesuah et al., 2004; Hewitt, 2016). Decolonization is not about mainstreaming practice. In other words, a truly decolonial project cannot seek legitimation and validation from the dominant!

Our de/anti-colonial educational practices must be open and clear for all learners to see what educational agenda is being pursued. Long ago, Linda Smith (2012) asked us to acknowledge "the reach of imperialism into our heads" (Smith, 2012, cf. Jackson, 2019, p. 109). What this also means is to recognize the metaphoricity of decolonization as also about developing the oppressor consciousness and an awareness of "cultural invasion" (Freire, 2000). This is what Ngugi wa Thiong'o referred to when he long posited that we must be aware of the severity of the problem of colonization, particularly as it has to do with the colonization of "the mental universe" of the colonized worlds (wa Thiong'o, 1981, p. 16; Dei & Lloyd-Henry, 2024).

Thus, we need to rethink global partnerships in higher education, by moving away from the "catching up" syndrome. Conventional partnerships (human capacity building; student and faculty mentorship and training; staffing and physical infrastructure resourcing; collaborations in academic research; knowledge mobilization & field dissemination; etc.) are framed within this "catching up" mindset. There is clearly the perils and desires of global knowledge mobilization. Among the perils is knowledge appropriations in the global marketplace of ideas (i.e., addressing the control of "intellectual property" through restrictive copyright legislation that benefits the West, reducing a global sharing of knowledge, and the impacts on African scholarship). The race to internationalization in African education also suffers from an emerging class and gender-based privileges (e.g., how higher education rewards the proximity to "Whiteness or the West" and the access that such proximity affords). There is also the "educational sector imbalance" where resources are disproportionately allocated to certain fields (e.g., natural sciences, technology, engineering and management at the expense of the arts & humanities).

There is clearly an urgency for African education to move beyond Eurocentric models of global partnerships driven by an agenda of competition, rivalry, maximization of benefits, and the race to internationalization. We have much to learn from what Indigenous African communities themselves do around building sustainable partnerships of trust, respect, acknowledging respective strengths and contributions and to share power. Knowledge is power and global partnerships in African higher education must lead to our academies gaining power and recognition, as well as legitimacy and validation on our own terms.

Thus, we must disrupt the race to internationalization with an African-centered paradigm of global partnerships that deploy Indigenous philosophies to subvert colonial hierarchies of schooling partnerships and the imposition of colonial systems of knowing and practice. We must critically ask: What does "global" in "Global Partnership" signify? These partnerships signify asymmetrical power relations and dynamics that most often serve the interest of the rich and powerful (e.g., mantra of the West—"what is yours is ours but what is mine is mine"). But what does it take to move from Eurocentric to African-centered models of sustainable partnerships? In a forthcoming text (Dei et al., 2024) we highlight an "African ElderCrit" that espouse values of community, cooperation, mutuality, solidarity, interpersonal and intergroup relations as a derived and informed knowledge base.

We ask for a reframing of what makes for sustainability in education. Sustainability is about custodianship and authenticity. It is more than creating conditions for long-term benefit. Educational sustainability raises fundamental questions of how we conceptualize the Land (i.e., understanding "Land" as more than a physical space)—a site of knowing, inclusive of metaphors, ontologies, literacies of seas, waters, Earth and sky, and reclaiming our social, psychic, cultural and spiritual memories as "living forces" to learn from (see Dei et al., 2022; Simpson 2011, 2014; Styres, 2019). The Land and Earthly teachings of relationality, sharing, reciprocity, connections, mutual interdependence, building relationships, social responsibility and accountability can ensure livable, workable and sustainable communities of ethical learners and an idea of schooling as community (see Dei, 2008). We can also learn from the twinning of Indigenization and Africanization in a project of global partnerships in African education. It will mean to challenge the colonial appellation of "Indigenous" (e.g., African Indigenous does not have to prove its existence). It also means learning from the Cartographies of Indigenous across multiple geo-spaces—Africa, Caribbean, Latin America, Asia, Europe, United States and Turtle Island—ways to build sustainable global partnerships.

As editors, we do bring an intellectual and political project to this book in the articulation of an intersectional African-centered analysis encapsulating specificities of African education in multiple contexts informed by the African and Black diasporic experience and historical connections with the Motherland (see also Asante, 1991). We insist the examination of African education must have a global lens. It must also encapsulate Black education and the connections of Black and African identities and educational politics. Africanness, like Blackness as it is raced, is also a cultural, political and sociohistorical construction, experienced differently on Black and African bodies, in different locations and geo-spaces. Issues of Black and African schooling and education intersect on a global landscape. Notwithstanding some specificities and uniqueness of the multi-geo-spaces, Black and African education share many considerations. In particular, the Black African experience in White supremacist contexts highlights the saliency of race and (anti)Blackness as lodged in skin color, body image and representation, culture, identity, and politics. But the Black and African identities are intertwined. So, we complicate understandings of Black and African community as complex, multifaceted, tensions filled, and contested, and yet still hold on to its political and spiritual force of coming to a collective Black African humanhood.

Within the global diaspora (and particularly in transnational mobility), Black existence is always in question and in dialectical opposition to Americanness, Europeanness, Canadianness, etc. (see also Harris, 2019; p. 219). Thus, as argued in Dei and Adjei (2024) in challenging Eurocentric definitions and articulations of Blackness and Africanness in White supremacist logics, there must be a simultaneous recognition that nowhere is safe for the African body to escape their Blackness. This must explain why we need to be skeptical of Black bodies who espouse the idea that race as color is meaningless because they only serve as a descriptor (i.e., "Black" is a meaningless category and/or as an imported label) and would prefer the identity of "African." The dehumanization and racialization of the Black humanhood does not happen solely on Blacks reaching the Indigenous Lands of North America or Europe. The colonial dominant has consistently sought to "mess up" or dispute Black and African identities and racially politicized identifications. For Black bodies who fail to question this, it is a Black betrayal and a Black race to innocence with a disavowal of the historic struggles of our Ancestors. We must acknowledge the continuing significance of the rich heritage of Black African intellectualism that fuses politics, militancy and advocacy. While "Black" has different multidimensional meanings and is context-bound on different Lands and geographies, the challenge is Black learners is to think through a collective approach to our education and our educational system for young learners. We must thus find and articulate our centeredness in conversations about race, Blackness, and Euro-modernity, and to build Black solidarities for new Afro-futurities (see Dei & Adjei, 2023).

We articulate new visions of African education lodged within an Indigenous African identity, outside of the identity constructed within Euro-American hegemony. The twinning of Black and African in our analysis is deliberate. It is to register the confluence of race, color, culture and history so as to implicate, invoke and advocate a global Black radical educational politics. This is important for emphasis given the European creation of Black pathology (see Cesaire, 1972; Fanon 1967) serves two purposes. First, to justify the sub-humanity of Blacks; and second, to separate Blackness from Africanness to reinforce the discourse of White dominance. An affirmation of a de/anti-colonial Africanness is an insistence on the authenticity of the Black African Self and the Black African Collective as foundational for constructing Black perspectivism.

Asking New Questions

What discursive lens do we use in our intellectual and political critiques and interrogations? How do we as African learners work toward the painful demise of Eurocentrism (Asante, 1991)? How do we develop a robust epistemological and ontological framework for understanding the global Black African existence and its inseparable connections to the Motherland, Africa? How do we subvert the internalizations, colonial oppressions and colonizing relations within our own communities and schooling systems? How do we read the African anti-colonial educational resistances in academia? What are the pedagogical lessons of African pluralities across Lands and geo-spaces for us to work with (multi-dimensionalities, intersections, and cartographies)? How are such pluralities of African geographies themselves, revealing of resistance (see also Bledsoe & Wright, 2019)?

The urgency of seeking answers to these questions calls for radical thinking and creative solutions. There is an Africanness rooted to the continent of Africa, but Africanness can also be located in the body, and it travels beyond time and space (i.e., One is African not because they were born on the continent but because Africa was born in the person). We need to re-trace our histories, cultural knowledges, experiences, and identity as they relate to a place, Africa. McKittrick (2021) argues that "referential beginnings and referential scaffolding shape conclusions" (p. 23). Our location and positionalities implicate what we see and do. In fact, knowledge presented by African humanhood should offer a particular reading and interpretation of our world. Re-envisioning African schooling and education start by advancing and embracing education within counter and/or oppositional African theorizing, "designed to give voice to those denied the competency to theorize, to overturn the epistemic norm that validates the conceptual erasure of societies that existed before the European imagination" (see McLeod, 2022). We cannot continue to sustain the very colonial structures that oppress us in the structures of educational delivery that is teaching, learning and administration of education. We must utilize African philosophies of community and social responsibility to subvert Western liberal conceptions of individual hard work, meritocracy, individual achievement and success, by promoting ideals of relationality, connections, sharing, generosity, spiritual and cultural anchorage, and collective social responsibility. It is here that the idea of unchaining minds (Womack, 2013) becomes most significant. As educators and learners, we need to think in circles rather than thinking in hierarchies.

Schools are and can be carceral places that produce ethnic/racial, class, gender, sexual, disability, etc. inequities, disparities, and violence. Re-envisioning African education must address questions of social difference as fundamentally about issues of power, identity, and representation. Schools often work with the expectations of domination as revealed in the push for conformity, policing, surveillance, discipline and punishment. Our decolonization cannot be a way to uphold dominance in our schools, colleges and universities. We cannot approach decolonization in ways that end up becoming an "an arm of the [nation] state" to control the education of African learners (see also Hill 2022). We must question the hetero-patriarchal normativity upon which understandings of excellence is built and critically reflect on who is automatically assumed to be the speaker, author, to be that voice, or the knowledge creator, and knowledge consumer. Similarly, when we valorize integration, we must also ask, "integrating into what"? Our education requires a subversion of dominant conceptions of human, humanity, knowledge, as these have traditionally influenced schooling in terms of how we teach and learn.

We must strive for African-centered education which is about resistance and being action-oriented to work toward new educational futures. As educators this will necessitate that we continually embrace a politics of fleeing from without leaving (Harney & Moten, 2013), that is, to flee from carceral logics without leaving the possibilities of creating critical spaces in which we work to subvert, transform and abolish. There must be a new vision of African education. The intellectual politics of the African educator and learner must draw on history, culture, psychic memories, Spiritualities and politics to advance an African humanhood. Our de/anti-colonial work must interrogate colonial institutions such as conventional school systems to heal their dehumanizing effects of African mental psyche and trauma. This is the essence of making African spirituality a backbone of African education transformations.

The Place of African Spiritual Ontologies in the Search for New African Educational Futures

In re-envisioning African schooling and education, we place African spirituality and spiritual ontologies as the bedrock, the foundation for any transformation. African spiritual ontologies represent philosophies of life and customary ideologies that guide human social action and everyday practice, helping us as a people to heal our colonial wounds (see also Dei et al., 2024). African spiritual ontologies challenge "imperial cultural worldviews" (Smith 2012) espousing counter knowledge needed for "cultural decolonization" (Mazrui, 2003)—with significant implications for African & Black global Indigeneities. African spiritual ontologies are to be analyzed and understood within the framework of their own rationality and cultural logics to challenge Eurocentrism (see also Mudimbe, 1988, in another context; Mazama, 1998, 2001).

But the key question to ask is, what type of African education is made possible if the spiritual is placed at the center of schooling (see also Cajete 1994, 2000)? What are the potentialities and possibilities of pursuing schooling as emotionally and spiritually felt experiences to ensure educational transformation and subversion? The school space can be a hostile, unfamiliar place, with dismemberment and depersonalization of learners such that young learners are not always true to our/their authentic selves. We mimic and perform for legitimation, validation and acceptance. Such psychic and emotional wounding calls for spiritual resistance to heal selves and bodies to make us whole again (see also Anzaldua, 1987; Anzaldua & Moraga, 1981). There is a case to be made for African authenticity that grounds the search for new educational futurities.

Increasing the question of sustainable quality education in Africa has been raised. We need to rethink how educational innovations in place actually enhance quality education and particularly what other interventions are called for. We must rethink African education in more creative ways that work with counter knowledges and must ask critical questions of how these counter knowledges grounded in African philosophical thought intersect with the new call for sustainable quality education espoused in the United Nations sustainable development goal #4. We must critically interrogate how quality education looks like, how it is defined, and how it is theoretically grounded to ensure that quality education is disruptive and that it does not advance contemporary neocolonial education rooted in neoliberalist theories of globalization and educational internationalization policies and narratives of education (Majee & Ress, 2020). For quality education to be meaningful, it must center and be grounded within Indigenous African philosophical thought, and within an African-centered epistemological and pedagogical framework that foregrounds African spiritual ontologies, identities and the Land as sites of knowing and Knowledge production (Dei et al., 2022). We must ask critical questions like; how do we define quality education? How do we deliver quality education that is responsive to both local realities and global realities? How does quality education address questions of gender, for example?

Conventionally, the question of gender and education has been approached without serious consideration of ways to center African women's access and control over Land and processes of gender relations and gendered violence as significant in colonial analysis. How do we teach our learners to acknowledge women's cultural resource knowledge base for learners' empowerment? Teaching Land rematriation and African education will focus on African mothers' roles in nurturing, sustenance, Mothering, respect, sacredness and veneration of Land and Environment. Such spiritual rematriation is "an intersectional knowing of soil, soul, and solidarity; a re-imagining of life beyond (colonial) logics"; a search for "liberated well-being" (Tyler, 2020; p. 418), as well as an analysis that returns to the Land as a process of cultural continuance through Mothering (see also Dei, 2024b). Educators can connect the pursuit of such knowledge in schools with the integration of African Elders teachings. These teaching will include African rites of passage, naming ceremonies, telling cultural stories (e.g., Ananse) stories, engaging proverbs, fables, folktales and riddles n classroom pedagogies and instruction, including the art of African drumming and other folkloric productions. As Dei and Adjei (2024) argue, we drum and dance not as a form of entertainment, but as a way of reconnecting to our African traditional values, worldviews and spiritual knowledge. The African talking drum communicates ancestral languages and cultural metaphors. When played, it carries the rallying voices of the Ancestors calling on the living for action. One critical action is to engage in de/anti-colonial work that will make education relevant to people and help in solving the challenging problems of everyday living for people to actualize their hopes and dreams.

The chapters in this book offer decolonial perspectives on education in Africa and urge the reader to examine and interrogate the coloniality embedded in contemporary education in Africa. The book offers anti-colonial and decolonizing perspectives for making African education more relevant and meaningful for Indigenous African through decolonization of the school curriculum, language and pedagogy that speaks to the African experience, situatedness and local realities. The book challenges colonial education and the ongoing colonialism embedded in contemporary education in Africa to argue that for education to be decolonized, there is need to rethink western definitions of science. For example, the use of English as learning in schools and how embodied knowledge and ways of knowing have been negated and silenced in the curriculum.

Ali Abdi and Bathseba Opini write their chapter, *The Potentialities of African Indigeneity in East Africa's Harmonized Curriculum Structure and Framework*, while acknowledging decolonization of education efforts in the East African region and urge us to cast our gaze to how these education reforms have continued to silence or have failed to consider the criticality of Indigeneity and the need to center Indigenous African knowledges and perspectives in decolonizing the curriculum, to address issues of epistemic injustice in education.

The call for the decolonization of education and the school curriculum in Africa is followed up by Maureen Kanchebele-Sinyangwe and Ann Lopez. In their chapter, *Creating Space for African Indigenous Knowledges and Indigeneity in Teaching Through Counting Songs in Early Childhood Education*, Kanchebele-Sinyangwe and Ann Lopez speak to the colonization of language and African Indigenous epistemologies to call for the reimagining of a decolonized K-12 curriculum as a form of resistance to colonial education policies and practices that have continually excluded local Indigenous knowledges. They offer possibilities for decentering Western Epistemologies in education and schooling by centering Indigenous pedagogies and curriculum. It is crucial, they argue, for critical scholars to develop decolonized education curricula in African education systems to challenge prevailing universalist-centeredness of knowledge production and validation based on Eurocentric knowledge systems.

The theme of an African-centered education and educational philosophy is taken up by Kofi Poku Quan-Baffour in his chapter, *Indigenizing the Curriculum Integrating Indigenous Knowledge into Sub-Saharan African Schools: Curriculum*

Transformation for Socio-Economic Freedom and Maintenance of African Identities. Quan-Baffour argues that education is a tool for development and people must be given the opportunity to acquire relevant quality knowledge and skills to improve their lives and to enable them to contribute to the socio-economic development of their respective communities and countries. Calling for a more African-centered education that is "brewed in an African pot," he decries the role of colonial education and Western religion in the demonization of African Indigenous knowledge systems, identities and the exploitation of the continent's natural resources and argues that Africanization and Indigenization of education requires education to be decolonizing and transformative; and for an urgent need to incorporate in school curricula, relevant Indigenous philosophies and practical knowledge, skills and values. For Quan-Baffour, this would be transformative in that it would help open people's eyes to the subtle tactics of the oppressor, advance African values and identity and ultimately, decolonize people's minds.

Challenging universalist-centeredness of knowledge production and validation aligns with Nyerere's vision and philosophy of African-centered education. Njoki Wane, Sein Kipusi and Rachael Kalaba examine Mwalimu Nyerere's philosophy of education and self-reliance to explore the intricate connections to African cultural, historical, and sociopolitical contexts of education and self-reliance. In their chapter, *Mwalimu Nyerere: The Philosophy of Self-Reliance from an Afrocentric Perspective*, Wane, Kipusi and Kalaba delve into self-reliance and Afrocentrism to extricate their theoretical foundations and explore their symbiotic relationship with Nyerere's philosophy to illuminate how the ongoing dialogue on African philosophies of development and liberation can shed light on the enduring significance of Nyerere's philosophy of education and its potential for inspiring transformative change in African communities and governance.

Yelkpieri follows up on the issue of decolonization through curriculum reform and reflects on the basic school curriculum in Ghana. In his chapter, *Contextualization of the Basic School Curriculum: Reflections of the Ghanaian Situation*, he contends that for a curriculum to meet societal needs, it must be guided by the sociocultural and economic needs of the community for it to meet the needs and aspirations of the people. He speaks to the coloniality of Ghana's school curriculum to argue that for the education system in Ghana to be decolonized, stakeholders in curriculum development must be guided by the principles of worthwhileness, relevance, the characteristics and needs of learners and intended outcomes.

Embodied knowledge is manifested and enacted in the daily lives of people. In *Conceptual Connections for Endogenous Science in Low-income Everyday Life: A Kenyan Exploration of Makerspace*, Wanja Gitari offers a practical example of how endogenous science in Africa can be applied to advance the decolonial project for science education in Africa to challenge global modernity/coloniality theories of education through knowledge diffusion to offer possibilities for the co-construction of knowledge, expansion of possibilities of meaning making through self-determination and affordances in the sociocultural environment, the exemplification of situated universal knowledge and curiosity for knowledge creation and ways of knowing. Drawing from findings from a local endogenous science project in a rural school in Kenya, Gitari calls for an acknowledgment of the richness of knowledge and skills found in everyday life and the validation of the role of the learner as a co-knowledge producer to challenge the prevailing dominant expert/novice paradigm in knowledge production. This, she argues, enables the integration of a multiplicity of ideas including know-that and know-how perspectives from Indigenous contexts.

But curriculum reform must also address and break down the hegemony and coloniality of English language in schools. Avea Nsoh and Helen Atipoka Adongo in their chapter, *Linguistic Social Injustice in the Upper East Region of Ghana*, explore the decolonization of language through the universal human rights framework to maintain that linguistic human and language rights of Indigenous peoples have been grossly abused and that this abuse has continued unabated due to the failure or neglect of international and local actors and to elaborate on an implementation framework for the enforcement of language rights laws in the educational system. They maintain that the denial of Indigenous language rights in education is a form of linguistic social injustice that denies the learner to develop to the learner's full potential not only in school but also in their socio-economic participation in society. No decolonization of education would be complete without wrestling with the question of gender and the violation of Black bodies, especially on the issue of anti-black gender-based violence.

For Elmarie Constandius and Shelley Pride, a key feature of Indigeneity and Indigenous knowledge production as the acknowledgment that knowledge is also embodied and that embodied knowledges are sites of knowing and knowledge production. Elmarie Constandius' chapter, *Embodied Cognition and Anti-colonial Education in Higher Education*, is poignant in that it reminds the reader that embodied knowledge can be engaged in foregrounding educational practices that draw from local contexts. Elmarie argues that such knowledge includes relational and sensory embodied experiences in teaching and learning and sees Indigenous practitioners as knowledge holders and teachers of relational mind—body practices, relational and dualist thinking. Elmarie argues that Immersive embodied practices have the potential to decolonize the body—mind, and interface with the possibility of enhancing teaching and learning practices. For Elmarie, incorporating embodied and relational learning perspectives in education practices are critical pathways toward the decolonization of education.

References

Asante, M. (1991). The Afrocentric idea in education. *Journal of Negro Education*, 60(2), 170–180.

Anzaldúa, G. (1987). *Borderlands/La frontera: The new Mestiza*.

Anzaldúa, G., & Moraga, C. (Eds.). (1981). *This bridge called my back: Writings by radical women of color*. Kitchen Table.

Bledsoe, A., & Wright, W. J. (2019). The anti-Blackness of global capital. *Environment and Planning D: Society and Space*, 37(1), 8–26.

Bhabha, H. K. (1994). *The location of culture*. Routledge.

Cajete, G. (2000). *Native science: Natural laws of interdependence*. Clear Light Publishers.

Cesaire, A. (1972). *Discourse on colonialism*. Monthly Review Press.

Christensen, R. A., & Poupart, L. M. (2013). *Connective pedagogy: Elder epistemology, oral tradition, and community*. Aboriginal Issues Press.

Dei, G. J. S. (2024a). *The Black scholar travelogue*. Peter Lang.

Dei, G. J. S. (2024b, in press). Foreword: Subversive knowledge: The educational curriculum and indigenous wisdom traditions. In. E. d. Abdou & T. G. Zervas (Eds.), *Historical and living indigenous wisdom traditions in curricula and textbooks: Towards more balanced and inclusive global representations*. University of Toronto Press.

Dei, G. J. S., Adjei, P., Garlow, G, Haydarian, I., & Cacciavillani, A. (2024, in press). *African ElderCrit*. (2024, in press). Routledge.

Dei, G. J. S., & Lloyd-Henry, P. (2024). The possibilities of an indigenist anti-colonial research praxis: A response to "The False Promise of Decolonial Research: The Complexities and Limitations of Decolonizing Methods and Methodologies" by Leon Moosavi. Published in the Special Issue of the *International Journal of Social Research Methodology*.

Dei, K., & Erger, G. (2022). *Elders' cultural knowledge and the question of Black/African indigeneity*. Springer.

Dei, K., & Adjei, P. (2023, in press). ElderCrit as a building framework for Blacks-Indigenous' solidarities. *Canadian Journal of Education*.

Dei, K., & Adjei, P. (2024, in press). Convergences of "Blackcentricity" and "Africentricity" and implications of African spiritual ontologies.

Dei, K., Nsoh, A., & Yelkpieri, D. (Upcoming, 2025). *Decoloniality and African Education: Contested Issues and Challenges*. Myers Publishers: Cambridge, Massachusetts.

Denzin, N. K., Lincoln, Y. S., & Smith, L. T. (Eds.). (2008). *Handbook of critical and Indigenous methodologies*. Sage.

Emeagwali, G., & Shizha, E. (2016). *African indigenous knowledges and the science: Journey's into the past and present*. Sense Publishers.

Emeagwali, G., & Dei, G. I. S. (Eds.), (2014). *African indigenous knowledge and the disciplines*. Sense Publishers.

Ezati, A. B. (2016). The recent history and political economy of basic education curriculum reforms in Uganda. Kampala: Not published.

Fanon, F. (1967). *Black skin, white masks*. Grove Press.

Freire, P. (2000). *Pedagogy of the oppressed* (30th anniversary ed.). Continuum.

Harney & Moten (2013) The Undercommons: Fugitive Planning and Black Study. (New York: Minor Compositions).

Harris, C. I. (2019). Of Blackness and Indigeneity: Comments on Jodi A. Byrd's "Weather with You: Settler Colonialism, Antiblackness, and the Grounded Relationalities of Resistance." *Journal of the Critical Ethnic Studies Association*, 5(1–2), 215.

Hewitt, J. (2016). *Indigenous restorative justice: Approaches, meaning & possibility*. University of New Brunswick Law Journal. Retrieved November 27, 2022, from https://journals.lib.unb.ca/index.php/unblj/article/view/29082

Hill, J. (2022). *Pedagogies and Politics of Hope and Refusal in Higher Education and Beyond*. Unpublished course paper, SJE 1921Y: Principles of Anti-Racism. Ontario Institute for Studies in Education, University of Toronto.

Jumba, H., & Mwiti, F. M. (2022). Teachers' perception on integration of indigenous knowledge systems in competence based curriculum at selected primary schools in Buuri East Sub-County. International Journal of Public Policy, 10(1), 1–15. https://doi.org/10.31686/ijier.vol10.iss10.3558

Jackson, M. (2019). In the end "The Hope of Decolonization." In *The handbook of indigenous education* (pp. 101–110). Springer. https://doi.org/10.1007/978-981-10-3899-0_59

Majee, U. S., & Ress, S. B. (2020). Colonial legacies in internationalization of higher education: Racial justice and geopolitical redress in South Africa and Brazil. *Compare: A Journal of Comparative and International Education*, 50(4), 463–481. https://doi.org/10.1080/03057925.2018.152126

Mazama, A. (1998). The Eurocentric discourse on writing: An exercise in self-glorification. *Journal of Black Studies*, 29(1), 3–16.

Mazama, A. (2001). The Afrocentric paradigm: Contours and definitions. *Journal of Black Studies*, 31(4), 387–405.

Mazrui, A. (2003). Towards re-Africanizing African universities: Who killed intellectualism in the post-colonial era? *Alternatives: Turkish Journal of International Relations*, 2(3&4).

McLeod, M. (2022). Unpublished paper. Ontario Institute for Studies in Education, University of Toronto.

McKittrick, K. (2021). *Dear science and other stories*. Duke University Press.

Mihesuah, D. A., & Waziyatawin. (2004). *Indigenizing the Academy: Transforming scholarship and empowering communities* (D. A. Mihesuah & A. C. Wilson, Eds.). University of Nebraska Press.

Mudimbe, V. Y. (1988). *The invention of Africa: Gnosis, philosophy, and the order of knowledge.* Indiana University Press.

Muyanda-Mutebi P (1996). An Analysis of the Primary Education Curiculum in Uganda including a framework for a Primary Education Curriculum Renewal, UNESCO pp. 4–6.

Ndlovu-Gathsheni, S. J. (2015). Decolonization as the future of Africa. *History Compass, 13*(10), 485–496.

Odora-Hoppers, C. A. (2001). Indigenous knowledge systems and academic institutions in South Africa. *Perspectives in Education, 19*(1), 73–86.

Odora-Hoppers, C. A. (2002a). Indigenous knowledge and the integration of knowledge systems: Towards a conceptual and methodological framework. In C. A. Odora hoppers (Ed.), *Indigenous knowledge and integration of knowledge systems towards philosophy of articulation.* New African Books Limited.

Odora Hoppers, C., & Richards, H. (2011). *Rethinking thinking: Modernity's "Other" and the transformation of the university.* UNISA Press.

Parry, B. (1994). Resistance theory/theorising resistance, or two cheers for nativism. In F. Barker, P. Hulme, & M. Iversen (Eds.), *Colonial discourse/postcolonial theory* (pp. 172–196). Manchester University Press.

Simpson, L. (2011). *Dancing on our turtle's back: Stories of Nishnaaberg recreation, resurgence and a new emergence.* Arbeiter King Publishers.

Simpson, A. (2014). *Mohawk interruptus: Political life across the borders of settler states.* Duke University Press.

Smith, L. T. (2012). *Decolonizing methodologies* (2nd ed.). Zed Books.

Smith, L. T., Tuck, E., & Yang, K. W. (2019). Introduction. In. L. T. Smith, E. Tuck, & K. W. Yang (Eds.), *Indigenous and decolonizing studies in education: Mapping the long view.* Routledge.

Tyler, S. (2020). Rematriating to the wombs of the world: Toward Black feminist agrarian ideologies. In *Routledge handbook of gender and agriculture* (pp. 410–420). Routledge.

wa Thiong'o, N. (1981). *Decolonizing the mind.* Heinemann.

Womack, L. (2013). *Afrofuturism: The world of Black sci-fi and fantasy culture.* Lawrence Hill Books.

· 2 ·

THE POTENTIALITIES OF AFRICAN INDIGENEITY IN EAST AFRICA'S HARMONIZED CURRICULUM STRUCTURE AND FRAMEWORK

Bathseba Opini and Ali A. Abdi

Introduction

Local community and regional cooperation are not new endeavors in African contexts. Prior to independence, East African nationalist leaders envisioned building an East African Federation as a gateway to the United States of Africa (Katembo, 2008; Magu, 2014; Ogola et al., 2015). The idea was to establish a regional powerhouse that would stimulate collaboration and economic prosperity (Katembo, 2008; Magu, 2014). This initial plan failed because the member nations (Kenya, Uganda, and Tanzania) had different political interests and development goals and aspirations (Katembo, 2008; Ogola et al., 2015). Kenya, under Jomo Kenyatta's leadership, had a free-market economy that stressed capital accumulation, whereas Tanzania, led by Julius Nyerere, prioritized socialist principles, and Uganda, led by Milton Obote and later Id Amin, was somewhere in the middle but leaning toward the left. These ideological conflicts hampered early partnerships and continued to do so long after independence (Ogola et al., 2015).

Given these constraints, Maathai (2009) argued that the legacy of colonialism in Africa's newly independent states selectively bound the African people, particularly the leaders, to their colonial oppressors politically, economically, and socially. The leaders clung to the politico-economic ideologies of their colonial rulers rather than seeking the benefits of robust regional collaborations (Sylvester & Anthony, 2014). Although the initial vision of a unified East Africa did not come to fruition, the desire for unification persisted (Ogola et al., 2015). Following discussions that were aimed at resolving the ideological differences, the then heads of state—Kenya's Jomo Kenyatta, Uganda's Milton Obote, and Tanzania's Julius Nyerere—founded the East African Community (EAC) in 1967.

The formation of the East African Community at that time promoted trade between the three countries. Unfortunately, the union was disbanded in 1977 due to economic and ideological differences. This is because the three countries were not enjoying the same level of economic growth, and there were fears that unification might favor Kenya over Tanzania and Uganda (Katembo, 2008; Ogola et al., 2015). In 1999, Kenya, Uganda, and Tanzania reached an agreement to re-establish the East African Community (EAC), and the EAC was re-established in 2000 (Magu 2014; Odebero, 2011). The EAC expanded further in subsequent years, when Burundi and Rwanda joined in 2007; South Sudan joined in 2016; the Democratic Republic of the Congo in 2022; and Somalia in 2023 (East African Community, 2023; Magu, 2014). The original EAC's objectives of collaboration were purely economic. Education received little attention until 2012, when EAC member states proposed a unified curriculum for the partner states.

In 2014, the members created a harmonized curriculum structure and framework to ensure quality and consistency in education, which would help in regional integration and human resource mobility throughout the Community (East African Community Secretariat, 2014; Jowi, 2020). The harmonized curriculum prioritizes curriculum, standards, assessment, and evaluation of educational programs. Much of the existing works on the EAC harmonized curriculum focus on secondary and postsecondary education levels (Arik et al., 2020; East African Community, 2015; Karuku & Tenant, 2016; Nyangena et al., 2022; WHO, 2002). This is even though primary schools are critical building blocks for children's learning. This chapter looks at the potential of African Indigenous knowledges within the harmonized curriculum, with a particular focus on primary school curricula (Grades 1 to 7) in Kenya, Uganda, and Tanzania. It does so through the prism and possibilities of decolonization. The chapter considers ways in which decolonial education approaches may enhance the harmonized curriculum and thereby respond to the local needs of the member nations. We examine the curriculum because it is currently an important tool for the privileges of Euro-American knowledge and values in the education system in Africa. It is important to note that the terms Indigenous knowledges and African knowledges are used interchangeably in this discussion. African knowledges are experiential, are rooted in a relational worldview and culture, are deeply ingrained in cultural values, and place a strong emphasis on wholeness, community, and harmony (Dei, 2000, 2002; Mkabela, 2005; Shizha, 2008). African Indigenous knowledges emphasize the role of Elders as holders/guardians of knowledge, as sage philosophers as well as communal ideals, harmony, interdependence, and interconnection, and are acquired and practiced through collective and community-oriented processes (Dei, 2000; Emeagwali, 2003; Mkabela, 2005; Odera Oruka, 1990; Owusu-Ansah & Mji, 2013).

We write this chapter as Black African scholars situated in a Canadian academy. We work, live, and learn on the traditional, ancestral, and unceded territory of the xwməθkwəy̓əm (Musqueam) People. Both of us were born and raised in East Africa (Ali in Somalia and Bathseba in Kenya). Our writing is informed by our experiences growing up in the African context, as well as our working in primarily Eurocentric postsecondary institutions in Canada. Our work is focused on decolonizing education. We are the products of a formal Eurocentric education provided in post-independent Somalia and Kenya respectively, in which we learned more about other knowledges and regions of the world than about our own local settings. We nonetheless benefited from the gift of learning our Indigenous languages and knowledges passed down to us by our parents and extended family members and this is what has continued to anchor us. In writing this chapter, we acknowledge the complicated and long-lasting impact colonialism has had and continues to have on education and the people of Africa, as well as how education plays a vital part in sustaining and consolidating those effects. Thus, we attempt to engage in a critical examination of the harmonized curriculum, interrogating Eurocentric paradigms that privilege Western knowledges over African Indigenous knowledges, in the hope of fostering deeper conversations and reflections that will push for an education system that honors the humanity, knowledges, contributions, and significance of African Indigenous knowledges and systems.

Framing the Discussion

Many African scholars looking at education in the continent have argued that colonialism is an ongoing project and did not end with just the physical independence of African nations (Bayeh, 2015; Mamdani, 2015; Nwanosike et al., 2011). This is because colonial epistemologies continue to inform and are ingrained in education systems and structures in the continent (Dei, 2010; Ndlovu-Gatsheni, 2013, 2015; Nyamnjoh, 2012, 2019; Wane, 2006, 2008). The continued domination of colonial epistemologies has allowed little room for African communities to chart social, economic, and political development predicated on their own self-defined terms. Sadly, colonialism has continued to obstruct, or suppress, the social, economic, political, and spiritual development of Africa (Sylvester & Anthony, 2014). It continues to destroy Africa's innovative educational, industrial, and technological foundations, rendering them subordinate to Western knowledges (wa Thiong'o, 1992). As such, the decolonization process has to involve acknowledging, understanding and challenging colonial structures, institutions and systems (Abdi, 2012; Dei, 2002, 2010). This requires not only physical transformation, but also paradigm and cultural shifts to acknowledge, value and validate African Indigenous knowledges, practices, ideologies, and philosophies, which are often relegated to the margins. Decolonization is also about dismantling the oppressive and unequal power relations.

Ndlovu-Gatsheni (2013) calls for a decolonial approach in which decolonization moves beyond a mere reversing of institutions of colonialism to challenging the history and configuration of the modern world which places coloniality at the center. Maldonado-Torres (2007) described coloniality as the long-standing patterns of power that emerged because of colonialism, but that define culture, labour, intersubjectivity relations, and knowledge production well beyond the strict limits of colonial administrations (p. 243). Maldonado-Torres (2007) further argued that "we breathe coloniality every day because it is endemic in books, in the measurement of academic success, in cultural patterns, in common sense, in the self-image of people and their aspirations and many other aspects of our modern experience" (p. 243). Ndlovu-Gatsheni (2013) added that coloniality is global and supports unequal power relations between the Euro-American world and the Global South to the extent that, despite the end of formal colonial administrations, colonial arrangements continue to govern contemporary societies through various relations. As Abdi (2012) has observed, colonialism is physical, technological, and psychological, and the latter is endemic. Psychological colonization is complex and pervasive in knowledge production across the globe and is pervasive in former colonized nations. A decolonial approach focuses on deconstructing colonial thinking and detaching African epistemologies and educational practices from colonial dependency and structures (Abdi 2012; Dei, 2000; Dei et al., 2022; Ndlovu-Gatsheni, 2013; wa Thiong'o, 1986). Decolonial perspectives offer opportunities to examine curricula in Kenya, Tanzania, and Uganda for possibilities of producing and enacting knowledge that will contribute to centering the African people's experiences and amplifying their knowledges. We consider what a decolonial framework might do for the primary school harmonized curriculum in the East African Community.

In addition to decolonial debates, other African scholars talk about Africanizing the curricula, arguing that, "for the most part, education in Africa has been a journey fuelled by an exogenously initiated and disguised feeling of inadequacy in Africans, and blessed with the mission of depreciation or destruction of African imagination, organization, and esteem frameworks" (Enaifoghe, 2019, p. 67). Makgoba (1997) describes Africanization as a learning process and a way of life for Africans that entails fusing, modifying, and coordinating multiple civilizations into, and via, African aspirations to provide the dynamism, growth, and flexibility so essential on the global arena (p. 199). Many educational programs that were inherited from the colonizers remain sources of "estrangement because they don't address student encounters or reflect the philosophical, social substances of their groups" (Enaifoghe, 2019, p. 66). Africanization therefore calls for a renewed focus on African histories, cultures, needs and aspirations, which should affect the recovery of what has been taken from Africa in terms of educational systems with the right content of values, structures and institutions. It is about creating scholarship and research in African scholarly conventions (Enaifoghe, 2019). Despite the slightly varying approaches, the end goal is to free African curricula, education systems, and values from European/Euro-American dominance and cultural imperialism (Abdi, 2012; Dei, 1998; Shizha, 2007).

We also draw on Afrocentric constructs of identity, African culture, transmission and adoption of African values, community control, and institution building to inform our discussion (Shockley & Frederick, 2010). Afrocentricity is a way of thinking and acting in which African interests, values and perspectives are centered in all African peoples' experiences (Asante, 2003; Dei, 1994). The Afrocentric constructs allow for centering the learning needs of African students and their communities with the goal of preparing graduates who believe in the self-respect of Africans, who are focused on the best interests of Africans, and who are devoted to generating solutions to local challenges (Asante, 1990, 2003). There are parallels between Afrocentricity and the African philosophy of Ubuntu (as referred to in South African contexts) or Utu (as known in East Africa). Ubuntu philosophy is based on values of justice, responsibility, equality, collectiveness, kinship, reciprocity, love, respect, helpfulness, community, caring, dependability, sharing, trust, honesty, selflessness, and social change. Ubuntu is about humanness and emphasizes that people's identity is constantly evolving in the context of their relationships with others. Therefore, by supporting and caring for others, one's own identity and quality of life also improve (Mayaka & Truell, 2021; Mugumbate & Chereni, 2019). Ubuntu focuses on the inclusion of everyone in the community, responsibility to others, and the well-being of the environment to ensure success for future generations (Mayaka & Truell, 2021; Mugumbate & Chereni, 2019). Ubuntu is about how Africans see themselves, interact with others, their environment, and spiritual beings, and how outsiders should interact with them (Mugumbate & Chereni, 2019). Ubuntu is about liberation; it is about bringing back ownership of ancestral lands as opposed to expropriation; it is about freedom; autonomy, respect, recognition, justice, togetherness, forgiveness, and community among other virtues (Mugumbate & Chereni, 2019). To decolonize is to free the African from the shackles of Eurocentrism (Abdi, 2012) and bringing back lost Ubuntu as an inter-humanizing philosophy of life, that is, unconditionally seeing and practicing your being through the being of the other (Abdi, 2022), both in everyday living and in the educational system.

With the above in mind, we consider in this analysis, ways in which the harmonized curriculum could bring back the African learners' needs and perspectives to the center; empower them to critically examine subjects related to Africa; restore African knowledge, history, and creative and innovative skills; and prioritize Afrocentric and Ubuntu values of collaboration, community responsibility, spirituality, equity, and justice. Additionally, we consider opportunities for the harmonized curriculum to help students to understand and appreciate their culture and those of others; promote economic, political, technological, spiritual and social empowerment and sovereignty of the African people and their nations (Akua, 2020). We focus on primary education because we believe that for the decolonial efforts in education to be sustained, the process must be conceptualized and implemented from an early age to allow African children to be reared and educated with strong anchorage in their own cultural and ancestral value systems (Boukary, 2018).

Education and Primary School Curricula in Kenya, Uganda and Tanzania

Upon their independence in the 1960s, Kenya, Uganda, and Tanzania inherited a racially segregated educational system with separate schools for people of European, Asian, and African descent (Akala, 2021; Galabawa 1990; Ochieng', 1989). The existing Indigenous African educational systems and local languages were disregarded. The education system for Black Africans, which was mostly administered by European missionaries, prepared them for menial jobs and was aimed at "civilizing" and evangelizing the Africans (Akala, 2021). After independence, African countries worked to reform education and identify development trajectories that were relevant to Africa (wa Thiong'o, 1992). In particular, the Addis Ababa conference on education for Africa held in May 1960 was a major inspiration for nations to re-evaluate educational goals (Akala, 2021). This led to the updating of curricula, teaching resources, and pedagogical techniques to better serve the needs of local populations and address local challenges. We now offer a summary of each country's primary school curricula.

Kenya

After independence in 1963, Kenya committed to reforming the country's education away from colonial and racist education. This included introducing national education goals and Africanization of the curriculum, changing curriculum, revision of education objectives and policies among other initiatives (Republic of Kenya, 1988; 1999). Kenya's educational goals are to promote nationalism, patriotism, and national unity; foster social, economic, technological, and industrial needs for national development; promote individual development and self-actualization; foster positive attitudes toward good health and environmental protection; promote social equity and responsibility; promote global knowledge and favorable attitudes toward other nations; and foster respect for, and development of, Kenya's rich and diverse cultures (Kenya Institute of Curriculum Development, 2017).

Since attaining independence, the country has revised its curricula several times to include the relevance of education in addressing the needs of the nation, youth unemployment and skill development. The revisions have also paid attention to the expansion of higher education, and the creation of happy youths who uphold national values and are ready to serve their country (Sifuna, 1990; Sifuna & Obonyo, 2019). Kenya's primary education curriculum framework goals are supported by three fundamental pillars: values, theoretical approaches, and guiding principles (Kenya Institute of Curriculum Development, 2017). Kenya's 2010 Constitution mandates the Ministry of Education to incorporate values such as responsibility, respect, excellence, care, compassion, understanding, tolerance, honesty, trustworthiness, and ethical behavior into curricula (Kenya Institute of Curriculum Development, 2017).

In January 2018, the Ministry of Education introduced a competence curriculum that consists of three phases: (i) early years education (kindergarten to grade three); (ii) middle years education (grade four to nine) and (iii) senior years education (grade ten to twelve) (Kaviti, 2018; Kenya Institute of Curriculum Development, 2017). In primary school (kindergarten to grade 6), during the preschool and kindergarten years, students do language activities, mathematical activities, environmental activities, psychomotor and creative activities, religious education activities, and pre-Braille activities. The latter is an impressive revision as not many spaces in Africa offer this at such an early age. In lower primary (Grades 1, 2, 3) students are taught literacy activities or Braille literacy activities, Kiswahili language activities or Kenya sign language, English-language activities, mathematical activities, environmental activities, hygiene and nutrition activities, religious education activities, and movement and creative activities. In upper primary (Grades four to six), students are taught English, Kiswahili or Kenya sign language, home science, agriculture, science and technology, mathematics, religious education (Christian religious education or Islamic religious education or Hindu religious education), creative arts, physical and health education, and social studies. Optional subjects include Indigenous languages, Kenya sign language, Braille literacy and foreign languages such as Arabic, French, German and Mandarin (Kenyayote, 2021; Kenya Institute of Curriculum Development, 2017). The new curriculum includes Indigenous language teaching and learning, which is a requirement in lower primary but is optional in upper primary (Kenya Institute of Curriculum Development, 2017). Literacy and fluency in Indigenous languages are promoted with the purpose of changing the social, intellectual, and psychological attitudes of both instructors and students toward their cultural heritage and worldview. It is hoped that this would create alternative educational and linguistic paradigms and gradually result in decolonization of teaching, learning, and information transmission both within, and outside of, academic institutions (Kaviti, 2018).

While the new curriculum has yet to be thoroughly evaluated due to its ongoing implementation, the limited studies that have been conducted show that some teachers may not be aware of Indigenous knowledge systems, making its integration into the new curriculum impossible (Jumba & Mwiti, 2022). When compared to other subject areas, Indigenous knowledges was best integrated in grade one history and culture (Jumba & Mwiti, 2022). The lack of implementation across all grade levels and across subject areas likely to impede its integration in the aftermath of the new curriculum's implementation, so more support, training, and resources are needed to advance the place of indigeneity in the Kenyan curriculum (Jumba & Mwiti, 2022).

Tanzania

The goal of education, as the first president of Tanzania Julius Nyerere put it, is to pass on the wisdom and knowledge of society to the next generation, and to prepare the next generation for their future participation in society and their active part in its upkeep or development (Nyerere, 1982). Colonial education, according to Nyerere, did not meet local people's needs because it accentuated human inequalities and Western culture's social, political, and economic superiority. Colonial education also deliberately altered Tanzanian identity, culture, knowledge, and values in order to replace them with Western culture and knowledge. Nyerere's vision of education was one that centered Africa, its peoples, and perspectives, as well as restored African identity (Akua, 2020; Nyerere, 1967).

In 1967, Julius Nyerere proposed a plan for education in Tanzania which remains the guiding principle for educational objectives in the country today. The objectives of the plan were to: (a) equip learners with the skills, knowledge, and attitudes necessary to address societal challenges; (b) prepare them for employment in the predominantly agricultural economy of Tanzania; and (c) enable them to recognize, value, and cultivate a Tanzanian cultural identity that emphasizes national traditions, individual liberty, accountability, tolerance, and esteem (Ministry of Education, 1982; cited in Sanga, 2016 p. 2). Thus, in Nyerere's view, education should be relevant to society's past, present and future. Educated individuals must serve society, education must be problem-solving, and education must be work-focused (Sanga, 2016). The objectives of Education for Self-Reliance were clearly centered on Tanzania's best interests and align well with the Afrocentric constructs of identity, African culture, dissemination and acceptance of African values, community management, and institution development (Asante, 2003; Sanga, 2016; Shockley & Frederick, 2010).

Tanzania has pursued educational reforms, including curricular revisions, to enhance learning results and build an effective educational system, which we will not delve into in this discussion. For example, in 2005, a competence-based curriculum was introduced, and in 2014, the 3Rs (reading, writing and arithmetic) reform was implemented to strengthen basic skills. Despite these changes, there is still criticism that education in Tanzania fails to promote skills that are relevant to the twenty-first century (such as critical thinking, problem-solving, creativity, and collaboration) (see Kombo & Shukia, 2023). However, these criticisms are very Western-centric. Missing from that critique is a discussion of the continued marginalization of Indigenous knowledge and values, and thus a lack of analysis of how African Indigenous knowledge enriches twenty-first-century skills. African knowledges continue to be used and influence the lives of many African peoples, which is a reality that cannot be ignored (Abidogun & Falola, 2020; Adeyemi & Adeyinka, 2002; Heto & Mino, 2022; Maunganidze, 2016).

Nonetheless, the philosophy of Education for Self-Reliance continues to be the foundation of Tanzania's current primary education curriculum (Tanzania Institute of Education, 2019). The primary curriculum places emphasis on developing critical thinking and an inquiring mind, learning through both theory and practice, and developing self-confidence, decision-making, and respect for human values (Tanzania Institute of Education, 2019). It emphasizes the balance between education and the needs of the community or target groups. The primary curriculum also stresses the role of culture in shaping Tanzanians' sense of national identity and integrating teaching and learning about traditional values, practices, and taboos (Tanzania Institute of Education, 2019). Additionally, the curriculum aims to help students understand and respect their own culture as well as those of other groups (Tanzania Institute of Education, 2019, p. 6). Language instruction is prioritized at all levels of Tanzanian educational delivery. The Education and Training Policy (2014) acknowledges the use of Kiswahili, English, sign language, and other foreign languages in education and training. English, French, Arabic, and Kiswahili are also taught (Tanzania Institute of Education, 2019, p. 6).

In terms of core competencies, the grades one and two curricula are designed to help students improve reading, writing, numeracy, communication, health, physical activity and working with others. The aims of the curricula are to strengthen attitudes toward learning, environmental protection and talent development. They also focus on students' moral and spiritual growth according to their chosen religion (Tanzania Institute of Education, 2019). In Grades three to seven, students learn to respect and use the Swahili language, reading, writing, mathematics, rule of law, appreciation of Tanzanian culture, critical thinking, creativity, problem-solving, ethics, honesty, responsibility, community service, and science and technology. Parental involvement in education is strongly promoted. Family and community play a crucial role in a child's growth and development. Educating students is highly dependent on family and community involvement in promoting education (Tanzania Institute of Education, 2019). Some scholars have lauded the government's efforts to improve education access in Tanzania and make it more relevant locally and globally (Mosha, 2018). The challenge with the curriculum reforms, particularly at the primary and secondary school levels, remains to be the lack of coordinated efforts to match the changes with pre-service and in-service teacher training, which has a negative impact on quality (Lupeja & Komba, 2021; Mosha, 2018).

Uganda

The primary school curriculum in Uganda has undergone a number of revisions since independence, with the intention of raising the quality of education for students in primary schools. Before colonization, Uganda had Indigenous educational systems that primarily aimed to prepare children to promote societal harmony, promote cultural heritage, allow youth to acquire and apply life skills to solve individual and societal problems, and develop character and respect for Elders (Muyanda-Mutebi, 1996). Elders were critical in the education of the youth, and they freely shared their knowledge, wisdom and experiences (The Republic of Uganda, 2018). Colonization changed the country's education. Between 1900 and 1924, missionaries built educational institutions and curricula that focused on basic writing, arithmetic and religion. The Bible was the principal resource for teaching. The curriculum was foreign to the Indigenous people and access to education was unequal. These inequities paved the way for the issues of access and irrelevance which plague Uganda's education today (The Republic of Uganda, 2018).

After independence, Uganda began focusing on providing all Ugandans with good quality education. Various commissions have been created over the years to examine and provide suggestions on how to enhance Ugandan education's response to societal problems. For instance, the Castle Commission was established soon after independence to revamp the nation's education system to fulfill societal demands. In 1965, the Commission recommended the creation of the first post-independence primary school curriculum which covered 12 subjects including science, math, music, physical education, religion, English language, mother tongue, history, geography, and civics (Muyanda-Mutebi, 1996). Since then, Uganda's primary curriculum has undergone multiple reforms in 1967, 1990, 1999, and 2007–2010, which resulted in minor modifications in scope, sequencing, relevance, and language (Ezati, 2016). Therefore, there is little difference between the 1967 curriculum, which included the 12 subject groups, and the present curriculum (2007–2010), which combined and repackaged topics to reduce them to 9 (The Republic of Uganda, 2018).

Uganda's education system has been designed with several goals. It aims to promote national unity, patriotism, and cultural heritage while considering international ties and positive interdependence. It also aims to instill moral, ethical, and spiritual values, self-discipline, honesty, tolerance, and human fellowship. It seeks to foster a spirit of service, responsibility, and leadership in Ugandans through group and community activities. It is intended to eliminate illiteracy and provide individuals with basic skills for self-development and national growth, which includes improving health, nutrition, family life, learning capacity and preparing to contribute to an integrated, self-sustaining, and independent national economy. It also focuses on fostering scientific, technological, and cultural knowledge, skills, and attitudes for individual and national growth (Uganda National Curriculum Development Center, 2022).

The emphasis for primary education in Uganda is to help students learn how to read, write, and to communicate in English and Kiswahili, and at least one Ugandan language; to develop mentally and physically; to instil the values of working together with others and taking care of others in the community; to promote cultural, moral, and spiritual values and recognize the richness of the country's different cultures and values; to protect and use the natural environment with scientific and technical knowledge and skills; to understand their rights and civic responsibilities; to develop patriotism, nationalism, and national unity in a variety of ways; to develop prerequisites for continuing education and a range of practical skills so they can make a living as a multi-skilled person; to equip students with knowledge, skills, and values which they need to be responsible adults; to develop problem-solving skills in different life situations; and to learn how to manage time and finance and how to respect private and public property (Uganda National Curriculum

Development Center, 2022). The subjects that are taught in elementary school include English, integrated science, local languages, math, religious studies, social studies, music, dance and drama, physical education; and art and technology (The Republic of Uganda, Ministry of Education and Sports, 2022a, 2022b, 2010). While these subjects are well-described in the curriculum, scholars have identified gaps in how the curriculum is implemented and how this affects educational quality (Kagoda, 2009; Nyenje & James, 2016). It is critical to make curriculum more relevant to the needs of the local population. Learner assessment inconsistencies vary across the country. According to Nyenje and James (2016), having a curriculum without support and training teachers to implement it may have an impact on educational quality. Kagoda (2009) urged the Ugandan government to improve teacher education and fund research into Indigenous knowledges for incorporation into school curricula. This will enable capacity building and promote the mainstreaming of Indigenous content in curriculum and practice.

Opportunities for Indigeneity in the Move Toward a Harmonized Curriculum

Addressing coloniality of knowledges in East Africa—the privileging of European and Euro-American knowledges and experiences and worldviews—is complex and needs a deep awareness and re-evaluation of what knowledges are produced and taught in educational contexts, starting from the primary school level. This could ensure that the knowledge which is taught would be rooted in the community's experiences and needs. A close look at the structure of the core curricula of the three countries—Kenya, Tanzania and Uganda—shows that all the curricula are built around core competencies to work toward harmonized curricula in the region. Efforts have been made in the curricula to center the learning and appreciation of the local people's culture and their languages, especially for preschool children and Grades one to three.

The curricula also emphasize inclusion of Afrocentric and Ubuntu values of responsibility, respect, excellence, caring, compassion, understanding, tolerance, honesty, trustworthiness, spirituality and ethical behavior (Chawane, 2016; Mayaka & Truell, 2021; Mugumbate & Chereni, 2019). Indigenous knowledges are central in the aims and competencies of the countries' curricula. Kenya lays emphasis on Indigenous language teaching and learning. Literacy and fluency in Indigenous languages is seen as one of the many steps to decolonization of teaching and learning (Kaviti, 2018; Mugumbate & Chereni, 2019). Tanzania stresses the appreciation of Tanzanian culture, including the use, appreciation and teaching of the Swahili language, the teaching of traditional values, culture and practices, and teaching the role of culture in shaping the country's identity and spirituality and moral development. Uganda does not necessarily use the term Indigenous but emphasizes appreciation of culture and its role in society, including promoting cultural heritage, and fostering cultural knowledge, skills, and attitudes for both individual and national growth.

In all countries, music, dance, oral traditions, proverbs, and stories are emphasized, and their roles are seen as being as modes of education. As noted by Omolewa (2007), music and dance are central to the African way of life. They equip students with skills to work effectively in other areas of learning, including language learning, speech therapy, literacy, numeracy and other subjects. They are also simple ways to activate students' prior knowledge and experiences and incorporate them into the curriculum. Oral tradition continues to be the bank of knowledge from which Africans learn about their origins, history, culture and religion, and the meaning and reality of life, morality, norms and survival techniques (Ngara, 2007; Omolewa, 2007). Idioms, legends, folklore, stories, proverbs and myths are rich sources of some of African orality, wisdom and philosophy (Abdi, 2009; Adeyemi & Adeyinka, 2002; Dei et al., 2022; Ngara, 2007). The curricula of all three countries recommend using these approaches in teaching and learning. They also emphasize the role of spirituality and Elders in developing self-disciplined and ethical citizens with strong moral values (Kenya Institute of Curriculum Development, 2017; Tanzania Institute of Education, 2019; Uganda National Curriculum Development Center, 2022).

Learning through Indigenous languages is a crucial component of the curriculum. This is consistent with Wa Thiong'o's (1986) assertion that language informs and carries culture, and that it is central to identity and how people see themselves. Colonial languages imposed foreign ideals on Africans, and distorted their identity and history, resulting in the loss of their cultural values and self-esteem (Wa Thiong'o, 1986). According to UNESCO (2003), local languages are an important means of preserving, transmitting, and implementing Indigenous knowledges in schools. Emphasizing the teaching of local languages and culture, including technology, science, arts and music, helps students develop a strong identity, appreciate their communities' ingenuity, and participate fully in their education. All of these are important steps to ensure that content is not culturally disenfranchising and alienating students but is relevant to them and their communities (Asante, 1990). These steps are conscious efforts to activate the learners' Africanness, their ideals and their values (Asante, 1990; Chawane, 2016). Given the intergenerational impacts of psychological colonization and the implications on Africa's conceptual, cognitive, procedural and programmatic contexts and prospects (Abdi, 2009, 2020), an important discussion needs to happen relating to the extent to which these learnings challenge Euro-America supremacy, elevate African ways of knowing and being, and empower students to see themselves as agents, actors and participants in knowledge creation and dissemination (see Chawane, 2016). Similarly, Mazrui (1978) noted that very few educated Africans are even aware that they are also in cultural bondage. All educated Africans are still prisoners of Western culture, and the curriculum is still a powerful form of imperialism (p. 13). This means that the education system still keeps Africans and their scholarship trapped in a colonial mindset that requires thoughtful solutions. Otherwise, curricula and schools will continue to lose their potential to be cultural spaces and centers where reclamation and revitalization of African knowledges and identities should take place (Mazrui & Mazrui, 1993).

It is promising to see an emphasis on Afrocentric and Ubuntu principles in the harmonized curriculum, with a focus on place-based learning and environmental management from an early age. In Indigenous African knowledges environmental justice is woven into the practice of Ubuntu. This is because each person is responsible for their mutual relationship with the environment around them (Mayaka & Truell, 2021; Wane, 2003; Wane & Chandler, 2002). In Indigenous African societies, traditional use of Land and natural resources required that each community take responsibility for common land, water, forests and other natural resources (Mayaka & Truell, 2021; Mulat, 2013; Wane, 2003; Wane & Chandler, 2002). Their use was not extractive, but they were to be used responsibly and nurtured for the next generation (Mulat, 2013). These lessons are very much aligned with STEM education and could be extended to conversations about Africa and technology. For example, students can be taught and encouraged to study stone tools. In fact, the people of the Lake Turkana region in Kenya were some of the first to use stone tools (Kibunjia, 1994, cited in Burbanks IV et al., 2020, p. 16). This is an important understanding that locates the emergence of STEM on the continent of Africa more than 4 million years ago, and that Africa is the birthplace not only of technology but also of mathematics, astronomy, navigation, architecture and engineering (Burbanks IV et al., 2020). Discussions of the origins of STEM education often ignore the important role that Africa has played in world history. Credit has been given to Greeks, yet we know that Greek mathematicians like Euclid and Pythagoras studied under priests (professors) at African universities (Asante, 1990). Educating children from a young age in this knowledge would foster the institutionalization of the knowledge in African educational systems and institutions. It would also enable students to embrace scientific communication that would strengthen African knowledge and contributions, and challenge dominant Euro-American culture and ideologies (Rasekoala, 2022). As Mawere's (2015) has stated, "with Indigenous knowledge and conventional science in the curriculum, learners are better empowered to shake off the chains of imperial domination, make their own decisions, and chart their own destiny based on what they learn at home and at school" (p. 62).

There are additional opportunities to advance and transform the curricula by centering African ways of knowing. For example, we consider Zavala's (2016) recommendations to reclaim and revitalize the role and place of African knowledges through counter storytelling, healing and reclaiming across all levels. Counter-storytelling involves the practices of naming and remembering. Healing involves social/collective and spiritual/psychological healing, and reclaiming encompasses practices, identities, and spaces (Zavala, 2016, p. 2). Therefore, we argue that in all curricula, African knowledges should be embedded throughout all subject areas not only in geography, history and music where most cultural teachings are emphasized. We encourage more cross-curricula learning which center local communities and peoples, their languages, systems of government, and responsibilities and rights of community members from an affirming and not a deficit lens. Drawing more on African knowledges, approaches and learnings applying to taking care of natural features of the environment and their importance, as well as the medicines and technologies of various communities, should be prioritized. Conscious efforts must be made to embed more learnings and discussions on place and Land in relation to urgent needs such as developing and nurturing responsible African entrepreneurship based on Afrocentric and Ubuntu philosophies which pay attention to caring for the environment, the people, the Land and the waters.

Furthermore, although the curriculum for students with disabilities in much of Africa has been heavily influenced by the medical model of disability, there is a lot of room for African Indigenous knowledge to benefit students with disabilities. As noted by Owusu-Ansah and Mji (2013), African Indigenous peoples with disabilities have something to contribute to the knowledge acquisition process. The introduction of pre-Braille and Braille activities in Kenya's revised curriculum is a step in the right direction. There is a need to explore other ways of creating, producing, teaching and sharing new knowledge with students with disabilities, and Indigenous research offers new possibilities in Africa.

Also, more time should be allocated to the learning of Indigenous languages. In Kenya, for instance, in a week of learning, which is equivalent to 40 lessons, local languages are assigned two lessons while English has four, Kiswahili four, Math five, Physical Health and Education five, Science and Technology four, Religious Studies three, Agriculture three, Art and Craft two, Music one, Social Studies three, Home Science three and Pastoral Instruction one (Education Newshub, 2022). This allocation of time to each subject shows the hierarchy of knowledge in the curriculum. Looking at the attention, which is given to local languages and English, it is clear that there is a strong message about the relative importance of the English language compared to Kenyan local languages (Adzahlie-Mensah & Dunne, 2018, p. 52). In Tanzania, the Kiswahili language is allotted three hours and 20 minutes per week, while English is allotted four hours and 40 minutes, Mathematics is allotted four hours, Science and Technology is allotted three hours and 20 minutes, Social Studies is allotted two hours, Civic and Moral Education is allotted three hours and 20 minutes, Vocational Skills has no hours identified, Religious Education has 40 minutes allotted, and French and Arabic have one hour and 20 minutes allotted (Tanzania Institute of Education, 2019). The time distribution for Uganda is relatively like that of Kenya. English is the predominant language of instruction for all subjects except Kiswahili, local languages, and other foreign languages such as French, German and Mandarin. Therefore, despite efforts to embed Indigenous knowledges into the curriculum, "the basic curriculum structure and emphasis still bears the traces of its colonial history that has not significantly interrupted the sustained epistemic damage" (Adzahlie-Mensah & Dunne, 2018, p. 52).

Further emphasis should also be laid in African Indigenous foods to address nutrition-related non-communicable diseases in the country, ethical and sustainable food production systems that ensure food security, and the realities of climate change challenges. Seeking knowledge from Elders and cultural experts to enrich learnings in STEM (managing fires, geometric shapes, African fractals, etc.) should also be prioritized. The same applies to traditions and celebrations, history and stories of family, including ancestors, contributions, and the importance of preserving and transmitting knowledge from one generation to the next.

Conclusion

With the above observations and analysis, we go back to the questions which Nyerere asked in 1967, and which are very pertinent today: What is the purpose of education? What kind of graduates would the education system produce? (Sanga, 2016). If East African nations (and as applicable to the rest of Africa) are to chart their own development, what kind of knowledges are they transmitting to their children to advance the goal of self-reliance and decolonial education? How might educators, researchers, policy makers, and political leaders continue to create, nurture and support such an education? These questions call for a deeper engagement and re-evaluation of curricula, and particularly the proposed harmonized curriculum. If members of the East African Community are serious about change and promoting regional collaborations and self-reliance, then they must consider, among other issues, the role of indigeneity in the harmonized curriculum. By meaningfully centering Indigenous knowledges in the curriculum, students will have opportunities to compare and contrast different forms of knowledge for their own benefits and those of the communities to which they belong (Mawere, 2015). If these critical reflections do not continue to happen, Africans will continue to be chiefly consumers not only of goods and services which are imported to their own spaces, but also, more disappointingly, of imported knowledge which barely speaks to the needs of the people or addresses the local problems (Tshindoli, 2018). Graduates of the education systems will remain firmly anchored in Eurocentric theories, ideologies and practices which will continue to demean the richness of African knowledges, and they will remain active participants in the continued African human, material and technological resources that should, but likely won't remain in the region and be used to advance the economies and well-being of the EAC member states.

We recognize the existence of misplaced critiques about African Indigenous knowledges as being simple, even simplistic in their constructions and related outcomes by some educators (Dziva et al., 2011; Michie, 2002). Literature shows though, that many of those teachers have limited understanding of African Indigenous knowledges and therefore consider it as being of lesser value, especially in science subjects, and that it cannot be subjected to proof testing (Dziva et al., 2011). The authors concluded that what these teachers failed to understand is that African Indigenous knowledges provide "some similar and some different theories about the material world, derived from the processes which parallel Western scientific thought but operates within a different framework and therefore it sometimes comes to different conclusions" (Dziva et al., 2011, p. 99; see also Emeagwali, 2003). More work needs to be done at the teacher education levels to educate and sensitize teachers about African Indigenous knowledges and the centrality to student learning. Additionally, and as suggested by Thomson (2003), K to 12 science teachers should integrate action research, with communities surrounding their schools, into their work and document Indigenous knowledges and their development for classroom learning. This is lacking in many local African contexts (see also Michie, 2002). We agree with Mawere (2015) that, "as long as Indigenous knowledge fails to find full recognition within and real integration into curricula and the mainstream knowledge discourse, the lofty pan-African ideals of collective self-reliance, self-sustaining development, and economic growth will remain an unrealized dream" (p. 67). We want these ideals to be actualized and hope that they will be.

References

Abdi, A. A. (2009). Oral societies and colonial experiences: Sub-Saharan Africa and the defacto power of the written word. In D. Kapoor (Ed.), *Education, decolonization, and development* (pp. 39–56). Brill.

Abdi, A. A. (2012). Decolonizing philosophies of education: An introduction. In A. A. Abdi (Ed.), *Decolonizing philosophies of education* (pp. 1–13). Brill.

Abdi, A. A. (2020). Decolonizing knowledge, education and social development: Africanist perspectives. *Beijing International Review of Education*, 2(4), 503–518.

Abdi, A. A. (2022). Freireian and Ubuntu philosophies of education: Onto-epistemological characteristics and pedagogical intersections. *Educational Philosophy and Theory*, 54(13), 2286–2296.

Abidogun, J. M., & Falola, T. (Eds.). (2020). *The Palgrave handbook of African education and Indigenous knowledge*. Springer International Publishing.

Adeyemi, M. B., & Adeyinka, A. A. (2002). Some key issues in African traditional education. *McGill Journal of Education*, 37(2), 223–240.

Adzahlie-Mensah, V., & Dunne, M. (2018). Continuing in the shadows of colonialism: The educational experiences of the African child in Ghana. *Perspectives in Education*, 36(2), 44–60.

Akala, B. M. M. (2021). Revisiting education reform in Kenya: A case of competency-based curriculum (CBC). *Social Sciences & Humanities Open*, 3(1), 100107. https://www.sciencedirect.com/science/article/pii/S2590291121000036

Akua, C. (2020). Standards of Afrocentric education for school leaders and teachers. *Journal of Black Studies, 51*(2), 107–127. https://journals.sagepub.com/doi/abs/10.1177/0021934719893572

Arik, M., Bamenyekanye, E., Fimbo, A., Kabatende, J., Kijo, A. S., Simai, B., ... & Delano, T. (2020). Optimizing the East African community's medicines regulatory harmonization initiative in 2020–2022: A roadmap for the future. *PLoS Medicine, 17*(8), e1003129, 1–11. https://journals.plos.org/plosmedicine/article?id=10.1371/journal.pmed.1003129

Asante, M. K. (1990). *Kemet, Afrocentricity, and knowledge.* Africa World Press.

Asante, M. K. (2003). *Afrocentricity: The theory of social change.* People's Publishing Group.

Bayeh, E. (2015). Eastern Africa standby force: An overview. *International Journal of Research, 2*(1), 492–499.

Boukary, H. (2018). Putting the cart before the horse? Early childhood care and education (ECCE) the quest for Ubuntu educational foundation in Africa. In E. J. Takyi-Amoako & N. T. Assié-Lumumba (Eds.), *Re-visioning education in Africa: Ubuntu-inspired education for humanity* (pp. 135–145). Palgrave Macmillan.

Burbanks IV, S. M., Shockley, K. G., & LeNiles, K. (2020). The need for African centered education in STEM programs for Black youth. *Journal of African American Males in Education (JAAME), 11*(2), 12–24.

Chawane, M. (2016). The development of Afrocentricity: A historical survey. *Yesterday and Today, 16,* 78–99. https://www.scielo.org.za/pdf/yt/n16/06.pdf

Dei, S. J. G. (1994). Afrocentricity: A cornerstone of pedagogy. *Anthropology & Education Quarterly, 25*(1), 3–28.

Dei, S. J. G. (1998). "Why write back?": The role of Afrocentric discourse in social change. *Canadian Journal of Education, 23*(2), 200–209.

Dei, S. J. G. (2000). Rethinking the role of Indigenous knowledges in the academy. *International Journal of Inclusive Education, 4*(2), 111–132.

Dei, S. J. G. (2002). African development: The relevance and implications of Indigenousness. In G. J. S. Dei, B. L. Hall, & D. G. Rosenberg (Ed.), *Indigenous knowledges in global contexts: Multiple readings of our world* (pp. vii–x). University of Toronto Press.

Dei, S. J. G. (2010). *Teaching Africa: Towards a transgressive pedagogy.* Springer.

Dei, S. J. G., Karanja, W., & Erger, G. (2022). *Elders' cultural knowledges and the question of Black/African Indigeneity in education* (Vol. 16). Springer Nature.

Dziva, D., Mpofu, V., & Kusure, L. P. (2011). Teachers' conception of Indigenous knowledge in science curriculum in the context of Mberengwa district, Zimbabwe. *African Journal of Education and Technology, 1*(3), 88–102.

East African qualifications framework for higher education. https://www.knqa.go.ke/wp-content/uploads/2019/05/East-Africa-Qf.pdf with - https://www.gfmd.org/pfp/ppd/19631

East African Community. (2023). *EAC partner states.* https://www.eac.int/eac-partner-states

East African Community Secretariat. (2014). *Draft harmonized curriculum structures and framework for the East African Community—Primary education.* https://kicd.ac.ke/wp-content/uploads/2017/11/DraftHarmonisedCurriculumStructureandFrameworkforPrimaryEducation070814.pdf

Education Newshub. (2022). *Grade 4 to 6 time table, time allocation and lesson distribution for all primary schools: Ministry of Education guidelines.* https://educationnewshub.co.ke/grade-4-to-6-time-table-time-allocation-and-lesson-distribution-for-all-primary-schools-ministry-of-education-guidelines/

Emeagwali, G. (2003). African Indigenous knowledge systems (AIK): Implications for the curriculum. In T. Falola (Ed.), *Ghana in Africa and the world: Essays in honor of Adu Boahen.* Africa World Press.

Enaifoghe, A. O. (2019). The decolonization of African education and history. *African Renaissance (1744–2532), 16,* 61–84.

Galabawa, J. (1990). *Implementing educational policies in Tanzania.* World Bank.

Heto, P. P. K., & Mino, T. (2023). (Dis)continuity of African Indigenous knowledge. *AlterNative: An International Journal of Indigenous Peoples, 19*(1), 71–79. https://journals.sagepub.com/doi/pdf/10.1177/11771801221138304

Jowi, O. J. (2020). *The East African qualifications framework for higher education* (EAQFHE). 6th ACQF Peer Learning Webinar. https://www.etf.europa.eu/sites/default/files/2020-10/session_5_eaqfhe_6th_plw_22oct.pdf

Karuku, S., & Tennant, G. (2016). Towards a harmonized curriculum in East Africa. In A. Halai & G. Tennant (Eds.), *Mathematics education in East Africa* (pp. 9–25). Springer.

Katembo, B. (2008). Pan-Africanism and development: The East African Community model. *Journal of Pan African Studies, 2*(4), 107–117. https://www.jpanafrican.org/docs/vol2no4/2.4_Pan_Africanism.pdf

Kagoda, A. M. (2009). Integrating appropriate Indigenous knowledge in the geography lessons in secondary schools of Uganda. *Current Research Journal of Social Sciences, 1*(3), 117–122.

Kaviti, L. (2018). *The new curriculum of education in Kenya: A linguistic and education paradigm shift.* University of Nairobi.

Kenyayote. (2021). *Subjects taught in CBC Grade 1 to 12, pp 1, pp 2 in Kenya.* https://elimukenya.co.ke/subjects-taught-in-cbc-grade-1-to-12-pp1-pp2-in-kenya-2022/

Kenya Institute of Curriculum Development. (2017). *Basic education curriculum framework.* https://kicd.ac.ke/curriculum-reform/basic-education-curriculum-framework/

Komba, A., & Shukia, R. (2023). *An analysis of the basic education curriculum in Tanzania: The integration, scope, and sequence of 21st century skills.* https://riseprogramme.org/sites/default/files/2023-02/An%20Analysis%20of%20the%20Basic%20Education%20Curriculum%20in%20Tanzania_0.pdf

Lupeja, T., & Komba, S. (2021). Implementation of competence-based curriculum in the context of colonial education system in Tanzania. *International Journal of Research Studies in Education, 10*(5), 33–43.

Maathai, W. (2009). *The challenge for Africa.* Arrow Books.

Magu, S. M. (2014). Dilemmas of collective action: Explaining East African regional integration and cooperation. *International Journal of Political Science and Development, 2*(4), 58–67.

Makgoba, M. W. (1997). *Mokoko: The Makgoba affair: A reflection on transformation.* Vivlia.

Maldonado-Torres, N. (2007). On the coloniality of being: Contributions to the development of a concept. *Cultural Studies, 21*(2–3), 240–270.

Mamdani, M. (2015). Settler colonialism: Then and now. *Critical Inquiry, 41*(3), 596–614. https://www.journals.uchicago.edu/doi/abs/10.1086/680088?journalCode=ci

Maunganidze, L. (2016). A moral compass that slipped: Indigenous knowledge systems and rural development in Zimbabwe. *Cogent Social Sciences, 2*(1), 1266749. https://www.tandfonline.com/doi/pdf/10.1080/23311886.2016.1266749

Mawere, M. (2015). Indigenous knowledge and public education in sub-Saharan Africa. *Africa Spectrum, 50*(2), 57–71. https://journals.sagepub.com/doi/full/10.1177/000203971505000203

Mayaka, B., & Truell, R. (2021). Ubuntu and its potential impact on the international social work profession. *International Social Work, 64*(5), 649–662. https://www.socialserviceworkforce.org/system/files/resource/files/Ubuntu.pdf

Mazrui, A. (1978). *Political values and the educated class in Africa.* University of California Press.

Mazrui, A. M., & Mazrui, A. A. (1993). Dominant languages in a plural society: English and Kiswahili in post-colonial East Africa. *International Political Science Review, 14*(3), 275–292.

Michie, M. (2002). Why Indigenous science should be included in the school science curriculum. *Journal of Cognition and Culture, 4*(3–4), 409–450.

Mkabela, Q. (2005). Using the Afrocentric method in researching Indigenous African culture. *The Qualitative Report, 10*(1), 178–189.

Mohammed, M., Halai, A., & Karuko, S. (2016). Issues for quality enhancement and harmonization of education in East Africa. In A. Halai & G. Tennant (Eds.), *Mathematics education in East Africa* (pp. 1–8). Aga Khan University Press.

Mosha, H. (2018). The state and quality of education in Tanzania: A reflection. *Papers in Education and Development, 31,* 148–162.

Mugumbate, J., & Chereni, A. (2019). Using African Ubuntu theory in social work with children in Zimbabwe. *African Journal of Social Work, 9*(1), 27–34. https://www.ajol.info/index.php/ajsw/article/view/184222

Mulat, Y. (2013). Indigenous knowledge practices in soil conservation at Konso people, southwestern Ethiopia. *Journal of Agriculture and Environmental Sciences, 2*(2), 1–10.

Ndlovu-Gatsheni, S. (2013). Why decoloniality in the 21st century? *The Thinker, 48,* 10–15.

Ndlovu-Gatsheni, S. (2015). Decoloniality as the future of Africa. *History Compass, 13*(10), 485–496.

Ngara, C. (2007). African ways of knowing and pedagogy revisited. *Journal of Contemporary Issues in Education, 2*(2), 7–20. https://journals.library.ualberta.ca/jcie/index.php/JCIE/article/view/1025

Nyangena, J., Some, K., Kuria, M., Nangulu, A., Kasasa, S., da Costa Vroom, F., ... & Were, M. C. (2022). Developing harmonized benchmarks for the Master of Science in health informatics for the East African Region. *Studies in Health Technology and Informatics (MedInfo 2021).* https://pdf.usaid.gov/pdf_docs/PA00ZQ31.pdf

Nyamnjoh, F. (2012). Potted plants in greenhouses: A critical reflection on the resilience of colonial education in Africa. *Journal of Asian and African Studies, 47*(2), 129–154.

Nyamnjoh, F. (2019). Decolonizing the University in Africa. In N. Cheeseman (Ed.), *Oxford research encyclopedia* (pp. 1–36). Oxford University Press.

Nyenje, A., & James, N. L. (2016). Institutional dynamics of education reforms and quality of primary education in Uganda. *Journal of Education and Practice*, 7(32), 113–122.

Nwanosike, O. F., Onyije, L. E., & Eboh, L. (2011). Colonialism and education. *Mediterranean Journal of Social sciences*, 2(4), 41–47.

Nyerere, J. (1967). *Education for self-reliance*. United Republic of Tanzania.

Nyerere, J. K. (1982). On rural development. *Habitat International*, 6(1–2), 7–14.

Ochieng', W. R. (1989). *A modern history of Kenya 1985–1980*. Evans Brothers Kenya.

Odebero, S. O. (2011). Education inequalities and opportunities in the East African region. *East African Integration*, 51.

Odera Oruka, H. (1990). *Sage philosophy: Indigenous thinkers and modern debate on African philosophy*. Brill.

Ogola, F. O., Njenga, G. N., Mhando, P. C., & Kiggundu, M. N. (2015). A profile of the East African Community. *Africa Journal of Management*, 1(4), 333–364. https://www.tandfonline.com/doi/abs/10.1080/23322373.2015.1106719

Omolewa, M. (2007). Traditional African modes of education: Their relevance in the modern world. *International Review of Education*, 53, 593–612.

Owusu-Ansah, F. E., & Mji, G. (2013). African Indigenous knowledge and research. *African Journal of Disability*, 2(1), 1–5. https://journals.co.za/doi/abs/10.4102/ajod.v2i1.30

Rasekoala, E. (2022). Responsible science communication in Africa: Rethinking drivers of policy, Afrocentricity and public engagement. *Journal of Science Communication*, 21(04), C01. https://jcom.sissa.it/article/pubid/JCOM_2104_2022_C01/

Republic of Kenya (GOK). (1988). *Report of the presidential working party on education and manpower training for the next decade and beyond* (Kamunge Report). Government Printer.

Republic of Kenya. (1999). *Report of the inquiry into the education system of Kenya (TI QET)* (Koech report). Government Printer.

Republic of Uganda, The. (2018). *Comprehensive evaluation of the universal primary education (UPE) policy: Thematic Report 2: Efficacy of the primary school curriculum in supporting the realization of UPE*.

Republic of Uganda, Ministry of Education and Sports, The. (2010). *Primary school curriculum*. https://edumedia-depot.gei.de/bitstream/handle/11163/5417/803267207.pdf?sequence=1

Republic of Uganda, Ministry of Education and Sports, The. (2022a). *Implementation of the abridged curriculum for primary and secondary levels of education*. https://www.mediacentre.go.ug/sites/default/files/media/THE%20REPUBLIC%20OF%20UGANDA.pdf

Republic of Uganda, Ministry of Education and Sports, The. (2022b). *Primary level—Abridged curricula from NCDC*. https://uneb.ac.ug/abridged-curricula-from-ncdc-primary/

Sanga, I. (2016). Education for self-reliance: Nyerere's policy recommendations in the context of Tanzania. *African Research Journal of Education and Social Sciences*, 3. http://arjess.org/education-research/education-for-self-reliance-nyereres-policy-recommendations-in-the-context-of-tanzania.pdf

Shizha, E. (2007). Critical analysis of problems encountered in incorporating Indigenous knowledge in science teaching by primary school teachers in Zimbabwe. *Alberta Journal of Educational Research*, 53(3), 302–319.

Shizha, E. (2008). Indigenous? What Indigenous knowledge? Beliefs and attitudes of rural primary school teachers towards Indigenous knowledge in the science curriculum in Zimbabwe. *The Australian Journal of Indigenous Education, 37*(1), 80–90.

Shockley, K. G., & Frederick, R. M. (2010). Constructs and dimensions of Afrocentric education. *Journal of Black Studies, 40*(6), 1212–1233.

Sifuna, D. N. (1990). *Development of education in Africa: The Kenyan experience.* Initiative Limited.

Sifuna, D. N., & Obonyo, M. M. (2019). Competency based curriculum in primary schools in Kenya -Prospects and challenges of implementation. *Journal of Popular Education in Africa, 3*(7), 39–50.

Sylvester, O. A., & Anthony, O. I. (2014). Decolonization in Africa and Pan-Africanism. *Yönetim Bilimleri Dergisi, 12*(23), 7–31. http://acikerisim.comu.edu.tr/xmlui/bitstream/handle/20.500.12428/770/Ogba_Sylvester_Makale.pdf?sequence=1

Tanzania Institute of Education. (2019). *Curriculum for primary education standard I—VII.* Ministry of Education, Science and Technology. https://www.tie.go.tz/uploads/files/Curriculum%20for%20Primary%20Education%20STD%20I-VII%20English%20Medium%20Schools.pdf

Thomson, N. (2003). Science education researchers as orthographers: Documenting Keiyo (Kenya) knowledge, learning and narratives about snakes. *International Journal of Science Education, 25*(1), 89–115.

Tsindoli, S. (2018). Teachers' perception towards integration of Indigenous knowledge in teaching of mathematical concepts in primary schools in Kenya. *International Journal of Education and Research, 6*(10), 1–14. https://www.ijern.com/journal/2018/October-2018/01.pdf

Uganda National Curriculum Development Center. (2022). *Resources.* https://ncdc.go.ug/resources/

United Nations Educational, Scientific and Cultural Organisation (UNESCO). (2003). *Education in a multicultural world, UNESCO Educational Paper.* Fontenoy.

wa Thiong'o, N. (1986). *Decolonizing the mind: the Politics of language in African literature.* Heinemann.

wa Thiong'o, N. (1992). *Secret lives and other stories.* Heinemann.

Wane, N. (2003). Embu women: Food production and traditional knowledge. *Resources for Feminist Research, 30*(1–2), 137–149.

Wane, N. N. (2006). Is decolonization possible? In G. J. S. Dei & A. Kempf (Eds.), *Anti-colonialism and education* (pp. 87–106). Brill Sense Publishers.

Wane, N. N. (2008). Mapping the field of indigenous knowledges in anti-colonial discourse: A transformative journey in education. *Race Ethnicity and Education, 11*(2), 183–197.

Wane, N., & Chandler, D. J. (2002). African women, cultural knowledge and environmental education with a focus on Kenya's indigenous women. *Canadian Journal of Environmental Education (CJEE)*, 86–98.

World Health Organization. (2002). *Harmonization of undergraduate pharmacy curricula in Southern and Eastern Africa: Future trends: Report of a workshop in Kariba, Zimbabwe,*

8–11 April 2001. WHO/EDM/PAR/2002.4. WHO IRIS. https://apps.who.int/iris/handle/10665/67717

Zavala, M. (2016). Decolonial methodologies in education. In M. A. Peters (Ed.), *Encyclopedia of educational philosophy and theory* (pp. 1–6). Springer. https://doi.org/10.1007/978-981-287-532-7_498-1

· 3 ·

CREATING SPACE FOR AFRICAN INDIGENOUS KNOWLEDGES AND INDIGENEITY IN TEACHING THROUGH COUNTING SONGS IN EARLY CHILDHOOD EDUCATION

Maureen K. Kanchebele-Sinyangwe and Ann E. Lopez

Introduction

Indigenous African music has not received the same primacy in education as Eurocentric music has and concerns are growing that Indigenous African children's songs are disappearing and could be lost (Nompula, 2011). Research has shown that children's literacy development is enhanced when they are grounded in their historical and cultural traditions. Due to colonization Indigenous music and arts education in many countries on the continent of Africa have been viewed in stereotypical ways as backward and as such Western music is still the dominant form of education in the music section of the Arts and Culture curriculum. Indigenous music is an oral tradition that aims to transmit culture, values, beliefs, and history from generation to generation (Nompula, 2011).

This paper examines the role of using songs as a pedagogical tool in Early Childhood Education (ECE) within the African context. Early Childhood Education (ECE) is the foundational stage for formal education and plays a significant role in the introduction of basic learning skills which are relevant for the child's education in the later stages of life. Early Childhood Care, Development and Education (ECCDE) in Zambia focuses on holistic development of children (ZECF, 2013). The ECE curriculum forms the foundation for primary education (National Numeracy Framework 2020; ZECF, 2013) and as such plays an important role in literacy development. Children's oral language and early literacy development serve as an important foundation for later reading abilities and overall academic success in school (Snow et al., 1998). Research has shown that children with low oral language abilities are at risk for poor educational outcomes as they progress through school. Children in ECE are expected to learn through play and songs, and children in ECE in Zambia are expected to be taught through local Indigenous Zambian language as their language of instruction. The Ministry of Education (formerly Ministry of General Education) introduced early childhood education policies focused on using familiar languages as a medium of instruction when teaching all subjects within the Zambian curriculum from ECE to Grade 4' (National Numeracy Framework, 2020). The following is an excerpt from that policy document:

> There is evidence that children learn more easily and successfully through languages that they know and understand well ... Furthermore, the use of ... Zambian language as a medium of instruction will support and aid effective comprehension of numerical and mathematical concepts among learners in the early grades of early childhood to Grade 4. (p. 5)

It is partly against this background and the need to facilitate the development of "interest and curiosity about the environment and nature through mathematics" (NNF, 2020, p. 8) that this study sought to examine whether teaching counting through songs can be made more context specific. Research over the years has shown that some forms of musical activity support and stimulate improvements in intellectual performance, spatial–temporal reasoning and other skills advantageous for learning (Hallam, 2015). For example, studies by Raucher and Hilton (2011) found that children under seven years old who received musical instruction had their numerical skills improved.

Within the Zambian experience at ECE level teaching is largely informal through guided and unguided play (ZECF, 2013). The Curriculum Development Centre (CDC, 2013) suggested the use of songs is one of the key suggested teaching methods in supporting ECE development. For many years, singing what is described as counting songs and the use of number rhymes have helped early childhood educators to teach number concepts to learners. Counting songs and number rhymes are a fun way that children learn through mathematical concepts and skills through repetition. Number songs provide an opportunity to practice counting in a fun and playful way

(Susperreguy et al., 2020). They help to develop number sense, counting and counting skills (King & Purpura, 2021). Further, they give learners an opportunity to learn counting in a variety of ways that include their real-life contexts and draw on their lived experiences. To support children to better understand numbers they are encouraged to count real objects and draw on their experiences and contexts. This should include songs, games and stories (Kesicioglu, 2021). For a long time, due to colonization, children in many countries on the continent of Africa did not value the songs from their local and Indigenous communities and these were not valued in the curriculum. Music permeates into all the various aspects of the lives of Africans. In folk tales or storytelling, Africans have always indulged in music to entertain and recreate themselves, and to challenge injustices and oppression of the Africans, either by the white man or by dictatorial African leaders (Mbaegbu, 2015) and is an important pedagogical tool in the teaching of math especially in the early years.

Trinick et al. (2016) argue that there is an opportunity for developing deeper understanding of underlying mathematical concepts when learners make connections across learning areas, draw on their lived experiences and contexts. As children sing, they are given an opportunity to develop a deeper understanding of the counting concept. This study sought to explore how teaching counting through the use of counting songs could be made more contextual or context specific within Zambia ECE educational curriculum. The following questions guided the study:

1. How are songs included in pedagogy and the number counting to young children?
2. How can local songs to support the teaching of counting be made more context specific?
3. What are the challenges associated with making teaching counting through counting songs more context specific?

Theoretical Framework

African Indigenous knowledge perspectives undergird this study. There is an urgent need to make education on the continent of Africa relevant to its people given the history of colonization and the role education plays. According to Faruqui et al. (2017) up to 40% of children in Sub-Saharan Africa fail to meet basic numeracy and literacy targets that impact their life chances of a productive life and perpetuates a cycle of poverty. The continued reliance in elementary and secondary education on models left by the colonizers has thwarted progress. In education systems across Sub-Saharan African countries not much has changed in the curricula since they gained independence from colonial rule in the 1960s and many of them still retain colonial legacies (Falola, 2020). Given the demands of a new generation calling for greater relevance of education grounded in African ways of knowing. For Africans and other colonized populations, colonialism was a psycho-cultural and educational process that disparaged African knowledge, rendered Africa and Africans as ahistorical, uneducated, and underdeveloped (Abdi, 2020, Rodney, 1982). Abdi (2020) states, "This discrediting of Africa on the historical, educational, and developmental fronts also carried the denial of its philosophical and educational philosophy achievements which formed the continent's livelihood and learning dynamism and trajectories. . . . And contrary to European misreading and demeaning of African traditional education, different types of learning and practices were contextually conceived and designed for needs of the community" (pp. 202–205). As Abdi further argues precolonial traditional African education was well endowed with communally constructed systems of teaching and learning. More and more educators, policy makers and community members are coming to realize that an education system grounded in colonialism will not serve the students of Africa, a youth population that is growing the fastest in the world, and its own future development. There needs to be an improvement in the quality of education at all levels starting with early childhood education.

There are growing calls in many African countries including Zambia for rethinking education drawing on local Indigenous knowledges. African educational researchers, educators, and educational policymakers need to rethink ways of re-centering local Indigenous ways of knowing and African epistemologies in African spaces of teaching and learning (Abdi, 2020). Indigenous knowledge in the form of culture represented through songs, storytelling is also a process of generating a national identity and as Coe (2020) argues when African countries promote Indigenous knowledge schools and education are usually involved. According to Coe, "[African] Indigenous knowledge or culture is historical involving town and family history as well as ritual practices and wisdom of the ancestors and elders" (p. 220). Coe argues further that the incorporation of Indigenous knowledge into schools involves three transformations to the meaning, communicative form, and content of that knowledge and to the local hierarchical relationships between young people and adults. These include: (1) experiential knowledge about cultural practices is codified and systemized as it becomes part of school knowledge; (2) construction of cultural practices as cultural knowledge to be taught in schools; and (3) creating space where relationships between teachers and students are negotiated.

The power of colonizing knowledge and the potential to take hold in schooling practices must be challenged (Lopez, 2021). African Indigenous opens space in education and schooling for new forms of knowledge and ways of learning. Dei (2017) argues educators must question Western philosophies and colonial discourses, repositioning African people as holders and custodians of territorial and cultural rights and not subjects of Euro-colonial knowledges. As such Indigenous African knowledge can be conceptualized as home-grown knowledge, about the ways local peoples have understood their presence on the Land and how they function in their everyday lives (Dei, 2014; Gumbo, 2017) and we argue this includes education and schooling.

Methodology

The study examines how teaching counting using counting songs in early childhood education in Zambia can be made more contextual and context specific. The study employed a qualitative research paradigm which examines phenomena in their natural settings and attempts to make sense of it (Denzin & Lincoln, 2017). The study is also informed by the interpretivism paradigm Vygotsky's (1978) sociocultural context framework. Better understanding of human thoughts and actions requires researchers to consider sociocultural contexts. Purposeful sampling (Msabila & Nalaila, 2013) was used to select the research study participants. Participants in the study included five student teachers who were in a cohort for Distance Education Early Childhood Education Degree at a University located in the central region of Zambia. The participants were all females and who had prior teaching experience. They enrolled in the program to upgrade their teaching qualifications from Diploma to Degree. The participants had prior teaching experiences in the early years that were in keeping with the goals of the study. Their experiences provided a platform for contextualizing the teaching of counting through counting songs, as well as exploring and developing possibilities of including local Indigenous knowledges.

Data were collected using semi-structured interviews (Creswell, 2013) and document analysis (Corbin & Strauss, 2008). Semi-structured interviews allow researchers to collect open-ended data, explore thoughts, feelings and beliefs about a particular issue (Josselson, 2013). Document analysis allows for deeper understanding of the phenomenon and is often used in conjunction with other qualitative research methods (Bowen, 2009). The documents reviewed were the students' written songs that they sang during the teaching of counting in math classes. Data analysis involved coding reading and rereading of participants' narratives using open, axial, and selective coding for themes.

Findings

The findings are discussed below in response to the research questions that guided the study. The findings from the data revealed that children knew more counting songs in English than for example Bemba, one of the local languages spoken widely in Zambia. Most of the songs shared in class were in English with very few in the local language and that songs in English in particular, were easily accepted and easily accessible than songs in local languages. This speaks to the ongoing influence of colonization on education systems in Zambia, and one could argue in most African countries. In exploring the kinds of songs, the participants used in their classes when teaching counting, the study revealed that they paid attention not only to the rhythm of the song but the lyrics. The songs the student teachers engaged the students in counting included both recorded songs and those written down on paper. The chart below shows the songs included in English, local language, and both. Of the 26 songs, four were in local languages, 21 in English, and in one in both languages. This shows the predominance of Eurocentric knowledge that still dominates in teaching and learning.

Participants (pseudonyms)	Songs and mode of sharing of the song	Language		
		English	Local	Both English and local
P1—Tiwonge	5 written down songs	4	1	—
P2—Mutinta	4 Audio recorded songs	3	—	1
P3—Mukuma	8 Audio recorded songs	6	2	

CREATING SPACE FOR AFRICAN INDIGENOUS KNOWLEDGES

Participants (pseudonyms)	Songs and mode of sharing of the song	Language		
		English	Local	Both English and local
P4—Lushomo	3 Audio recorded songs and 3 written down	5	1	
P5—Thandiwe	3 Audio recorded	3	–	
Total	26	21	4	1

Participant Mutinta noted, "I know more counting songs in English than I know in Bemba" while Mukuma stated, "I am more comfortable with singing the songs that are in English than the ones that are in the local language." This speaks to the need for African Indigenous knowledge in schools where both teachers and students learn to decenter Eurocentric knowledge and center African tradition. The student teachers also indicated that songs in English were more readily accepted than local ones and this made it easier to work use with the students and that could be because, "that is what we are used to singing … the songs in English … they are easier to find and easier to sing … that is what we know, what others know and they are a lot easier to share, easier to sing than the local ones …". The effects of colonization on culture and traditions cannot be underestimated. One of the many sites of decolonization of education in Africa is for schools to engage in the cultural custodians of local cultural knowledge (Dei, 2020).

During the interviews, participants shared their views about the nature or forms of songs as well as the words making up the songs. Participant Thandiwe noted:

> Songs such as "man and a dog walking to Lusaka" do not mean much … in terms of the words used. They don't share real issues happening here in Zambia … people generally take buses, but it is like we want the learners to believe they walk and walk with dogs to Lusaka.

Another participant, Lushomo argued, "songs that include phrases like 'catching a fish alive', or 'buckle my shoe' are fun to sing but I am not sure the learners in towns for example even know what it means to catch a fish alive from the river or a lake … or whether the child in the deep rural areas of Zambia knows what a shoe with a buckle looks like and what to buckle one's shoes really means."

Based on the data collected and analyzed, it was evident that the counting songs commonly sung were generally in a foreign and not in Indigenous language. The National Numeracy Framework (NNF) recognizing the importance and relevance of local language and culture states that songs and rhymes in local languages that enhance teaching and learning are highly recommended while suggesting English for grade two and up. The NFF states, "From ECE ... songs and rhymes, in the local languages that enhance teaching and learning are highly recommended so that they tally with the language of instruction at this level and that songs in English are highly recommended for grade two upwards when oral English would have been introduced" (NNF, 2020, p. 30). Singing more songs and rhymes in English than in Indigenous local language does not align with current Zambia Education Curriculum Framework (2013) and language guidelines given regarding the medium of instruction for children in ECE. Additionally, it is argued that Indigenous songs "are an integral part of the children's cultural heritage" (Campbell, 1991, p. 14). Not including the Indigenous songs in teaching children counting can negatively affect or distort children's cultural heritage as they sing songs that preschool children cannot personally identify with based on their context and experiences.

Singing has a role to play in exposing children to a wide range of vocabulary and to helping children develop language skills (Sarrazin, 2016). This implies that learners have opportunities to learn a wide variety of vocabulary as they sing the counting songs. However, when the content of the song is foreign and largely overlooking the rich environments surrounding the learners, it can contribute to alienating learners from their environment. wa Thiong'o (1986) argues that this kind of education alienates one from their own local and Indigenous knowledge and language. David and Ozakai (2006) present a similar argument and suggest that the consideration of the superior standing of English language against Indigenous language and its dominant use could contribute to one devaluing their Indigenous language and shunning their Indigenous roots. There is a need to make the knowledge in counting songs be more relevant, more representative of the real experiences of diverse learners and representative of different their cultures, languages, identities, and histories (Tikly, 2021). Meaningfulness and relevance of the counting songs and words to learners' lived experiences is advocated. Not paying particular attention to the selection of the song content contributes to creating a weak foundation for future learning of vocabulary in Indigenous language and language skills in general, as well as lack of or no appreciation of one's local environment.

In terms of efforts to make teaching counting through counting songs more context-specific the findings revealed that participants were intentional in seeking spaces to act in their agency and actively search out opportunities. They looked for songs that children were receptive to singing and that supported the curriculum goals. In terms of children's receptiveness to singing participants noted that children are generally willing and open to learning through songs, liked and enjoy singing. Participant Mukuma noted, "children are excited about singing . . . this makes it easier to teach through songs" while Lushomo said, "It is fun for children to sing . . . we need to give them a chance to continue enjoying themselves in singing as we teach . . . especially singing about things their little minds can easily understand." Mutinta noted, "I find that singing is a way of playing for the children . . . they love it and one can see this in the way they dance and stretch their small bodies to follow through with the activities that go with the songs."

Relevance to the curriculum offered an avenue to make counting songs more context specific by connecting to broad curriculum goals and expectations. Mukama noted, "the curriculum recognizes singing songs when teaching the little ones . . . probably because the curriculum designers acknowledge singing makes learning fun and it is good for helping children with their learning." While Mutinta said "singing and counting songs is part of learning counting . . . and it is there in the curriculum . . . preschoolers learn better through play. Singing . . . is part of play. They cannot learn counting without it . . . it is there in the curriculum and so by singing we are putting the curriculum to real life." The data revealed children enjoyed singing songs in keeping with findings of Sarrazin (2016) who argues that singing is fun for children and can at the same time be highly educational. Early years are important years in a child's development and what happens to a child in these years can affect their physical development, mental development, and success in life (Li, 2023). It is best to seize every opportunity during this stage of children's lives to facilitate the acquisition and development of fundamental concepts and process skills in mathematics through active involvement with their environment (Lind, 1998). Liao & Campbell (2016) urge that "an understanding of the nature of the songs by and for children, their . . . contextual components can illuminate their use in the education of young children' about school related content and their cultural heritage". This suggests that a critical reflection of counting songs, the words making up the counting songs could be a starting point toward making counting more meaningful and relevant to the already receptive children.

There are challenges associated with making teaching counting through counting songs more context specific. This included attitude and mindset, acceptability, and accessibility, as well as ability with respect to singing, composing, or translating counting number songs. Attitude and mindset toward singing local songs posed challenges with making teaching counting through counting songs more context specific. Participant Tiwonge noted, "I don't think it is as fun to sing in the local language as it is to sing the songs in English . . . . Counting songs which are in English seem to sound better and classy . . . one singing such presents to be very educated . . ." This speaks to the ongoing influence of colonization that erased and devalued Indigenous knowledge. The power of colonizing knowledge to take hold and move through generations is evident in. schooling practices and what is valued (Lopez, 2021). The manifestations of settler colonialism in education is the stripping away from local communities their identities and forms of cultural initiation.

Acceptability and accessibility of songs proved to be a challenge in making teaching counting through counting songs more context-specific due in part to the ability to locate songs, especially local songs. Thandiwe noted that "English songs are easier to learn than local ones. I can easily find them than those songs that are in the local language." Mutinta noted that she had, "learnt the counting songs in English while at college and these are the ones I teach, not the ones in local languages."

There were also challenges encountered with the inability to sing counting songs in local languages. Lushomo noted that "I struggle with the counting songs in the local language . . . I would rather stick to the ones in English . . . I would rather spend my time perfecting singing counting songs in English than start learning the ones in the local language because I know it will be a real struggle." This is the result of the undervaluing of local knowledge in the education system due to colonization and the superiority of English in education and schooling. There was also a desire to draw on counting songs that already exist and those oftentimes were in English. Some participants thought it was too challenging to create new songs in local languages, "It is difficult to make songs . . . too much hard work for nothing . . . I just want to sing the songs that are there . . . the ones that are in English" (Mukama). Tiwonge noted that she was not trained to compose in the local language "I am not able to do it . . . I am not trained to compose songs, not even translating . . . it is not as straightforward as some would think." There were also challenges in translating counting songs in English into the local language, "I don't think I can do this translation thing from English to a local language . . . it would be very difficult for me especially that I am not even that good in Tonga". Tonga is one of the seven main local languages in Zambia.

Participants' mindset about the pedagogy of singing counting songs in local languages may be aligned with the view that English language is superior to local language, a view held by many and the prominence that English is given in assessment. It could be participants' inability to communicate in various local languages. While the MOE expectation is that learners from ECE be taught using the local language as a medium of instruction, some teachers still prefer to use English. This preference could be because of a state of mind where what is Western is considered the best or superior. The conflict between what is being implemented by the teachers in this case and what is recommended by the Ministry of Education remains an unresolved issue. Ways of developing a positive realization of the complementary roles of Indigenous languages and English is crucial (Adegbite, 2003) in the teaching and learning context. The findings of the study show that songs in English are more acceptable, easily accessible and are generally considered superior to local Indigenous ones. As earlier stated, this contributes to teachers and student teachers devaluing their Indigenous language and shunning their Indigenous roots (David & Ozakai, 2006). The NNF (2020) acknowledges the challenges raised under the themes of accessibility and ability to sing, compose, and translate songs in local languages and suggests that, "there are still a lot of local songs ... that can help teach, but they have not been documented" (p. 30). The recommendation by NNF is that teachers need to take advantage of such songs, even if they may not have been documented, but contain approved language and procedure used in that given environment.

Analysis of the data reveals that there is not a single challenge to using local songs in counting songs in ECE in Zambia, but a combination of challenges associated with making teaching counting through counting songs more context specific. The choice of counting songs to sing remains a teacher's responsibility and as such they have influence not only on pedagogy but curriculum. Teachers have the freedom, and agency to choose songs that are age, content, and context-appropriate, that are relevant and meaningful to learners' lives and experiences. This creates space for the intentional inclusion of Indigenous songs drawing on children's cultural heritage. It is imperative that teacher education programs and policymakers in Zambia decolonized the curriculum centering African Indigenous knowledge. Dei (2020) argues: In the broader politics of new educational futurity, we must be able to place certain ideas on the table informed by the teaching of African Indigeneity and Indigenous knowledges: First, there is need for a critical reflection on our practice as educators, both individually and collectively ... the urgency of engaging in subversive pedagogies, asking new decolonial questions, thinking through classroom teaching practices that center (not merely include) counter texts, books, and discourses. The curriculum must embrace the idea of co-creation of knowledge where we work with our students and their off-school, street, and community knowledges, as well as cultivating a place for Elders and their cultural knowledges in the school system (p. 291).

As many decolonial scholars argue education and schooling is a site of contestation in the anti-colonial struggle for freedom and justice, and no place like pedagogy and curriculum.

Conclusion

This study sought to explore whether teaching counting through counting songs could be made more contextual or context specific. The specific questions asked were: (1) How are songs included in pedagogy and the number counting to young children? (2) How can local songs to support the teaching of counting be made more context specific? (3) What are the challenges associated with making teaching counting through counting songs more context specific? The findings show that songs in English, and not local language, have dominated and generally shaped knowledge of counting and counting songs. The content of the counting songs is, "somewhat foreign" and generally overlooking the rich local environments surrounding the learners, contributing to alienating learners from their local environment and context. The findings also reveal that opportunities to make teaching counting through counting songs more context specific exist. These include children's receptiveness to singing as a way for learning as well as the broad curriculum goals and expectations. Further, the study has shown that there are challenges and a combination of challenges associated with making teaching counting through counting songs more context specific. These include, attitude and mindset, accessibility and acceptability related issues as well as limited ability such as that associated with linking the content of the counting songs to what learners could personally identify. The study recommends that both capacity and resource constraints need to be addressed in the process of Indigenization and contextualizing at the level of teaching counting through counting songs in ECE in Zambia. While the research was conducted in Zambia there are implications of other African countries as they seek to make education more relevant to them and throw away the legacies of colonial education that has not served the continent in developing a sustainable future for its people.

References

Abdi, A. A. (2020). Reconstructing African philosophies of education: Historical and contemporary analyses. In J. M. Abidogun & T. Falola (Eds.), *The Palgrave handbook of African education and indigenous knowledge* (pp. 201–213). Palgrave Macmillan.

Adegbite, W. (2003). Enlightenment and attitudes of the Nigerian elite on the roles of languages in Nigeria. *Language Culture and Curriculum, 16*(2), 185–196.

Bowen, G. (2009). Document analysis as a qualitative research method. *Qualitative Research Journal, 9*(2), 26–40.

Campbell, D. J. (1991). Goal levels, complex tasks, and strategy development: A review and analysis. Human Performance, 4(1), 1–31.

Coe, C. (2020). African Indigenous knowledge: African state formation, and education. In Reconstructing African philosophies of education: Historical and contemporary analyses. In J. M. Abidogun & T. Falola (Eds.), *The Palgrave handbook of African Education and indigenous knowledge* (pp. 215–222). Palgrave Macmillan.

Corbin, J. and Strauss, A. (2008) Basics of Qualitative Research: Techniques and Procedures for Developing Grounded Theory. Sage, Thousand Oaks.

David, E. J. R., & Okazaki, S. (2006). Colonial mentality: A review and recommendation for Filipino American psychology. *Cultural Diversity and Ethnic Minority Psychology, 12*(1), 1.

Dei, G. J. S. (2014). African Indigenous Proverbs and the instructional and pedagogic relevance for youth education: Lessons from the Kiembu of Kenya and Igbo of Nigeria. *Journal of Education and Training, 1*(1), 1–28.

Dei, G. J. S. (2017). *Reframing Blackness and Black solidarities through anti-colonial and decolonial prisms*. Springer.

Dei, G. J. S. (2020). Elders' cultural knowledges and African Indigeneity. In J. M. Abidogun & T. Falola (Eds.), *The Palgrave handbook of African education and indigenous knowledge* (pp. 279–301). Palgrave Macmillan.

Creswell, J. W. (2013). *Qualitative inquiry and research design: Choosing among five approaches*. SAGE Publications.

Denzin, N. K., & Lincoln, Y. S. (2017). *The SAGE handbook of qualitative research* (5 ed.). SAGE Publishing.

Falola, T. (2020). Introduction to Africa's wealth. In J. M. Abidogun & T. Falola (Eds.), *The Palgrave handbook of African education and indigenous knowledge* (pp. 3–38). Palgrave Macmillan.

Faruqui, D., Laad, S., Abdo, M., & Thapar, P. (2017). *Is private education in Africa the solution to a failing education aid? Stanford Social Intervention Review: Informing and Inspiring Leaders of Social Change*.

Gumbo, M. T. (2017). Alternative knowledge systems. In J. Williams & K. Stables (Eds.), *Contemporary issues in technology education: Critique in design and technology education* (pp. 87–105). Springer.

Hallam, S. (2015). *The Power of Music: A research synthesis of the impact of actively making music on intellectual, social and personal development of children and young people*. International Music Education Research Centre.

Josselson, R. (2013). *Interviewing for qualitative inquiry: A relational approach*. Guilford Press.

Kesicioglu, O. S. (2021). Investigating of counting skills of preschool children. *International Journal of Progressive Education, 17*(4), 262–281.

King, Yemimah, A & Purpura, David J. (2021): Direct numeracy activities and early math skills: Math language as a mediator, Early Childhood Research Quarterly, Volume 54, Pages 252–259.

Li, P. (2023). *Formative years—why are they important in child development?* https://www.parentingforbrain.com/formative-years/

Liao, M. Y., & Campbell, P. S. (2016). Teaching children's songs: A Taiwan—US comparison of approaches by kindergarten teachers. *Music Education Research, 18*(1), 20–38.

Lind, K. K. (1998). *Science in early childhood: Developing and acquiring fundamental concepts and skills*.

Lopez, A. E. (2021). *Decolonizing educational leadership: Exploring alternative approaches to leading schools*. Palgrave MacMillan.

Msabila, D. T., & Nalaila, S. G. (2013). *Research proposal and dissertation writing: Principles and practice*. Nyambari Nyangwine Publishers.

Mbaegbu, C. C. (2015). The effective power of music in Africa. *Open Journal of Philosophy, 5*, 176–183.

National Numeracy Framework 2020; ZECF, 2013

Nompula, Y. (2011). Valorising the voice of the marginalised: exploring the value of African music in education. *South African Journal of Education, 41*, 369–380.

Prakash, Madhu Suri & Esteva, Gustavo (2008); Escaping Education: Living as Learning in Grassroots Cultures (2nd Edition) (New York: Peter Lang Publishing)

Rauscher, F. H., & Hinton, S. C. (2011). Music instruction and its diverse extra-musical benefits. *Music Perception, 29*(2), 215–226.

Rodney, W. (1982). *How Europe underdeveloped Africa*. Howard University Press.

Snow, C. E., Burns, M. S., & Griffin, P. (1998). *Preventing reading difficulties in young children*. National Academy Press.

Saldana, J. (*2013*). The Coding Manual for Qualitative Researchers (2nd ed.). London: Sage.

Sarrazin, N. (2016). *Music and the child*. Open SUNY Textbooks.

Silverman, S. (2015). The colonized mind: Gender, trauma, and mentalization. *Psychoanalytic Dialogues, 25*(1), 51–66.

Susperreguy, M. I., Douglas, H., Xu, C., Molina-Rojas, N., & LeFevre, J. A. (2020). Expanding the home numeracy model to Chilean children: Relations among parental expectations, attitudes, activities, and children's mathematical outcomes. *Early Childhood Research Quarterly, 50*, 16–28.

Tikly, L. (2021). Racial formation and education in England: A critical analysis of the Sewell report. *Ethnicities, 22*(6), 857–881.

Trinick, R., Ledger, G., Major, K., & Perger, P. (2016). More than counting beats: Connecting music and mathematics in the primary classroom. *International Journal for Mathematics Teaching and Learning, 17*(3).

Wa Thiong'o, N. (1986). The Writer in a neocolonial state. *The Black Scholar, 17*(4), 2–10.

Wiredu, K. (2005). On the idea of a global ethic. *Journal of Global Ethics,* 1(1), 45–51.

Vygotsky, L. (1978). *Mind in society: the development of higher psychological processes*. Harvard University Press.

Zambia Education Curriculum Framework. (2013). CDC.

· 4 ·

INTEGRATING INDIGENOUS KNOWLEDGE INTO SUB-SAHARAN AFRICAN SCHOOLS: CURRICULUM TRANSFORMATION FOR SOCIO-ECONOMIC FREEDOM AND MAINTENANCE OF AFRICAN IDENTITIES

Kofi Poku Quan-Baffour

Introduction

The socio-economic and political advancement of any society is completely tied to relevant education. This realization that education is a tool for development encourages governments to open schools to equip their citizens with relevant quality knowledge and skills for better life and to contribute to the socio-economic development of their respective communities and countries. Quality education is defined here as the kind of school learning that makes its graduates productive citizens. The value of quality education therefore cannot be overemphasized as it equips citizens with the relevant knowledge, skills, and values for better life and adequate contribution to the socio-economic development of their respective communities and countries. As Whitehead (1962, p. 2) affirms:

> Education should aim at producing people who possess both culture and expert knowledge in some special direction. Their expert knowledge will give them the ground to start from, and their culture will lead them as deep as philosophy and as high as art.

Western [formal school] education was introduced to Africa over four hundred years ago by the colonialists in cahoots with the missionaries. School education was not established by the colonialists and missionaries as a favor for the *natives* but to enhance the exploitation of the continent's human and natural resources and for the evangelization to convert the so-called *savage* and the *heathen* to Christianity. Apart from the Christian interests, missionary education had economic importance to the expansion of trade and the administration of the colonies. In line with this motive, education the school curriculum was skewed towards the production of half-baked educated *natives* to serve as messengers and interpreters for the self-imposed colonial administration and to win souls for Christ. Datta (1987) attests that in content the colonial and missionary education had a definite European bias and had a heavier stress on liberal arts to the neglect of vocational, technological, and professional instructions. Christianity and education went together, with the general belief that the most rudimentary knowledge of the 3 Rs was necessary for conversion to Christianity (p. 16). This kind of education which is devoid of practical knowledge for job creation does not serve the development and emancipation agenda of contemporary Sub-Saharan Africa because it is education for socio-economic frustration and retardation. With the arrival of colonialism all African systems of learning and modes of development were derided as useless and not fit to be used. During the colonial era all the reliable and tested African projects of learning were perforce rescinded from all learning contexts, and European education, languages, educational philosophies, and epistemologies were imposed on the colonized populations (Abdi, 2011). Thus, education, culture and alien way of life were imposed on the being of the persona Africans. The formal school education as inherited from the colonialists does not suit the needs of contemporary Sub-Saharan Africa hence the continent must re-assert itself by transforming it to obtain the kind of education that prepares its products to be job creators who can contribute to economic growth and not seekers of jobs. In citing Spencer (1861), Curzon, (1990) has this to say, "To prepare us for complete living is the function which education has to discharge and the only rational mode of judging of educational course is to judge in what degree it discharges such function."

Contrary to the noble aims of education as noted above, the postcolonial school curriculum does not adequately prepare Africans for a better living; instead, it churns out in their droves *job hunters* and not job creators. Despite this appalling situation African education policymakers somehow missed the crucial point that colonial education was not going to develop Africa as it was designed and implemented with the intention to underdevelop it. The formal school systems and their learning experiences have not been Africanized by our leaders and policy makers and we still mimic the West with regards to education provision. As Abdi (2011) appropriately points out, one of the main plunders of the postcolonial African elite was the continuation of colonial philosophies and epistemologies as the main definers of education and development in the continent. The postcolonial situation continued to be dominated by the colonial curriculum, colonial languages and colonial structuring and distribution of educational resources.

The outmoded school curriculum based on imperialist philosophies cannot liberate Africa from its current socio-economic and political doldrums. It is time we, Africans, re-looked at what should be done to make school education more relevant to our current socio-economic situation and interests. Political and socio-economic emancipation for Africa's true and sustainable renaissance requires education which is based on Indigenous philosophies of the continent and its people. School education must not continue to churn out passive consumers and technocrats of the apparent stagnant socio-economic contexts of today's Africa. There is a need for emancipation and the need to change the way in which we regard knowledge (Higgs & Letseka, 2022) and its production through school education. Our formal school learning should be contextualized to make it relevant to its recipients and their communities. Nyerere (1968, p. 268) appropriately states that the educational systems in different kinds of the world have been, and are, very different in organization and content. They are different because the societies providing the education are different, and because education, whether it is formal or informal, has a purpose. The [main] purpose is to transmit from one generation to the next, the accumulated wisdom and knowledge of society, and to prepare the young for their future membership of that society and their active participation in its maintenance and development.

The above affirms my claim that we need to decolonize education through the Africanization of the curriculum of our schools to make education more relevant to our current socio-economic needs and context. In the context of developing countries, most people believe that school education would eradicate poverty, but the current economic crisis demonstrates that education is not living up to expectation (van Niekerk, 2013) because as pointed out in this discussion it does not equip learners with job creation knowledge and skills. An African-centered education system may not only open people's eyes to the subtle tactics of the oppressor and the exploiter but can decolonize the minds of educated Africans and equip them with the relevant knowledge and skills for self-employment. The lack of transformation in the Sub-Saharan African school curriculum has created a general perception among the youth, parents, and some community members that all citizens who complete school should seek work from the government, instead of creating their own jobs. One may argue that to some extent, the perception of youth or parents can be valid because of governments' inability to transform the school curriculum since political independence. This book chapter advocates for the practical transformation of the African school curriculum to secure socio-economic freedom and maintain African values and identity. To achieve the above, we need to make a *backward gaze* to our Indigenous philosophies and knowledge to reclaim those that are very relevant and integrate them into the school curriculum to speed up decolonization, enhance job creation and maintenance of our African identities. The thesis of the chapter is that Africa's socio-economic and political regeneration and emancipation depend on appropriate school curriculum brewed in an African pot and unless we decolonize our school system and its curriculum our socio-economic emancipation will remain a dream. As Magesa (1997) remarks, "No sane society chooses to build its future on foreign cultures, values and systems. Every society is obliged to search deep into its own history, culture, religion and morality in order to discover the values upon which its development and liberation, its civilization and identity should be based. To do otherwise is nothing less than communal suicide" (p. 9).

Chapter Objectives

The chapter was crafted to:

1. Advocate for the integration of African Indigenous knowledge, skills, and values into the Sub-Saharan African school curriculum.
2. Emphasize the importance of education transformation to make school education relevant to the socio-economic realities of today's Sub-Saharan Africa.
3. Conscientize Africans the need to reject the legacy of colonial education because of its anti-African-ness.

Indigenous Education in Precolonial Africa

Education, which is the process of imparting relevant knowledge, skills, and values for individuals to play a productive role in their respective communities has been an important institution in human life since time immemorial in all kinds of societies. In its broader sense, education covers both informal and formal training and induction of people into the social, economic, and political life of their respective communities and societies. Before colonization and the arrival of the missionaries there was an Indigenous form of education in Africa which worked very well for the African people in their specific contexts. The Indigenous education fitted the context and realities of the African people as it produced all-round citizens who were never in want of work. Indeed, it is through this form of learning that Africans have thrived and managed their lives since time immemorial. From both historical and contemporaneous terms, African education was steeped in Indigenous philosophies that were not necessarily structured as Europe's but were put into place to serve the situation-specific needs of the African people (Abdi, 2011). The Indigenous or traditional education prepared the youth for meaningful family and community life before the advent of colonization and its concomitant Western school education. I argue that education is broader than literacy [reading and writing] and formal schooling. Therefore, it is invalid for anyone to think that education was started in Africa by the colonialists and their missionary collaborators. If education is just literacy and numeracy, then one would be right to say it was brought from the West by the colonialists and the missionaries, but education is more than schooling. In precolonial times education was pragmatic and prepared the children for life because there was no separation of education and the socio-economic endeavors of people. The Indigenous education which was socially most effective learning systems shaped the developmental and general life management schemes of the African people (Abdi, 2011).

In most cases however, knowledge acquisition was cyclical in that the same crafts or profession were transferred from one generation to the other within a family or a community. The aim of education in precolonial Africa was to inculcate in the youth, economic knowledge, skills and values for better living and preservation of African identity.

While the emphasis on girls' education was on homemaking, knitting, gardening and good manners, the boy child learned practical job-oriented skills such as farming, gold and blacksmithing, weaving, cobbling, sculpturing and local customs to socialize them into manhood and good citizens. Much of the education took the form of apprenticeships where young men were attached to accomplished tradesmen in their respective communities for a few years to learn specific skills through observation and doing. Education was useful and critical for the socio-economic life of Africans before the advent of colonization, colonialism and its concomitant Western school education that eclipsed Indigenous job-oriented education. I emphatically say that if our Indigenous education was allowed to co-exist with or integrated into the Western formal schooling, Sub-Saharan Africa would be at par with most of the so-called first-world economies. The imposition of Western philosophies, theories, and knowledge [education] complemented by the denial that the ancient continent had any philosophy of education has done much damage as any other project of the imperial enterprise (Abdi, 2011). Putting it more succinctly, the ontological and epistemological colonization of Africa led to the ongoing de-development of the continent (Rodney, 2009).

Eclipse of Indigenous Knowledge by Western Schooling System: Consequences and Call for Curriculum Transformation

The colonial formal schooling system did not integrate African Indigenous knowledge, skills, values, and sensibilities into learning experiences because they were deemed backward and to avoid competition with Europeans for decent jobs. Rodney (2009, p. 293) affirms that "the main purpose of colonial school was to train Africans to help man the local administration at the lowest ranks and the capitalist firms owned by Europeans." I argue that its other aim was to protect European-made goods and services through the stifling of Africa's Indigenous industrialization. Furthermore, education was used to colonize the minds of Africans to pour scorn on their own values and to see everything European as the best. The colonial and the missionary school education rejected, overshadowed, and eclipsed African Indigenous knowledge and the traditional education system because of their ignorance of Africa and its people. The following statement from Hegel (1965) affirms how the colonialists and the missionary's lacked knowledge and respect for *persona Africana*; Africa is in a state of barbarism and savagery which is preventing him from being an integral part of civilization (p. 247). With this wrong perception the goal of colonial and missionary education was to *civilize* the *savage* Africans through school education. In pursuance of this *civilization of the savage* agenda, formal school, as Wolhuter (2000, p. 14) intones, educated the Indigenous populations outside the context of their own cultures and environment. Schools were used to serve colonial interests: the quantity and quality of education that colonial administrations were prepared to supply were just enough to train staff for auxiliary and subsidiary positions such as clerks, interpreters, and preachers.

The consequence of educating Africans outside their context was that they lost most of their Indigenous technical knowledge and skills such as sculpturing, brewing, smith works, food processing, sewing, knitting, leather works, pottery moulding and handicrafts. Technically and for all pragmatic undertakings, this is nothing short of an organized attempt in the total dehumanization of everything African (Abdi, 2011). The Indigenous knowledge system which was marginalized during the colonial era has better knowledge, skills, and values which when re-integrated into our current school system may not only enhance job creation and economic development and freedom but can also ensure the Africanization of education in Sub-Sahara Africa.

The schools established by the colonizers were isolated from the so-called "pagan" influences (McWilliam & Kwamena-Poh, 1975) because of the misunderstanding of African cultures which emphasized communalism. Akua (2020) asserts that the traditional African values were replaced with alien values that served alien interests, including hyper-individualism lack of respect for Black life and culture, distrust of other Black people and Black ideas. Anti-African, self-destructive and anti-human values. Recounting his own experience of how the colonial school education isolated its products from their African communal life, Busia (1969) had this to say,

> At the end of my first year at the secondary school (Mfantsipim, Cape Coast), I went home to Wenchi for Christmas vacation. I had not been home for four years, and on that visit, I became painfully aware of my isolation. I understood our community far less than the boys of my own age who had never been to school.
>
> Over the years as I went through College and University, I felt increasingly that the education I received taught me more and more about Europe and less and less about my own society.

Colonial education sought to destroy everything African—languages, Indigenous knowledge, skills, values, religion, and culture. It aimed at making African-educated people Europeans in black skins, people who would look down upon their own culture as backward. wa Thiongo (2005) attests that the educational terrain, especially the de-Africanization of that terrain, has affirmed the processes of mental colonization that are still afflicting the lives of Africans. Colonial education discouraged African industrialization efforts as a strategy to protect European markets and to ensure Africa's continuous dependence on the West. It was for this reason that the colonial education system did not integrate African Indigenous knowledge, skills, and values into the formal schools to teach new ways that could enhance and expand agro-based industries such as the production and processing of food for preservation and export all Indigenous technologies and skills for processing food, manufacturing of farm tools, iron, clothes, sandals, alcoholic drinks. The destruction of everything African was too overwhelming hence Wiredu (2005) summed it up that colonialism was not only a political imposition but also cultural one.

Although Sub-Saharan African countries gained political independence from the 1950s, they have not attained economic freedom largely because of the legacy of poor and unresponsive school curriculum which they have not been able to significantly transform to match the current needs of the African people. Davidson (1992) asserts that in their rush to liberation and their alienation from African culture which they viewed as savage and primitive, African leaders constructed their new nation-states on European models imposed on them by departing colonial authorities. This has created lots of socio-economic and political problems of which solutions must be envisaged within a historical framework, an Indigenous historical framework, no matter what contribution an external world may have made (p. 2). Most of our leaders pay mere lip service to decolonization of the school curriculum.

The transformation of the school curriculum has therefore become political rhetoric which explains the huge unemployment situation in the region and its concomitant crime, political instability, and exodus of the youth to Europe via dangerous means. Nyerere (1968) affirms that Africa's stunted progress in the past two centuries could be traced back to those moments when people's learning and social development platforms were deliberately destroyed by the colonial forces. To re-assert ourselves, socio-economically and politically we need to be pragmatic to revisit our Indigenous philosophies and knowledge systems, including our technologies, skills and values and incorporate them into the school curriculum to make education more relevant to our African contexts. As Odora Hoppers (2011, p. 15) appropriately points out, "when piles of unanswered questions heap up outside our door, it is time to undertake some radical action to unblock some of those blockages and release some of the knots to clear the 'nasal' passage."

The discussion here describes the concept curriculum as the planned teaching and learning activities for which an educational institution or the school is responsible. It covers all that is considered important to be taught to learners and represents the distilled thinking of society on what it wants to achieve through education. It spells out knowledge, skills and values a particular society considers useful for its development (Quan-Baffour, 2000). I submit that the learning experiences provided by the African school today must integrate Indigenous knowledge, skills, values, and relevant exotic knowledge to complement our school education. My view of decolonization of the school curriculum is a pragmatic one that seeks to intermesh the most relevant alien courses with our Indigenous knowledge, skills, and values to make school education more Africanized and more relevant to our current socio-economic and political needs.

While our schools must not continue to be Eurocentric, we should appreciate and retain alien knowledge and skills that are relevant to our current socio-economic interests and can complement the ideas and practices extracted from our African contexts, history, knowledge, values, languages, and culture. As an adage goes, slaves are named by their masters, but free people name themselves. Therefore, we cannot continue to outlaw our own relevant practical job-oriented knowledge, skills and values that emanate from African philosophies from our education systems. Our schools cannot teach irrelevant alien knowledge and values at the expense of Indigenous knowledge, skills, and values. Salia-Bao (1989, p. 3) maintains that "if curriculum is to serve its real purpose, it must assist the pupil to see the value of the past in relation to the present and the future. It must equip the child with the necessary skills for modern living; and it must help to keep the child a fully integrated member of his community." A decolonized education system can open people's eyes to the subtle tactics of the oppressor and decolonize the minds of educated Africans.

The absence of transformation in the Sub-Sahara African school curriculum has created a general perception among the youth, parents, and some members of the public that all citizens who complete school "demand" work from the government should, instead of creating their own jobs. The practical transformation of our education system may not only make school education African-centered and more relevant to Africans but also secure socio-economic freedom and maintain African values and identities. African governments and for that matter, education authorities, must integrate the most important Indigenous knowledge, skills, culture, and values into the school learning experiences to enhance employment creation, decolonization of the minds of educated people, and maintain African identities. I emphasize that Africa's socio-economic and political regeneration and emancipation cannot be achieved without an appropriate school system and curriculum *brewed in an African pot*.

Sankofa and Curriculum Transformation: An Agenda for Anti-Colonial Education

Sankofa comes from three Akan words—*San* (return), *Ko* (go) and *Fa* (take). It is an Indigenous African communal philosophical thought and cultural custom among the Akan of Ghana. *Sankofa* literally means, *go back and fetch it*. The Akan use proverbs and symbols extensively in their everyday expressions to convey important messages. The *Sankofa* symbol is a mythical bird that flies forward with an egg in the mouth, but its head turned backward. The thought behind this myth is that there is wisdom in learning from the past, both to understand the present and shape the future. Galloway (2004) insinuates that the egg in the mouth of the bird represents the "gem" or knowledge of the past upon which wisdom is based. The egg also signifies the generation to come that would benefit from the wisdom. The forward and backward gaze of the *Sankofa* bird is based on the Akan proverb, *Se wo were fi na wo sankofa a yenki* (i.e., it is not wrong or shameful to go back for something you have previously forgotten). The belief among the Akan is that the past illuminates the present and that the search for success is a lifelong process, in fact, a journey. Citing Dzobo (1976), Quan-Baffour (2022) attests that life is a journey, and sometimes as people undertake a journey, they might have left some very important things behind or at home and must turn back to fetch them before they continue their journey.

Sankofa is an Indigenous philosophy that has implications for Indigenization and transformation of African education and the school curriculum, in particular. As an Indigenous African thought *Sankofa* is based on the premise that no one can know where he is going unless he knows where he is coming from. People's past could hold sweet, bitter, positive, or negative memories, but whatever it might be, they can take some lessons from it to guide them to move forward. In life, sometimes people literally take steps backward to reclaim something important from the past to understand the present. The step into the past can assist them to realize why and how they have come to be where they are today and where to from here.

Africans had Indigenous forms of education which was eclipsed by the introduction of Western school education. The contemporary Africa is beset with huge unemployment among the economically active which threatens the stability of sub-Saharan African countries hence the need to do some introspection to ensure the delivery of relevant quality school education. Indigenous knowledge systems have a critical role to play in Africa's socio-economic development and the decolonization of school education should embrace their relevance and integration. In searching for a better educational future, Sub-Saharan Africa should take into consideration how education responds positively to local and global needs and aspirations. The onus is therefore on our political leaders, bureaucrats, and policymakers to make a *backward gaze* like the proverbial *Sankofa* bird into the past to reclaim the economically relevant Indigenous knowledge and skills to integrate them into the formal school programs to ensure job creation, self-employment, economic growth, and active participation in the fourth industrial revolution.

African renaissance cannot be realized without decolonization of education to suit the continent's current socio-economic and political realities and needs. To make the continent and its people socio-economic free, it is crucial to transform its education systems in line with African aspirations, interests, and values. A transformed education based on the teachings of *Sankofa* can give Africans confidence to resist foreign manipulations. In recent times, the economic upheavals seem to divide the continent. Some African leaders have become political hypocrites, sycophants and "boot lickers" of Russia and would not condemn its invasion of Ukraine, a sovereign state, because of their own parochial personal interests. A *backward gaze* to the past could have reminded them of the evils of colonialism which their own countries suffered. That would make them to refrain from supporting Russia's unwarranted invasion of Ukraine. African leaders should do some retrospection to take better decisions for the future of the continent and its people.

Sankofa also teaches that people's past is as important as their present and their future. Therefore, to make the best out of the present and plan for the future, African leaders and policymakers must *gaze backward* to the past for appropriate guidance to ensure positive forward movement for future success. No matter how *far away* Africans have traveled, it is prudent and crucial for them to *return home* to the past for lessons and guidance. In recent times the awareness and the need to reclaim some African identity has begun to grow among many Africans (both on the continent and in the diaspora). In Dzobo's (1976, p. 132) view,

> This apprehension of reality is the passport for our journey as a people. It represents what we Africans see as life and understand it to be because of the perspective of our environment and of the experiences we have gone through as a people.

This *apprehension of reality* could mean the various setbacks experienced by Africans throughout their history, such as colonialism, slavery, civil wars, dictatorships, diseases, and poverty—some of which still haunt the African people and impede their progress. This therefore calls on all Africans, especially our political leaders, to *gaze backward* for some retrospection, to study and analyze both the bitter and the good experiences of the past and to learn from them as Africa makes a leap forward into the present millennium.

Despite the European incursions and assaults made on Indigenous African education, Africans can make *a backward gaze* to reclaim its core knowledge, skills, values, and practices to integrate them into today's formal education to make it relevant to our current needs and contexts. Making education relevant to the needs and situations in Africa means firstly, that the school curriculum and textbooks had to be reformed to consider of the African economic context, environment, and cultural heritage and secondly, that education should be re-directed to make it more responsive to the needs of the people (Wolhuter, 2000). We cannot reflect on our present destiny without analyzing the grafting between the Indigenous values and the modern values in a context of accelerated globalization, fashioned by a boundless liberalism with its share of all types of trading (currencies, money, merchandise including migrants, men, women, children, drugs, and weapons). Africans need to take the historical evolution and hence lessons from the past, into account to be able to establish a viable educational system (Diop, 2000).

The school curriculum should promote learning of theory and practice, that is, knowledge and skills that can lead to employment or self-employment. Children need to be educated through an integrated curriculum that covers learning experiences from home, community and the school as well as a variety of courses such as basic mathematics, science, social science (i.e., Indigenous art, crafts, sculpturing, languages, ethics, civics, history, economics, management, marketing, co-operatives, accounting and geography), scientific agriculture (e.g., practical aspects of farming such as crop rotation and production, animal rearing, poultry keeping, soil conservation and farm technology where simple farm implements can be designed and manufactured) and applied science (e.g., building, carpentry, welding, basic electricity and engineering). These courses may not only broaden knowledge but are tied to skills that can lead to self-employment. When many school leavers can create their own jobs, unemployment and crime could decrease and Africans can be proud of their true Renaissance.

To redeem ourselves philosophically, epistemologically, and ontologically we must take a *backward gaze* to the past for lessons to re-indigenize both our philosophies of education and the content of what we teach our young ones. It is only when we take lessons from the past that we can transform our education to make us thrive in the contemporary selectively connected but developmentally divided world. By "looking back to the past" like the mythical *Sankofa* bird, the present educational systems can be transformed to incorporate teaching pupils the ideals of *Sankofa* which are humaneness, discipline, honesty, respect for life and human dignity, communicating appropriately and co-operating with others, fear of God and living and working in harmony with people from diverse backgrounds. When education is transformed, and pupils learn what is practiced in their communities they may grow to appreciate the acquisition and use of practical skills as very important means of survival in today's world. The countries in the global north that have managed to attain socio-economic advancement and infrastructural development could not have achieved those heights without using their Indigenous knowledge systems as the reference point or point of departure.

The views expressed on the Indigenous philosophy of Sankofa by many writers and Africanists including Dzobo (1976), Tedla (1995), Galloway (2004), and Quan-Baffour (2022) attest that *Sankofa* is not only an Indigenous African thought but a way of life and practice that has lessons for Africa's rebirth. Being a practice and heritage *Sankofa* brings Africans face to face with a new awareness of the historical realities and African identity. As the Akan adage goes, *tete wo bi* (the past has a lot of important lessons for today) hence the search for relevant education for Africa today must take lessons from *Sankofa*, an Indigenous African philosophy and epistemology.

Conclusion

The huge unemployment facing Sub-Saharan countries today is mostly due to the legacy of unresponsive school curriculum. The schools keep churning out unskilled graduates because African countries have not been able to decolonize or transform the school curriculum to incorporate Indigenous philosophies, knowledge, skills, and values for job creation. The chapter has emphasized the crucial need for education transformation in Sub-Saharan African schools in line with the current socio-economic and political realities of the region and its people within a globalized world. The de-colonization of education, and the school curriculum should move from political rhetoric to praxis to ensure socio-economic and political advancement, stability, reduction in desperate and dangerous journeys by the youth in search of "greener pastures" and above all maintain African identities. The transformed and decolonized school curriculum can defuse the time bomb emanating from huge unemployment among the economically active citizens. The devil, they say, finds job for the idle and as Whitehead (1962, p. 2) observes, "education with inert ideas is not only useless; it is above all things, harmful—C*corruptio, optimi, pessimal.*"

References

Abdi, A. (2011). African philosophies of education. Deconstructing the colonial and reconstructing the indigenous. *Indigenous Philosophies and Critical Education: A READER. Counterpoints, 379,* 80–91.

Akua, C. (2020). Standards of Afrocentric education for school leaders and teachers. *Journal of Black Studies, 51*(2), 107–127.

Busia, K. A. (1969). *Purposeful education for Africa.* Mouton Publisher.

Curzon, L. B. (1990). *Teaching in further education. An outline of principles and practice.* Cassel Educational Ltd.

Datta, A. (1987). *Education and society: A sociology of African education.* Macmillan.

Davidson, B. (1992). *The Black man's burden: Africa and the curse of the nation state.* Times Books/Random House.

Diop, B. (2000) African education: Mirror of humanity. In P. Higgs, N. C. G. Vakalisa, T. V. Mda, & N. T. Assie-Lumumba (Eds.), *African voices in education.* Juta and Co.

Dzobo, N. K. (1976). The courage to be an African in education. *The Oguaa Educator, 7*(1), 132–138.

Galloway, D. (2004). *Sankofa, Sasa and Zamani. The ongoing influence and spirituals on African American poetry.*

Hegel, G. W. F. (1965). *La raison dans l'histoire.* UGE.

Higgs, P., & Letseka, M. (2022). *Philosophy of education today; An introduction.* Juta & Co.

Magesa, L. (1997). *African religions: The moral traditions of abundant life.* Paulines Publication Africa.

McWilliam, H. O. A., & Kwamena-Poh, M. A. (1975). *The development of education in Ghana.* Longman Group.

Nyerere, J. (1968). *Freedom and socialism: Selection from writing and speeches, 1965–1967.* Oxford University Press.

Odora Hoppers, C. (2011). *Rethinking thinking: Modernity's order and transformation of the university.* UNISA Press.

Quan-Baffour, K. P. (2000). *A model for the evaluation of ABET programmes* [D.Ed. Thesis]. University of South Africa.

Quan-Baffour, K. P. (2022). *Sankofa* and restorative justice in South Africa. In R. L. Johnson & K. P. Quan-Baffour (Eds.), *Correctional education; An African panopticon* (pp. 1–180). University of South Africa Press.

Rodney, W. (2009). *How Europe underdeveloped Africa*. PANAF Publishing.

Salia-Bao, K. (1989). *Curriculum development and African culture*. Edward Arnold.

Tedla, E. (1995). *Sankofa, African thought and education*. Peter Lang.

Van Niekerk, L. J. (2013, January 25–30). The curriculum as a myth and narrative. In F. E. Gouws & C. C. Wolhuter (Eds.), *Educational research in South Africa: Practices and perspectives. Proceedings of the Southern African Educational Research Association Conference, Klein-Kariba Resort, Limpopo*, pp. 1–443.

Wa Thiongo, N. (2005). Europhone or African Memory: The challenge of the Pan Africanist intellectual in the era of globalization: In T. Mkandawire (Ed.), *African intellectuals: Rethinking politics, language, gender and development* (pp. 115–164). Zed.

Whitehead, A. N. (1962). *The aims of education and other essays*. Ernest Benn.

Wiredu, K. (2004). Prolegomena to an African philosophy of education. *South African Journal of Higher Education, 18*(3), 17–26.

Wolhuter, C. C. (2000). Strategies and initiatives for expansion and reform of education in Africa since independence. *Africa Insight: Giving Insight into Change in Africa, 30*(1).

· 5 ·

MWALIMU JULIUS NYERERE: THE PHILOSOPHY OF SELF-RELIANCE FROM AN AFROCENTRIC PERSPECTIVE

Njoki Nathani Wane, Sein A. Kipusi, and Rachael Kalaba

Introduction

"If real development is to take place, the people have to be involved" (Mwalimu Nyerere).
"A man/woman is developing himself/herself when [he/she] grows or earns enough to provide decent conditions for [himself/herself] & their family; s/he is not being developed if someone gives him/her these things" (Mwalimu Nyerere).

Mwalimu Julius Kambarage Nyerere (hereafter referred to as Mwalimu, which means teacher) was one of few African Presidents who saw that the political independence many African countries attained was not liberation. The two statements by Mwalimu speak to that. If actual development is to take place, the community needs to be involved. However, the former colonial masters wanted to control development, education, culture, politics, and governance from their seats in Europe with an African president leading the newly independent African country. Many of the African nations did not realize that running their own affairs would be a very difficult task, because the seeds of discord were planted when European nations drew the artificial boundaries of countries during the scramble for Africa, at the Berlin Conference of 1884. The agenda of the conference was purely that there were no Africans at the table—their opinions were not considered economics. Uzoigwe (1984) notes that: "Bismarck ... stated in his opening remarks that delegates had not been assembled to discuss matters of sovereignty either of African states or of the European powers in Africa." "It was no accident that there were no Africans at the table—their opinions were not considered necessary." The Berlin Conference was Africa's undoing in more ways than one. The colonial powers superimposed their domains on the African continent. American journalist Daniel De Leon (1886) described the conference as "an event unique in the history of political science ... Diplomatic in form, it was economic in fact." Few on the continent or in the African diaspora were fooled. A week before it closed, the Lagos Observer declared that "the world had, perhaps, never witnessed a robbery on so large a scale." Six years later, another editor of a Lagos newspaper comparing the legacy conference to the slave trade said: "A forcible possession of our land has taken the place of a forcible possession of our person." Theodore Holly, the first black Protestant Episcopal Bishop in the US, condemned the delegates as having "come together to enact into law, national rapine, robbery, and murder." As Professor Terence Ranger noted, the colonial period was marked "by systematic inventions of African traditions—ethnicity, customary law, 'traditional' religion. Before colonialism Africa was characterized by pluralism, flexibility, multiple identity; after it, African identities of 'tribe', gender and generation were all bounded by the rigidities of invented tradition" (Patrick Gathara, pulled from the internet, November 17, 2023). At the time of the conference, 80% of Africa remained under traditional and local control. What ultimately resulted was a hodge-podge of geometric boundaries that divided Africa into 50 irregular countries.

This new map of the continent was superimposed over the one thousand Indigenous cultures and regions of Africa. The new countries lacked rhyme or reason and divided coherent groups of people and merged disparate groups who really did not get along. By the time independence returned to Africa in 1950, the realm had acquired a legacy of political fragmentation that could neither be eliminated nor made to operate satisfactorily (H. J. de Blij and Peter O. Muller, *Geography: Realms, Regions, and Concepts* (1997), p. 340). That is, 135 years ago, 14 European nations sat around a horseshoe-shaped table to decide the fate of Africa and to divide her among themselves. The was done to continue exploiting African people and their land after Atlantic slave trade was abolished. As Uzoigwe notes that the only way one would find out why this "gathering of white men was hung on the wall—a large map of Africa 'drooping down like a question mark' as Nigerian historian, Professor

Godfrey Uzoigwe (1984)." The conference was created by Otto von Bismarck to settle disputes between the European powers with interests in Africa and to create pseudo-borders of ownership, allowing various European nations to claim almost the entire continent, including its resources and people. Ethnic groups were separate and placed in different countries. The Berlin conference has come to represent the late nineteenth-century European Scramble and Partition of African continent. At the time of the conference, only the coastal areas of Africa were colonized by the European powers. At the Berlin Conference the European colonial powers scrambled to gain control over the interior of the continent. The boundaries created a bedrock for wars, disunity, and perpetual crisis. Throughout Africa, nationalists came together to fight for their freedom. They got their independence; however, nothing much had changed, only the skin color of the head of state.

Mwalimu, speaking about the Berlin conference noted: "We have artificial 'nations' carved out at the Berlin Conference in 1884, and today we are struggling to build these nations into stable units of human society ... we are in danger of becoming the most Balkanized continent of the world." Mwalimu knew although his country had gained political independence, she was being controlled by Europe. President Kwame Nkrumah of Ghana knew that, and Samora Machel of Mozambique knew it too, so was Kenneth Kaunda of Zambi. To avoid this, Mwalimu decided to revisit the African Indigenous ways of knowing and advocate for self-reliance and self-determination, community collectivism and responsibility. He situated his leadership on the Ubuntu philosophy: *I am because you are*. He advocated returning to our African Indigenous governance, African languages, use of Ujamaa (cooperative economics), Nia (purpose), etc. The West isolated his country on many levels, but today, Tanzania is united by African culture, language (Kiswahili) and African philosophies. In this paper, we will focus on the Philosophy of Self-Reliance, a discourse that is deeply rooted in Afrocentric ideals.

Africa has some of the world's greatest civilizations that represent a rich diversity of knowledges, philosophies, and ways of knowing. Her Civilizations and ways of knowing have been suppressed, masked, and mocked. Currently, Africa is marked by postcolonial oppression and is struggling with many colonial legacies such as political, economic, cultural leadership, spiritual and mental enslavement. Mwalimu Nyerere was brave enough to introduce to his nation, Tanzania, one African Indigenous way of knowing:

The Philosophy of Self-Reliance. This philosophy has long been a central theme in the discourse surrounding African development and independence.

Among the prominent figures who championed this philosophy, few are as renowned and influential as Mwalimu Julius Kambarage Nyerere, the first President of Tanzania. Mwalimu's visionary leadership and unwavering commitment to self-reliance shaped his nation's destiny and left an indelible mark on the broader African continent.

This paper explores the philosophy of self-reliance as espoused by Mwalimu Nyerere, examining it from an Afrocentric perspective. By delving into Mwalimu's life, intellectual background, and political ideology, we seek to understand the intricate connection between his philosophy of self-reliance and the broader African cultural, historical, and sociopolitical standpoint. We offer the reader an analysis of Mwalimu's philosophy of self-reliance, highlighting its basic tenets and assessing its relevance and impact. In addition, the paper delineates the concepts of self-reliance and Afrocentrism to shed light on their historical evolution and theoretical underpinnings. A synthesis of these frameworks will uncover the unique intersections and symbiotic relationships between Mwalimu's philosophy, the principles of Afrocentric and Ubuntu thought, specifically in reclaiming African agency, cultural heritage, and socio-economic autonomy. The paper will contribute to the ongoing academic discourse surrounding African Indigenous knowledges and the quest for decolonizing our minds, body, and spirit. Ultimately, this paper endeavors to honor Mwalimu's legacy by contributing to the ongoing dialogue on Africa's future and the quest for self-determination. We also ask questions such as: How does his philosophy speak to issues of African Indigenization of education? If the African governments adapt Mwalimu's philosophy of self-reliance, will there be transformative change relatable to African people? How do we engage with self-reliance topics from an Afrocentric perspective from a place of sincerity, honesty, and openness? What is Afrocentricity? How can we use Indigenous (decolonial) ways of teaching and learning to decolonize our minds, body, and spirit? If Mwalimu were to speak to us today on Self-Reliance, what would he share with us? We shall not attempt to have explicit answers to these questions, but we provide them to engage in a dialogue with our readers. We shall first situate ourselves before we examine Mwalimu's life, who he was, what he stood for, and why. This will be followed by analyzing our understanding of self-reliance as Mwalimu advocates.

Situating Ourselves

Njoki Nathani Wane

Situating myself before I write any paper gives me fulfillment and a chance to revisit my rural upbringing and my education in both Kenya and the West. I am a Professor and Chair of Social Justice Education at the Ontario Institute for Studies in Education, University of Toronto. Situating myself enables me to show the glaring contradictions between my rural upbringing and my colonial education. In my early years of education, I did not even know I was going through an education that spoke nothing about African ways of knowing. I was happy to memorize about the Mississippi river in the United States, lumbering and wheat farming in the prairies of Canada. I learned nothing about the history of Africa before the enslavement of African people, nor about the Indian Ocean (Arab slave trade) or Atlantic slave trade that saw many of my ancestors shipped to the Americas or Europe to build those nations not as free people, but as enslaved and as other people's property. I learned nothing about the dehumanizing of people of African ancestry, African Indigenous ways of knowing, nothing much about Africa. What was emphasized was the notion that Africa was a dark continent needing rescue. Situating myself, therefore, allows me to reflect on colonial education and how I was steeped in it as a young African child and what it meant to me. As I have indicated elsewhere, "I took pride in attending colonial schools and memorized everything that we were taught. I wanted so badly to be westernized, a dream that my parents had" for me. I wanted to run as far as possible from the "dark" continent, my home, Africa, my motherland and the center of my world (quoted from Wane 2023). Elsewhere (quoted 2023) I have articulated how:

> My parents wanted me to acquire a European education, an education that would remove me from my rural upbringing and enable me to lead a different and supposedly "better" life.... Africans acquiring literacy in English or French quickly realized that a university education opened prospects for economic advancement and individual attainment and would ultimately provide keys to political power and self-government or self-advancement. (Wane, 2003)

Elsewhere (2014), I have reflected on how the teachings I gained from my parents and village elders sometimes felt like a contradiction. From my elders, I received African Indigenous ways of knowing, teachings that got ingrained in my psyche and were quickly available to me when I needed that education.

I was sent to a missionary boarding school from grade 5 to 12, and most of my teachers were European nuns. We followed a British curriculum and memorized material written by Western scholars to pass British-set examinations. Looking back, I often thought of Ngugi Wa Thion'go, who began in the 1970s to decry the "colonial mentality" and to promote the virtues of writing in African languages, as a whining, troublesome English professor. Today, Wa Thion'go is my hero. his scholarship on decolonization has paved the way for many scholars (Wane, 2003, p. 321; Wane, 2023).

I have learned a lot from the work of Thiong'o, which has pushed me to address my colonized mind and to search for my authentic self. Co-writing this paper on Mwalimu is to show my commitment to cultivating a scholarship that speaks to the core of my being and a way of honoring African Indigenous ways of knowing. "The emphasis on colonial education was to ensure there was complete erasure of traditional knowledges and ways of being. This has made decolonizing of education a very difficult task" (Wane, 2023).

Racheal Kalaba

My decision to relocate to Canada five years ago was propelled by an earnest desire to dissect the concept of "development" and to absorb Western viewpoints on this subject. This quest led me to pursue a master's degree in development studies, focusing on Indigenous Development. This academic phase was crucial in deepening my understanding of colonization, especially within Zambia's history as a former British colony. Reflecting on this, Wane (2011) cites Mama, who articulates the profound and lasting impact of colonialism on various facets of life in postcolonial African states (Mama, 1998, p. 47; Wane, 2011), citing Mama, notes that "being conquered by the colonizing powers, being culturally and materially subjected to a nineteenth-century European racial hierarchy and its gender Politics, being indoctrinated into all-male European administrative systems, and the insidious paternalism of the new religious and educational systems ... has persistently affected all aspects of social, cultural, political, and economic life in postcolonial African states" (Mama, 1998, p. 47). Additionally, Wane (2011) references Ama Ata Aidoo's critique of the problematic portrayal of Africa, a narrative that has historically cast a shadow over the continent and its people (Aidoo, 2000). Furthermore, Wane, 2011, citing Ama Ata Aidoo in confronting the problematic representation of Africa and its people, which I also see myself in (Wane, 2011, p. 16).

I grew up knowing that Europeans had dubbed Africa "The Dark Continent" ... That expression was first used in the nineteenth century. Since then, its ugly odor has clung to Africa, all things African, Africans and people of African descent everywhere, and has not faded yet. ... I am not a psychologist or a psychoanalyst. However, I do know that it has not been easy living with that burden. Africans have been the subject of consistent and bewildering pseudo-scholarship, always aimed at proving that they are inferior human beings. Even when there was genuine knowledge, it was handled perniciously by anthropologists and social engineers, cranial and brain-size scientists, sundry bell curves, doomsday, medical and other experts (Ama Ata Aidoo, 2000).

My scholarly awakening led me to re-evaluate established narratives critically and question traditional attitudes toward development, particularly those rooted in the colonial era. Currently, as a PhD candidate in Adult Education and Community Development, I engage with scholars who have helped me navigate my identity as a Black African Zambian woman; I am deeply grateful to continue my journey learning from Professor Njoki Wane, Ba Mulenga Kapwepwe, Nana Dei, Professor Lo, to mention a few. This journey is also influenced by Julius Nyerere's emphasis on the significance of Adult Education in Africa's quest for self-understanding. My relearning and re-engagement with my ancestral heritage have been pivotal in reshaping my cultural identity.

One of Nyerere's key contributions is that he declared 1970 to be Adult Education Year. Mwalimu Nyerere announced this in his New Year's speech to the nation, which can be found in the document *Elimu Haina Mwisho* (Learning Never Ends). Mwalimu noted that adult education has three objectives: (1) to shake ourselves out of resignation to the kind of life Tanzanians have lived for centuries; (2) to learn how to improve our lives; and (3) to understand our national policies of socialism and self-reliance. These objectives resonate with me as an emerging scholar and an adult learner. In my professional trajectory, from grassroots work to leading a development organization, the question of "what is development" has been a constant companion. The teachings of Julius Nyerere have been particularly transformative; he critically assessed the Western development model and defined development as freedom (Nyerere, 2009), underscoring the inseparable link between freedom and development. His Ujamaa philosophy, which advocates for cooperation and community spirit, greatly influenced my perception of development within the African context. Similarly, the emphasis on human dignity and a "man-centered" society by Kenneth Kaunda (Zambia's first president), through his ideology of humanism, deeply resonated with me. These philosophies, alongside the principles of Self-reliance and Ubuntu, underscore the necessity of centering humanity in our work and communal life.

This journey of learning, unlearning, and relearning has been rediscovering and reaffirming our heritage and culture. As discussed by Wane (2023), the decolonization concept involves a reconnection with our cultural roots, a principle that Nyerere and Kaunda championed long before "decolonization" became mainstream. I am immensely grateful for the opportunity to learn from and be inspired by the wisdom of these great African leaders, Mwalimu Julius Nyerere and Kenneth Kaunda. Their legacies continue to inform and shape my approach to development work—Natotela (Thank you) for their enduring wisdom and guidance.

Sein Kipusi

As a teenager, I left Canada to go to Kenya for high school in a British-curriculum school with notions of my self-identity as a racialized, gendered, "third world" privileged African girl. I discovered I entered Kenya with a vitality steeped in Eurocentric pedagogy that became problematic in my self-discovery journey of finding my roots due to the impact of colonization on my psyche. My education in Kenya was steeped in European history, geography, and literacy. When I sought to discover my ancestral history, governance, spirituality, and economic systems, I faced the detrimental impact of colonization on what I understood as a colonial subject in my own country. As Mazama affirms,

> Colonization was not simply an enterprise of economic exploitation and political control, as it was commonly held, but also an ongoing enterprise of conceptual distortion and invasion, leading to widespread confusion and, ultimately, mental incarceration. (Mazama, 2003, p. 3)

Mazama's quote is supported by Fanon's and Wa Thiong'o's work. They, among others, articulated the goal of colonizing colonial subjects was to break their spirit, subjugate their knowledge, then make them hate themselves, their languages, and their cultures. For instance, most colonial governments viewed Indigenous ways of knowing, their cosmology, their spirituality, and their ontological existence as "barbaric," "backward," "traditional," and "unscientific" (Shizha, 2013). A colonized subject's ways of knowing and their learning methods were portrayed as invalid; hence, the colonized people were forced to assimilate a hegemonic foreign culture. My concept of self-reliance, self-determination, and African Indigenous ways of knowing had been mentally hijacked, a tree whose roots had been uprooted and thrown into the abyss. My engagement with Mwalimu's philosophies is illuminating, educative and informative. Reading his work pushes me to yearn for more scholars and philosophers like him. His work paved the way for my PhD work, where I explored financial literacy for Black entrepreneurs in Canada. Many times, I would ask myself while I was listening to my research participants why they could not reproduce a Black Wall Street in Canada; I was pretty sure that the Canadian government would not burn it or bomb it down the way the American Black Wall Street was destroyed by the American government in 1922. However, this is where I saw the importance of Nyerere's work on communal cooperation for collective development. This principle aligns with the cooperative economics aspect of financial literacy, where individuals are educated on the benefits of collaborating with others for mutual financial growth. learning about cooperative ventures, community banks, or investment clubs can foster a sense of shared responsibility and economic interdependence. The Black Wall Street can be bombed down; however, what his philosophy of self-determination has taught me is that the self-determination that he advocated for us when he was still living is ingrained in my psyche. Pursuing a PhD with a focus on collective economics, I would like to say Mwalimu, asante sana for your legacy, for your teachings. Let me now turn the light to the life of Mwalimu Nyerere.

Mwalimu Julius Kambarage Nyerere: What He Stood for and Why

> Take every penny you have set aside for aid for Tanzania and spend it in the UK, explaining to people the facts and causes of poverty.
>
> Julius Nyerere

Mwalimu is widely recognized as a visionary leader and champion of African liberation was the first present of Tanganyika, which later merged with Zanzibar and took the name of Tanzania. Born in 1922 in Tanganyika (present-day Tanzania), Mwalimu was pivotal in the struggle against British colonialism and the promotion of Pan-Africanism. His unwavering commitment to African unity, social justice, and education as a means of liberation propelled him to become one of Africa's most influential leaders (Kanu, 2018). Mwalimu's early experiences and education influenced his worldview and political beliefs. He attended mission schools, where he was exposed to the marginalization of traditional African values and the prioritization of Western ideas. His education at Makerere University in Uganda and the University of Edinburgh in the United Kingdom broadened his intellectual horizons, shaping his philosophy and understanding of social and economic development (Ibhawoh, 2011). By analyzing his ideas within the broader framework of African intellectual thought and cultural heritage, we deepen our understanding of the multifaceted nature of self-reliance and its potential as a catalyst for Africa in her quest for the liberation of the mind, body, and spirit.

Mwalimu's many contributions to the liberation movements in Southern Africa included the supported African nations such as Zambia, Zimbabwe, Mozambique, and South Africa in their struggles against colonialism and apartheid regimes. He provided refugee space for fleeing people from the war-torn countries, diplomatic support, and resources in their liberation movements. He was emphatic in promoting his status as a symbol of African solidarity. Mwalimu openly promoted the importance of African socialism and commitment to Indigenous education (Ishemo, 2000; Otunnu, 2018). He believed African Indigenous education was a tool for empowering people and building a strong nation. Education for Mwalimu was key for social transformation, particularly the crucial role education played in societal progress. For Mwalimu, education was not for a few children but for all Tanzanian children. He implemented policies that expanded access to education, including free primary education and the use of Swahili as the language of instruction.

Regarding African socialism ideology or philosophy, Mwalimu advanced that socialism should benefit all people while acknowledging the importance of tailoring its implementation to the unique needs of each society (Nyerere, 1968). African Socialism, Mwalimu's political ideology, was a cornerstone of his vision for Tanzania. He aimed to combine socialist principles with African communal values emphasizing self-reliance, community development, and equitable distribution of resources. Mwalimu believed African societies should find their unique development path, distinct from Western capitalism and communism. At the core of his ideology lay the concept of self-reliance, which was intricately intertwined with economic development. He argued that Tanzania should reduce her dependency on foreign aid and develop its economy based on its resources. This was in addition to creating societies based on communal responsibility, egalitarianism, African ideals, and values

(Otunnu, 2018). He inspired generations of African leaders and contributed to the continent's pursuit of self-reliance, unity, and justice. He believed in the transformative power of education as a tool for liberation (Major & Mulvihill, 2009).

Major and Mulvihill's work points out how Mwalimu emphasized the importance of decolonizing our minds and restoring pride in our African cultural heritage.

Mwalimu wanted the people of Tanzania to acquire a relevant and empowering education. It is important to note that Mwalimu did not only advocate for Tanzania but the whole of Africa. He believed in Pan-Africanism, as this ideology would unite African nations and foster solidarity. He was pivotal in forming the Organization of African Unity (OAU), (Prasad, 2012). Pan-Africanism, as an ideological framework advocating for the unity and solidarity of African people, encourages the pooling of expertise, knowledge, and resources across borders. This shared commitment to collective advancement aligns with Mwalimu's vision of self-reliance, as it empowers nations to tap into their combined strengths and address common challenges together (Nunoo & Adu-Boateng, 2022).

Moreover, Pan-Africanism and regional cooperation substantially foster self-reliance by facilitating collaborative efforts and resource sharing among African nations (Nunoo & Adu-Boateng, 2022). Scholars of Pan-Africanism note that regional cooperation further enhances self-reliance by creating economic blocs and trade agreements. African nations can leverage their combined mutual growth and development capacities by establishing joint projects, infrastructural initiatives, and trade partnerships. The African Union (AU) could facilitate African regional cooperation, offering a platform for member states to collaborate on issues ranging from economic development to peace and security. The collaborative approach not only fosters self-reliance but also reinforces the idea that the collective progress of the continent is intertwined with the prosperity of individual nations (Sanga, 2016).

Self-Reliance As a Philosophy Advocated by Mwalimu Nyerere

> No nation has the right to make decisions for another nation; no people for another people.
>
> Julius Nyerere

Self-reliance is a philosophical concept deeply rooted in individualism, independence, and personal responsibility. It urges us to rely on our capabilities and judgment rather than on external sources for our well-being and decision-making. As a philosophy, self-reliance has been championed by great thinkers, writers, and leaders throughout history, from Julius Nyerere to Mahatma Gandhi, and it continues to shape the way we perceive ourselves and our roles in society. Self-reliance as a philosophy is a call to embrace individuality, trust oneself, and take personal responsibility for one's life. Its historical roots in transcendentalism and its enduring relevance in the modern world demonstrate its continued significance. While self-reliance encourages independence and personal growth, it's important to recognize that it coexists with the need for community, cooperation, and empathy. Ultimately, self-reliance can empower individuals to navigate the complexities of life with resilience, authenticity, and the courage to be their true selves.

Self-reliance has gained much attention in various philosophical and sociopolitical discourses. It is defined as a socio-economic and political philosophy within the African context. It underscores a nation's capacity for development, progress, and self-sufficiency by utilizing internal resources, capabilities, and collective endeavors (Sanga, 2016). Nwoke (2020) contends that the trajectory of Africa's development is negatively impacted by externally imposed definitions and strategies crafted by global entities like the World Bank and the International Monetary Fund rather than being shaped by African voices. He argues that reliance on foreign aid and externally directed trade policies are not mechanisms for genuine advancement but rather instruments of dominance and exploitation. Nweoke critiques the failure of Western-imposed development models to achieve real and independent growth in African nations, as these models violate African sovereignty. He calls for a reimagining of development that prioritizes the well-being of the African people over economic metrics.

Ultimately, Nweoke champions the principle of self-reliance as the foundation for a dignified and enduring model of African development. Additionally, "African Indigenous education systems inculcated self-reliance among members of society, and every individual had a specific defined role within the society." It was suggested that aspects of Indigenous African education need to be integrated into the education system to promote self-reliance among students, as noted by Sanga (2016). Mein (2003) delves into the concept of African socialism, emphasizing its role in fostering self-reliance during the nationalist movements of the 1960s. This ideological approach was seen as instrumental in supporting the self-determination and advancement of postcolonial African nations, positioning itself as an alternative to the capitalist systems linked with neocolonial influences.

Mein (2003) clarifies that unlike Marxist socialism, which is predicated on Western class struggles, African socialism is rooted in the continent's traditional communal structures, which inherently promote self-reliance through a system where community members contribute to and benefit from the collective based on their abilities and needs. This framework prioritized a strong work ethic and communal support for the vulnerable, aligning with self-reliance principles. Mein's analysis aims not to overhaul the understanding of African socialism but to re-examine it through a contemporary philosophical lens, thereby contributing to the broader discourse on the subject.

Mwalimu championed self-reliance for Tanzania and all African nations. He sought to counter reliance on external aid and cultivate a sense of empowerment and autonomy among African nations (Nyerere, 1967). Mwalimu believed that African countries should diminish their dependence on foreign aid and external influences, which he perceived as potential conduits for neocolonialism and exploitation. He advocated for promoting robust domestic economies, investment in education and human capital, and promoting cooperative community initiatives. This strategic approach aimed to empower African countries to effectively confront their unique developmental challenges and shape their own trajectories (Nyerere, 1967).

Mwalimu felt that education needed to speak to the learning needs of Africans. In his book: *Education for Self-Reliance* (1967), he examined the Western perspectives of education, their marginalization of African education, and he highlighted tenets of African Indigenous education. In his education speech of 1970, Mwalimu emphasized the importance of self-reliance in noting that human liberation and development are self-actualizing processes; one cannot be freed or advanced through the actions of others, as everyone is the architect of their existence. This distinct ability to make conscious, intentional choices for one's objectives is what sets humans apart from other creatures. The growth of one's awareness and the subsequent control over oneself, surroundings, and community is, in essence, the true meaning of development Nyerere (1967). Mwalimu showed how these principles could have a positive influence on African education and on self-reliance. Mwalimu argued that education in traditional African societies fostered self-reliance by emphasizing communal values, holistic development, and practical skills. Mwalimu emphasized the notion of people being free to pursue their talents for personal growth and realize their full potential, not for individual gains but to contribute to society meaningfully. Mwalimu advocated for an education relevant to the learner's community. He indicated that Europeans introduced foreign education and isolated individuals from their society. According to Sanga (2016), education for self-reliance meant "delivering knowledge about 'self-reliance'" (p. 1). This sentiment is captured by Mwalimu's words below,

> Education must foster the social goals of living together for the common good. It must prepare our young people to play a dynamic and constructive part in the development of a society where all people share equitably for the good of the group and in which its progress is quantified concerning human well-being, not cars, prestige buildings, or other such things, whether privately or publicly owned. Therefore, our education must teach a sense of commitment to the general society and help society to accept the standards suitable to a better future, not those appropriate to the colonial past. (Nyerere, 1968; qtd by Sanga, 2016)

African people's concept of education viewed people as integral parts of the community, nurturing a sense of responsibility and interdependence. According to Sanga (2016):

> The relevance of education advocated by Nyerere aims to ensure that the educated eventually become servants of society in the struggle to eradicate disease, famine, poverty, and ignorance. The learners should know that the community educates them so that they may become effective "and productive members of society". (p. 5)

The above quote emphasizes the importance of a cohesive community whose ideals are the commitment to live together as humans. The quote also indicates that success is not measured by material wealth but by how humane people are. The European way of living should not set our standards; we should not measure our quality of life by using outside standards. Mwalimu also emphasized the importance of learning by doing. According to Sanga: "The practical method recommended is not only to aim at manual labor but such learning by doing must be directed toward a productive, constructive or creative end which should lead in the long run to solving the problems of the society" (p. 5). Sanga, quoting Rahumbuka, continued to advance that "the concept of Education for Self-Reliance is also about self-confidence, independence, responsibility, and democratic involvement" (Rahumbuka, 1974). He argued further that education for self-reliance is supposed to provide learners with knowledge that would enable them to tackle societal problems. In addition, education should inculcate in learners an appreciation for African traditions and culture, particularly the importance of individual freedom, responsibility, collective responsibility, tolerance, and respect (Sanga, 2016). In other words, everything that speak for or about Africa, her resources, and people, should be centered on African land, her teachings, traditions, and ways of knowing, hence the Afrocentric ideals. Let's now turn to Afrocentricity, a theory and philosophy.

Afrocentricity: A Theory and a Philosophy

According to Asante (1990) Afrocentricity is an academic theory and approach to scholarship that seeks to center the experiences and peoples of Africa and the African diaspora within their own historical, cultural, and sociological contexts. In essence, Asante (1990), goes on to state that this theory asserts that African communities are active, fundamental, and central participants in shaping their historical narratives (p. 5). Karenga (2006) outlines the essence of Afrocentricity by identifying core cultural characteristics such as community centrality, respect for tradition, spirituality, ethical concern, harmony with nature, sociality of selfhood, veneration of ancestors, and unity of being. Bekerie (1994), advances that an Afrocentric theory is an approach that emphasizes the importance of examining Africa's cultures and history from its own vantage points. It is a concept aimed at validating, revitalizing, creating, and sustaining African life and existence, free from limitations shaped by a Western perspective or worldview.

As an intellectual pursuit, Afrocentricity has emerged as a catalyst in the spirited discussions and debates among a diverse range of thinkers and scholars, especially concerning the creation and application of knowledge, mainly what Kershaw refers to as liberating knowledge. The term "Afrocentricity" merges "Africa" and "center." "Africa" is a comprehensive and plural concept encompassing a rich tapestry of cultures and experiences, while "center" denotes a sense of place and rootedness. This notion of being centered evokes a sense of belonging. We contend that continental Africa constitutes the physical landmass and stands as a space of liberation for all African peoples. It is the core of their identity and cultural uniqueness, representing diverse shades and expressions. Africa, as the point of historical origin, serves as the wellspring of their cultures, belief systems, philosophies, family values, and self-awareness within the global context. This acknowledgment extends to the idea of multiple centers within a center, a concept introduced by Welsh-Asante (1985) in the Afrocentric framework.

Additionally, as explained by Asante (1991), the core concept of Afrocentricity is that it provides a framework for viewing phenomena through the lens of the African experience. This approach not only positions Africans as principal agents in their narrative but also actively engages in deconstructing and examining their dislocation in various spheres, such as culture, economics, psychology, health, and religion. Afrocentricity shifts the narrative from seeing Africans as victims to recognizing them as central figures in the intellectual discourse of history and current affairs. Essentially, this theory promotes an empirical investigation rooted in the African perspective, aiming to dismantle Western thought's psychological and intellectual hegemony. This liberation of the African mind is also seen as a step toward liberation in all other domains of life (Mazama, 2001).

Patricia Hill Collins (1991) posits that being Afrocentric involves engaging with a fundamental African value system and experiencing oppression, though being African does not automatically equate to being Afrocentric. Afrocentricity also emphasizes the development of a consciousness focused on triumph rather than oppression.

Molefi Asante (1988) distinguishes Afrocentricity from Eurocentricity, arguing that the latter claims universality, while the former acknowledges the legitimacy of diverse worldviews. Adams further categorizes Afrocentrists into groups such as the "Nile Valley" Afrocentrists, associated with Asante and labeled "pure Afrocentrists," and the Continental Afrocentrists, who are less narrowly focused. Keto (1994), in his pivotal work "The Africa-Centered Perspective of History," elucidated the notion of "polycentric" within the center by stating, "The Africa-centered perspective begins with Africa, which is historically connected to new derivative centers, which are legitimate in their own right for the construction of new knowledge" (p. 18).

For instance, Africa serves as a symbolic, metaphoric, and cosmological "homeland" for diasporic Africans, embodying a connection that surpasses mere territorial or physical boundaries. The macro geographical contours of Africa carry greater significance for diasporic Africans than the intracontinental regional, national, or ethnic divisions. The map of Africa, coupled with the narratives of heritage, forms the bedrock of cultural identity for most diasporic African communities. In essence, these elements constitute the derivative centers for diasporic Africans, further strengthening their interconnectedness with the core idea of Africa. Afrocentricity is an intellectual standpoint that places the African experience at the core of African people's worldview, a fundamental principle for anyone embracing Afrocentrism, according to Asante

(1990). Through an African lens, it demands a re-evaluation of all aspects of human activity, from daily habits to broader social practices.

Afrocentricity is set apart by its focus on African social and cultural experiences as the primary frame of reference, distinguishing it from other bodies of thought. Despite the retrospective application of the term to earlier thinkers who recognized the distinctiveness of the African experience, such as Blyden, Garvey, and DuBois, it is Asante who is credited with systematically formulating Afrocentricity as an operational principle. Similarly, Cheikh Anta Diop is acknowledged for establishing the African identity of ancient Egyptians as a scientific principle.

In conclusion, the term "Afrocentricity" encapsulates the intricate interplay between Africa and its center, a synergy that embodies the multifaceted cultural legacy of the continent. This paradigm acknowledges the centrality of continental Africa as the wellspring of identity while recognizing the concept of multiple derivative centers within diasporic African communities, as exemplified by Keto and Welsh-Asante's contributions to the Afrocentric discourse. Afrocentricity is an intellectual standpoint that places the African experience at the core of African people's worldview, a fundamental principle for anyone embracing Afrocentrism, according to Asante (1990). Through an African lens, it demands a re-evaluation of all aspects of human activity, from daily habits to broader social practices.

Self-Reliance from an Afrocentric Perspective

> As a people, our most cherished and valuable achievements are the achievements of spirit. With an Afrocentric spirit, all things can be made to happen; it is the source of genuine revolutionary commitment.
>
> Molefi Kete Asante

From an Afrocentric perspective, self-reliance is deeply rooted in the African concepts of education, unity, and communal collaboration. Afrocentricity highlights the precolonial Indigenous self-reliance systems and colonialism's disruptive effects. The Afrocentric perspective emphasizes the importance of cultural identity and the decolonization of knowledge systems in promoting self-reliance. It offers valuable insights into the concept of self-reliance in the African continent. By embracing African cultural identity, decolonizing knowledge systems, empowering Indigenous knowledge, and strengthening regional cooperation, African nations and communities can tap into their own resources, capabilities, and heritage to foster self-reliance and achieve sustainable development.

This section highlights the importance of recognizing and reclaiming African agency, promoting Indigenous knowledge systems, and working collectively towards a self-reliant and prosperous Africa. Moreover, it emphasizes the empowerment of African people but centering their African Indigenous knowledge systems. By reclaiming African agency and promoting Indigenous knowledge systems, African nations and communities can harness self-reliance to address their challenges and achieve sustainable development. It is crucial to recognize and draw upon the rich cultural heritage of Africa, which can foster a sense of pride and agency among Africans. Decolonizing educational curricula and including Indigenous African knowledge are essential in empowering individuals and communities to assert their agency and promote self-reliance.

Furthermore, integrating Indigenous knowledge into development strategies, such as sustainable agriculture, healthcare, and resource management, can contribute to the overall well-being of African societies. This issue requires valuing and utilizing the wealth of knowledge embedded in African cultures and traditions, as scholars like Mbiti (1977) and Ntongela Masilela (2017) advocate.

Regional cooperation enables sharing best practices and lessons learned, facilitating the adoption of successful strategies and policies in different contexts. This exchange of knowledge enhances the capacity of African nations to address their unique challenges and chart a path toward sustainable development. It also reinforces the concept of self-reliance by emphasizing the importance of building on internal strengths while learning from the experiences of neighboring countries (Sanga, 2016).

The synergistic relationship between Pan-Africanism and regional cooperation is pivotal in advancing self-reliance among African nations. These principles align with Nyerere's vision and contribute to a more empowered and collectively thriving continent by fostering collaboration, sharing resources, and promoting knowledge exchange. The unity between African nations, economic integration, and collective self-determination, as championed by Nkrumah (date) and Mazrui (date), can facilitate the sharing of resources, knowledge, and experiences, enabling African nations to overcome challenges collectively.

Unity and Self-Reliance

> And just as, in the First Scramble for Africa, one tribe was divided against another tribe to make the division of Africa easier, in the Second Scramble for Africa one nation is going to be divided against another nation to make it easier to control Africa by making her weak and divided against herself.
>
> Julius Nyerere

In his seminal address to the Congress of Youth seminar in Dar es-Salaam (1961), Julius Nyerere eloquently highlighted the profound significance of Pan-Africanism and unity as instrumental factors in attaining self-reliance. During this pivotal moment, Nyerere fervently cautioned against the perils of division within Africa and the potential repercussions of isolating African nations from the global community. His message resonated with the belief that unity was not only essential for the collective self-reliance of African nations but also for the liberation and advancement of humanity. Additionally, Nyerere's vision of self-reliance went beyond mere economic autonomy; it was deeply rooted in recognizing the interconnectedness of African nations and their shared dedication to common aspirations. This perspective underscores his conviction that the well-being of any single nation was intricately linked to the well-being of the entire continent (Nyerere, 1961).

Consequently, he championed collaboration and cooperation among African states, emphasizing the mutual benefits that could arise from collective efforts toward self-sufficiency and progress (Nyerere, 1961). In his speech, Nyerere's insights align with the broader discourse on the importance of unity in achieving self-reliance within the context of developing nations. Scholars such as Sanga (2016) have further emphasized the critical role of unity in fostering economic growth and sustainable development within the African context. Additionally, Nyerere's contributions to the discourse on Pan-Africanism and self-reliance are underscored in works by authors like Sanga (2016) who delve into the intricate relationship between collective action and self-determined development in Africa. Nyerere's 1961 address to the Congress is a cornerstone in understanding his profound advocacy for unity as a pathway to self-reliance. This perspective resonates through scholarly analysis and underscores the lasting impact of his ideals on the broader discourse surrounding African progress and global interconnectedness, particularly Ubuntu philosophy. Ubuntu, an African philosophy often associated with South Africa (the word means "humanity" in Zulu), provides insights into the Afrocentric understanding of community, commitment, and collaboration. Ubuntu emphasizes the interconnectedness of humanity, stating that "I am because we are." It promotes communal values, compassion, respect, and inclusivity. Ubuntu's philosophy fosters self-reliance by recognizing individuals' inherent dignity and contributions within a community. It advocates for social justice and the decolonization of African spaces, aiming to liberate Africans from oppression and establish harmonious relationships with the world. Within the Ubuntu philosophy, collaboration is an essential aspect of self-reliance from an Afrocentric perspective. It involves collective action, mutual support, and shared responsibilities within a community. Mugumbate and Nyanguru (2013) highlight the application of Ubuntu in various fields, including theology, management, computer science, and social work. Ubuntu-based collaboration enhances ethical practices, community engagement, and research conduct. It underscores the significance of working together to achieve self-reliance at both individual and societal levels. From an Afrocentric perspective, everything gets intertwined with elements of self-determination, African Indigenous education, communal responsibility, teachings from Ubuntu, and collaboration.

Another significant milestone of Mwalimu's teachings on Ubuntu Philosophy was the importance of commitment. From an Afrocentric perspective, commitment fosters self-reliance. In Ubuntu philosophy, commitment refers to a deep sense of responsibility and dedication to the community's well-being. Mwalimu's concept of Ubuntu concerning Ujamaa (Familyhood) in African socialism emphasized the importance of commitment to cooperative agriculture, racial and tribal harmony, and moral self-sacrifice (Nzemeka, 2021). The commitment to collective progress and community development helps cultivate self-reliance by fostering a sense of shared responsibility and collaboration. Ubuntu Philosophy and Collaboration are other critical elements in promoting self-reliance in the Ubuntu philosophy. Collaboration entails people working together harmoniously to achieve common goals. In Africa, collaboration extends beyond individual self-interests to encompass the entire community's well-being. Nyerere's emphasis on unity and Pan-Africanism highlights the significance of collaboration for self-reliance (Nyerere, 1974). By working together and pooling resources, African communities can address their challenges collectively and reduce dependence on external forces.

Ubuntu Philosophy and Education for Self-Reliance

> A person is a person through other persons. None of us comes into the world fully formed. We would not know how to think, or walk, or speak, or behave as human beings unless we learned it from other human beings. We need other human beings in order to be human. **I am because other people are.** My humanity is bound up in yours, for we can only be human together.
>
> Desmond Tutu

Education plays a vital role in promoting self-reliance from an Afrocentric perspective. Nyerere's concept of education for self-reliance emphasizes the importance of education in empowering individuals and communities to take control of their development (Nyerere, 1968). As described by Nyerere, precolonial African education systems focused on instilling values, practical skills, and a sense of responsibility towards the community. By valuing African education concepts and incorporating them into the modern educational framework, self-reliance can be nurtured and strengthened. Ubuntu's philosophy offers valuable insights into the development of self-reliance in Africa. African communities can foster a sense of agency, resilience, and empowerment through communal identity, commitment, collaboration, and education for self-reliance. Embracing Ubuntu principles allows everyone to recognize their interconnectedness and collective responsibility, leading to sustainable development and self-reliance. By drawing on the wisdom of African philosophical traditions and incorporating them into contemporary practices, the path toward self-reliance in Africa can be charted, acknowledging the continent's rich cultural heritage and collective aspirations.

The work of Mwalimu and his principles of Ubuntu philosophy provided valuable insights into the African understanding of self-reliance. Emphasizing communal values, interconnectedness, and collective responsibility, Afrocentric perspectives promote self-reliance to foster holistic development, social justice, and liberation from historical injustices. By embracing these perspectives, African nations can strive toward sustainable self-reliance and contribute to a more equitable and interconnected world.

Legacy and Criticisms

Mwalimu Julius Nyerere's legacy continues to shape Tanzania and resonates throughout Africa. He left a lasting impact by emphasizing unity, self-reliance, and social justice. Even so, Mwalimu Nyerere's enduring contributions to the liberation and development of Tanzania continue to be celebrated and acknowledged globally. His visionary leadership and unwavering commitment to self-determination, social justice, and economic progress have left an indelible mark on the nation's trajectory. Nyerere's pivotal role in leading Tanzania to independence and his steadfast dedication to uniting the diverse ethnic and cultural groups within the country underscore his legacy as a unifying figure. His guiding philosophy of "Ujamaa," which emphasized communal cooperation and collective responsibility, aimed to transform Tanzanian society into one that was equitable and self-reliant. Under his leadership, significant strides were made in sectors like education and healthcare, emphasizing ensuring access to these essential services for all citizens. Nyerere's commitment to education led to remarkable improvements in literacy rates and the development of a skilled workforce, contributing to the nation's overall progress.

Furthermore, his diplomatic efforts were crucial in mediating conflicts and fostering regional stability. Nyerere's advocacy for Pan-Africanism and his involvement in various international initiatives demonstrated his commitment to improving Tanzania and the African continent. Even beyond his time in office, Mwalimu Nyerere's legacy inspires leaders and citizens alike, serving as a beacon of hope for those striving for social justice, equality, and sustainable development. His contributions stand as a testament to the enduring impact of visionary leadership and dedicated service to the betterment of society (Rweyemamu, 1995). Mwalimu Julius Nyerere was a prominent leader, philosopher, and visionary who dedicated his life to the liberation and development of Tanzania and the African continent. His ideology of African socialism, emphasis on self-reliance, and commitment to Pan-Africanism continue to shape the African political discourse. While his policies faced challenges and criticism, Nyerere's contributions to education, social transformation, and the struggle for independence are essential aspects of Tanzania's history and the broader African liberation movement.

Conclusion

Mwalimu Nyerere was a visionary who was committed to African ways of governance. His philosophy of self-reliance was a message to all African nations—not to rely on foreigners to provide food, government, culture, and health. He knew that anything from outside would have no grounding, and the structures would be full of cracks that would continue bleeding the nations and their people. If Mwalimu were given a chance to come back, he would be very disappointed with the direction that most African nations have taken. Most nations constantly look out to the West or East for support, food for their people or experts in almost every field. Many of these nations have mortgaged their nations for the next 100 years. However, there is hope. At the grassroots level, organizations and individuals, scholars, and activists alike, are revisiting Nyerere's teachings. A growing movement is on the horizon, one that could see educational systems imbued with Nyerere's philosophy, shaping a generation ready to embody the principles of self-reliance and African autonomy he so fervently championed.

Reflecting on the implications of self-reliance as a philosophy, mainly through Mwalimu Nyerere's advocacy and its synergy with Afrocentricity, we see a beacon for the present and a blueprint for the future. As Nyerere envisioned, self-reliance weaves a rich philosophical tapestry into the essence of African growth, learning, and self-empowerment. It is a robust challenge to the lingering paradigms of postcolonial dependency, celebrating the profound richness of Indigenous knowledge, the power of communal effort, and the strategic use of local assets. This philosophy elevates the significance of personal and collective agency in charting one's course, emphasizing education's pivotal role in nurturing community-minded individuals committed to societal enhancement. The ethos of self-reliance, intertwined with Afrocentric principles, calls for a renaissance that respects Africa's cultural legacy and looks to its intrinsic values and dreams for inspiration. This call to action empowers Africans to chart a course of success defined by well-being and societal contribution, fostering a new generation capable of transforming challenges into opportunities with assuredness, innovation, and an intrinsic understanding of their heritage.

The conversation surrounding self-reliance and Afrocentricity signifies a critical shift from inherited external narratives toward reclaimed ownership of the African narrative in education, governance, and socio-economic development. Placing African experiences at the forefront, Afrocentricity dovetails with Nyerere's vision of self-reliance, advocating for an empowered mindset that overcomes past hardships and current obstacles. This intellectual revival, geared towards autonomy and the relevance of African contexts in education and policymaking, heralds the dawn of a new era in African intellectualism and ingenuity. Embracing these interconnected doctrines compels us to envision a future shaped by an Africa that is resilient, self-directed, and proudly anchored in its distinct identity and boundless promise.

References

Aidoo, A. A. (1992). The African woman today. *Dissent*, 39, 319–325.

Aidoo, A. A. (2000). What 'Hopeless Continent'?. *New Internationalist*, 327.

Asante, K. W. (1985). The Jerusarema Dance of Zimbabwe. *Journal of Black Studies*, 15(4), 381-403.

Asante, M. K. (1988). *Afrocentricity*. Trenton, NJ: Africa World Press

Asante, M. K. (1990). Kemet, Afrocentricity and Knowledge. Trenton, NJ: Africa World Press.

Asante, M. K. (1991). The Afrocentric Idea in Education. *The Journal of Negro Education*, 60(2), 170–180. https://doi.org/10.2307/2295608

Asante, M. K., & Karenga, M. (2006). *Handbook of black studies*. SAGE Publications, Inc., https://doi.org/10.4135/9781412982696

Bekerie, A. (1994). The four corners of a circle: Afrocentricity as a model of synthesis. *Journal of Black Studies*, 25(2), 131–149.

Collins, P. H. (1991). On our own terms: Self-defined standpoints and curriculum transformation. *Nwsa Journal*, 3(3), 367–381.

Ibhawoh, B. (2011). The Right to Development: The Politics and Polemics of Power and Resistance. Human Rights Quarterly, 33, 76–104.

Ishemo, S. L. (2000). "A symbol that cannot be substituted": The role of Mwalimu JK Nyerere in the liberation of Southern Africa, 1955–1990. *Review of African Political Economy*, 27(83), 81–94.

Kanu Y, 2011, Integrating Aboriginal Perspectives into the School Curriculum: Purposes, Possibilities and Challenges, University of Toronto Press, Toronto.

Keto, C. T (1994): *The Africa Centered Perspective of History and Social Sciences in the Twenty First Century 2nd Ed.*; Research Associates School Times Publications/Karnak House

Leon, D. De (1886). The conference at Berlin on the West-African question. *Political Science Quarterly*, 1(1), 103–139. https://www.jstor.org/stable/2139304

Masilela, N. (2017). *A South African looks at the African diaspora: Essays and interviews*. Africa World Press.

Major, T., & Mulvihill, T. M. (2009). Julius Nyerere (1922–1999), an African philosopher, re-envisions teacher education to escape colonialism. *New Proposals: Journal of Marxism and Interdisciplinary Inquiry*, 3(1), 15–22.

Mazama, A. (1998). The Eurocentric Discourse On Writing: An Exercise in Self-Glorification. *Journal of Black Studies*, 29(1), 3–16.

Mazama, A. (2001). The Afrocentric paradigm: Contours and definitions. *Journal of Black Studies*, 31(4), 387–405. http://www.jstor.org/stable/2668022

Mugumbate, J., & Nyanguru, A. (2013). Exploring African philosophy: The value of ubuntu in social work. *African Journal of Social Work*, 3(1), 82–100.

Mbithi, P. M., & Rasmusson, R. (1977). *Self-reliance in Kenya: The case of harambee*. Nordic Africa Institute.

Mama, A. 1998. Sheroes and Villains: Conceptualizing Colonial and Contemporary Violence Against Women in Africa. In Feminist Genealogies, Colonial Legacies, Democratic Futures, ed. M. Jacqui Alexander and Chandra Talpade Mohanty London: Routledge.

Mazama, A. (Ed.). (2003). *The Afrocentric paradigm*. Africa World Press.

Mein, K. (2003). *The concept of self-reliance and its relevance to freedom in Africa* [Doctoral dissertation]. University of Nairo.

Nwoke, C. N. (2020). Rethinking the idea of independent development and self-reliance in Africa. *African Review of Economics and Finance, 12*(1), 152–170.

Address by Julius Nyerere at the ceremony to mark the independence of Tanganyika (9 December 1961) - Retrieved from https://www.cvce.eu/s/h2.

Nyerere, J. K. (1967). *Education for self-reliance*.

Nyerere, J. (1968). *Ujamaa essays on socialism*. Oxford University Press.

Nyerere, J, K.; (1974): Man and Man and Development, *Oxford University Press paperback*

Nyerere, J. (2009) Technical and Vocational Education and Training (TVET) Sector Mapping in Kenya. Edukans Foundation, Amersfoort.

Nzemeka, Justus A. (2021). Socio-cultural status of 'barracks women' in Nigeria, 1905-1985: A historical perspective. Inkanyiso 13 (2).

Nunoo, I., & Adu-Boateng, E. (2022). Assessing agency in colonial Africa: Pan-Africanism as African agency. *The African Review, 49*(4), 399–427.

Otunnu, O. (2018). Mwalimu Julius Kambarage Nyerere's philosophy, contribution, and legacies. In *African political thought of the twentieth century* (pp. 18–33). Routledge.

Owuor, J. (2007). Integrating African Indigenous knowledge in Kenya's formal education system: The potential for sustainable development. *Journal of Contemporary Issues in Education, 2*(2).

Rahumbuka, G. (1974). *Towards Ujamaa: Twenty years of Tanu leadership*. East Africa Literature Bureau.

Sanga, I. (2016). Education for self-reliance: Nyerere's policy recommendations in the context of Tanzania. *African Research Journal of Education and Social Sciences, 3*.

Shizha, E. (2013). Reclaiming Our Indigenous Voices. The Problem with Postcolonial Sub-Sahara School Curriculum. Journal of Indigenous Social Development, 6, 1–18.

Uzoigwe, G. (1984) Reflections on the Berlin West African conference, 1884–1885. *Journal of the Historical Society of Nigeria, 12*(3/4), 9–22.

Wane, N. (2003). Anti-racism in teacher education: rethinking our practice. Orbit, 33(3), 6–8.

Wane, N. (2011). African indigenous feminist thought: An anti-colonial project. In *The politics of cultural knowledge* (pp. 7–21). Brill.

Wane, N. (2023). Black Canadian Women Leaders in the Academy: In Their Own Voice; An Intersectionality of Race, Gender, Class. *Canadian Woman Studies/les cahiers de la femme*, 36(1, 2).

· 6 ·

CONTEXTUALIZATION OF THE SCHOOL CURRICULUM: REFLECTIONS OF THE GHANAIAN SITUATION

Daniel Yelkpieri

Introduction

The school curriculum is generally described as all the planned learning activities and experiences that students undergo in the school that are worthwhile in the judgment of teachers, educators and society. This write-up examines the need for contextualizing the basic school curriculum based on context-based knowledge, and cultural resource materials relevant for the development of Ghana. The chapter discusses the meaning of curriculum, contextualization and relevance of culture in the development of a curriculum, key characteristics of a curriculum, relationship between education, culture and curriculum, standards-based curriculum for Basic 1–9 and its relevance, contextualizing teaching in the classroom, the way forward and conclusions.

This paper is to highlight the need for stakeholders of education to consider the relationship between the curriculum and education in Ghana and the need to contextualize the curriculum to suit the socio-economic needs, aspirations, values, culture and resource availability of the Ghanaian society. The paper tries to draw the attention of all stakeholders of education to the need to focus on what we have as a nation in terms of our cultural values, resources and where we aspire to be as a people and the need to do the right things by putting in place the relevant curriculum to drive the educational system of Ghana. In this way, our education will focus more on solving our problems by equipping the youth with problem-solving skills they need through practical and hands-on activities that will enable them tackle social, economic, political challenges among others that Ghanaians face in their everyday life. The writer wants to see the educational system becoming a training ground for the youth to train their minds and their hands in addition to their hearts which will make knowledgeable, skillful and patriotic individuals who are ready to contribute to the transformation of Ghana. This will help them contribute to solve societal problems so that they do not become problems themselves (unemployed graduates) after completing school. The contextualized curriculum has become necessary because the type of education bequeathed to Ghana by our colonial masters was too bookish and elitist which has not been helpful in our development effort.

Meaning of Curriculum

The term curriculum, like any other term, has been defined in many ways by different authors. The reason is that different authors define it from their perspectives which may be different from others. Even though no single definition has been generally accepted, however, all definitions that include valuable and worthwhile educational activities are more acceptable by most scholars. Some of these definitions are discussed in the next paragraphs.

According to Su the term curriculum usually relates to the knowledge and skills that students are expected to learn, including the learning standards or objectives they are expected to achieve, the units and lessons teachers teach, the tasks and projects of the students, the books, materials, videos, presentations and readings used in a course; and the tests, assessments and other methods used to evaluate students' learning. In sum, it is "all the experiences that a child has in school" (Su, 2012, p. 85).

A close look at the definition of Su gives a good idea of what a curriculum is all about. The definition helps us to understand that a curriculum has to do with a program that relates to "knowledge and skills that students are expected to learn" to prepare them for the future. This implies that a school curriculum is not planned for its own sake but to equip the youth with the necessary knowledge and skills that will be relevant to their lives and society. The definition also points out that the curriculum also sets out "learning standards or objectives" that students are supposed to achieve after a stipulated time. The curriculum, according to Su, includes all the tasks and projects of the students, the books, materials, videos, presentations, and readings used in a course to enable students acquire the desired knowledge and skills. The definition further points out that a curriculum is also about how the school uses test to assess the level of attainment of students' learning within a period. The definition summarizes a curriculum to be all the experiences that a student undergoes in a school irrespective of where the school is located.

Sweetland also describes a curriculum as made up of all the experiences children have under the guidance of the teacher (Sweetland, n.d.). This definition is similar to that of Su (2012). However, Su provided a detailed definition and later summarizes curriculum as all the experiences that a student undergoes in a school. These two definitions are in sync with the Ghanaian understanding and practice of a school curriculum.

A Ghanaian writer also defines a curriculum as a sum of educationally valuable experiences that learners undergo under the guidance of a school or other training institutions (Adentwi, 2005). His definition also emphasizes all educationally valuable experiences that students encounter in the school situation and similar training institutions. This definition agrees with the first two definitions presented.

A curriculum can be understood to mean whatever is purposively planned or selected by teachers or educationists as worthwhile knowledge and action in a society, to be taught with appropriate method to learners and evaluated with right techniques to ensure that learners achieve some stated objectives (Yakubu, 2000). This definition is from another Ghanaian scholar, and it agrees with the earlier definitions. This definition is also as detailed as Su's definition and emphasizes on whatever is planned or selected by teachers or educationists as worthwhile knowledge and needed in a society. The definition also highlights the importance of the right methodology to be used in teaching such a knowledge and/or a skill. Just like Su, the author also stresses the need to evaluate the students after a period to ascertain the achievement of the set objectives of the program.

In sum, one can say a curriculum is all the learning experiences planned by a school for students to undergo training to acquire worthwhile knowledge and skills necessary for their future lives and to meet the needs of society. By "all experiences," the writer means both teaching and learning experiences that a student encounters and extracurricular activities such as sports, drumming and dancing during cultural activities, art and craft among others that have impact on students during their education.

The Concept of Contextualization and Relevance of Culture in the Development of a Curriculum

Contextualization in this write-up means placing the subject content or material being taught by the school in a specific context that makes it relevant and worthwhile for learners and their society. The emphasis of this write-up is on the need to contextualize the Ghanaian school curriculum to reflect the societal aspirations, goals, culture, values and available resources. It is in view of this objective that the National Council for Curriculum and Assessment has been tasked to review the previous curriculum in order to meet the needs of the nation and ensure that the content of the curriculum is benchmarked to international standards (NaCCA, 2023). This is emphasized by the fact that the Standards-Based Curriculum is expected to respond to the national priority for shifting the structure and content of the education system from merely passing examinations to building character, nurturing values, and raising literate, confident and engaged citizens, with emphasis on mathematics and science as building blocks for success in either tertiary education or early entry in the workplace. (NaCCA, 2023, p. 1).

The focus of the current curriculum (Standards-Based Curriculum, [SBC]) is to develop a curriculum that is based on the culture and environment of the society bearing in mind their needs and aspirations as a people. In other words, it has become increasingly necessary to contextualize the Ghanaian school curriculum to equip the youth with the right values, strong character and the right attitudes that Ghanaians are known for. The concept of contextualization has been raised as a crucial factor in this write-up for the following reasons:

High Rate of Graduate Unemployment Among the Youth

The phenomenon of high graduate unemployment among the youth in Ghana should be considered a serious threat to national security which must be addressed to forestall high crime rate and other social vices. To address this problem as a nation, the writer feels, we need to revisit our curriculum to consider redesigning it to provide basic employable skills for learners at the basic school level as was envisaged in our education reform in 1987 but failed because of poor planning and implementation. This will help learners to acquire basic skills that they can depend on after completion of Junior High School and identify their career pathways to pursue at the secondary school level taking into consideration the introduction of the Technical and Vocational Education and Training (TVET). This is captured in Antwi (1992, p. 256), in the words:

> The new educational system advocates a broadening of the curriculum to include vocational and technical subjects to be taught in all junior secondary schools purposely to equip pupils with skills needed for the rural, urban or city economy.

This is the type of content recommended by the Saber-tooth curriculum (Yakubu, 2000). The opportunity should be there for those who want to pursue this career pathway to take advantage.

Available Resources and Opportunities in the Country

Ghana as a nation is endowed with many natural resources that are untapped and some of them are going waste or underutilized. For example, some communities have large quantity of clay deposits which can be utilized to produce ceramic wares, pots, plates and other dish wares for local use and export. Another area of opportunity is in communities in which our mothers and fathers weave kente clothes and smocks for the local market. These clothes have become so popular with Ghanaians and foreigners (tourists) that they can boost our tourist industry and Gross Domestic Product (GDP). The school system can introduce some of these trades as extra-curricular activities for pupils in Junior High Schools (JHS) whereby each class will use just an hour in a week to learn how to make these wares with identified master craft-men in the communities. However, to ensure its effectiveness, it must be part of the school curriculum for effective and efficient supervision and monitoring.

The Comparative Advantage We Have As a Nation Over Our Neighboring Countries

Ghana as a nation has a comparative advantage in the production of cocoa, coffee, rice, maize, millet, guinea corn among other agricultural products. In a similar way, Ghana has a large deposit of crude oil, gold, manganese, bauxites among others, that can be tapped to develop the nation. Therefore, there is the need to develop our middleman-power in these fields in order to play key roles in the agriculture and extractive industry so that we can take advantage of the large market in the sub-region of West Africa and Africa as a whole. When the petroleum industry started its operations in Ghana, the foreign companies needed the required manpower in areas of welding, electrical works among others but our youth did not have such skills to be employed. In light of these advantages and opportunities, there is an urgent need to take TVET very seriously in the country. It is in this regard that Paulo Freire and the Saber-tooth Curriculum suggest that our educational system should be problem-solving and not banking of knowledge into learners' heads (Yakubu, 2000).

Improve Indigenous Knowledge Through the Formal Educational System

There is a dire need for our formal educational system to improve the Indigenous knowledge of the Ghanaian society through the formal education. The scientific knowledge and principles of the formal educational system can complement our Indigenous knowledge to improve life for society. The Ghanaian Indigenous knowledge plays a significant role in the lives of people and must be enhanced to make life more comfortable for us as a nation. For instance, Ghana as an agricultural economy has high rate of post-harvest lost which cost farmers so much because of inadequate knowledge in preserving our farm products. Bumper harvests that should bring farmers extra income are lost because of poor preservation methods and storage of our products. Farmers and fishmongers still use the traditional way of preserving and storing fish and crops which are not helpful and as a result large quantities of such products go waste. Another example is the case of our mothers who brew pitoo (alcoholic beverage prepared from guinea corn in the northern part of Ghana) and related products. This is an alcoholic beverage that serves as food for most people in the northern part of Ghana and yet it cannot be preserved for a long time for use. Ghanaian scientists should take up the challenges in these areas and help improve upon our Indigenous knowledge to enable us to get the maximum from our efforts in the production of local food and other products.

In addition to the above reasons, Llego (2022, p. 5) has also assigned the following reasons for the contextualization of the curriculum:

- It enhances student-teacher collaboration in the classroom since both students and teachers can better understand the context of the material or topic and how it relates to their lives.
- It ensures that the material they are learning about is relevant to students' lives. When students note how important the material, they are learning is to their lives, they are more likely to be engaged and motivated to learn. For example, when a student is trained in how to keep bees or rear snails, grasscutters, rabbits, it makes so much direct impact on the society and therefore they are likely to show more interest in the learning process.
- This type of curriculum also ensures that the material is accessible to all students. When teachers take their time to prepare and ensure that all students have access to the material, it helps to promote equity and inclusion in the classroom. It can help improve academic achievement by providing all students with equal opportunity to learn.

These reasons among others should guide the construction of a school curriculum in any society considering their unique situations. In that context, educational factors are not isolated from the society's way of life but "are all inextricably connected with the life of any society" (Antwi, 1992, p. 208). Antwi notes that, very often the "nature of education, its' purpose and character are principally conditioned by society." This agrees with Jean-Francois' view that "education is a reflection of a society or is influenced by society" (Jean-Francois, 2015, p. 1). It is in the light of this argument that the writer is of the opinion that society should be considered first when it comes to decisions on the type of curriculum to design for learners in the society. In effect, there is an interconnected relationship between education and society which cannot be disputed.

The goal of education is to transmit knowledge, skills, attitudes, norms and values which are cherished by society to the younger generation to equip and make them functional members of society. It is further observed by other educationists that "what goes on outside the schools matters even more than what goes on inside them" (Antwi, 1992, p. 208). This seems to suggest that even though the school system is trying to train the youth through the formal educational system for the society, however, the society in its' own informal or traditional way provides even more training for the youth in various ways such as socialization and acculturation. Based on this argument, it will be out of place to design a school curriculum without considering the sociocultural needs, aspirations and resource availability of society. It is on this premise that, there is always the need to contextualize the school curriculum based on the culture of the people to make the school subjects or activities more relevant to the learners and the society. Based on this observation, the teaching in the classroom should be contextualized to suit the environment of the society and its culture.

Contextualizing Teaching in the Classroom

Teaching a contextualized curriculum implies that teachers have to prepare well in terms of getting their teaching and learning resources, plan fieldtrips, visit libraries and sites where they can easily have access to sample of materials they are teaching and try as much as possible to be familiar with the school communities so as to enable them cite examples and make references to some of the things they would be teaching about from the community. It is sad to note that some of the contents of our curriculum we inherited from our colonial masters were too foreign to us as learners because we could not relate directly to them. For example, in class one we learned about the Eskimos in North America and snow. We also learned about Alexander the Great of Macedonia and Napoleon Bonaparte of France and other heroes who we could not relate to at various stages of our education at junior classes, when we did not know about our own heroes in Ghana because the textbooks were prepared based on foreign content.

The availability of teaching and learning resources in the classroom enhances pupils' participation and when applicable, hands-on activities. In other words, the use of teaching and learning resources in the teaching and learning process will enhance teacher-pupils' interactions and communication so that it does not turn out to be the teacher trying to fill some empty receptacles as observed by Freire (2014). The interaction will benefit both the teacher and the pupils since they are already familiar with the lesson and therefore have some knowledge. This will enable the teacher and pupils to learn from each other. Unlike the lecture method where the teacher will spoon-feed the learners and thereby rendering the learners' passive recipients of knowledge.

Field trips will be an effective method in teaching some of the lessons because the curriculum is contextualized, and the topics are issues from society. Therefore, teachers can plan field trips to the sites or communities where they can easily have access to such facilities or materials. For example, a lesson on fishing in the sea or a site where local gin is distilled. The teacher can easily plan a field trip to the landing beach to observe how fishermen go to the sea in canoes and fishing boats. At the site, learners will observe and take notes and be briefed by one of the fishermen about the fishing expedition in the sea, after which pupils can ask questions. The class teacher may give a summary of all the briefings given by the fisherman and also ask questions for the pupils to answer.

Teachers can easily relate the concepts they are teaching with things learners are familiar with in the society. By so doing teachers will make the lesson or concepts so close to the learners and less daunting. In other words, contextualized learning can help students to understand complex concepts better (Llego, 2022). Aside this, Llego is of the view that contextualized learning can help students to develop critical thinking skills. As students think about how the material relates to their lives, they are motivated to think deeper and analyze what they are learning.

Characteristics of a Curriculum

Every school curriculum has certain qualities that make it qualify as a curriculum and some of these are discussed in the following paragraphs:

The first characteristic of a curriculum is that it is institutional based (Abroampa & Addai-Munnunkum, 2015). The reason is that a curriculum is a form of instructional program designed to achieve educational objectives in schools. It is a way of purposively transmitting knowledge, skills, and values that are regarded worthwhile and relevant for the promotion of human development by the society. Institutions that use that curriculum are usually state or privately owned that has the mandate to use it as prescribed by the curriculum developers. For instance, in Ghana, the Curriculum Research and Development Division (CRDD) and the Ghana Education Service (GES) jointly design the curriculum for pre-tertiary schools. At the tertiary level, institutions such as universities, university colleges and professional bodies that have accreditation from the National Accreditation Board (NAB) design their own curriculum to suit their missions.

Another characteristic of a curriculum is that it is a blueprint for educators and learners. It is a plan to guide the teaching of what is worthwhile and relevant to learners in society. The society in its effort to transmit its cherished culture, values and norms to the youth integrate such philosophies into the school instructional programs that are taught to learners. Usually, the aims, goals and objectives of such philosophies are spelt out in the curriculum. This is often presented in a systematic and a sequential arrangement of knowledge, principles, skills and values that translate into topics of different subjects which learners are taught to ensure that such cultural values are perpetuated (Abroampa & Addai-Mununkum, 2015). The curriculum also outlines the appropriate teaching and learning methods and resources required to ensure effective instructional delivery. In view of the expected outcome of the instruction, assessment techniques or tools are designed to assess the level of achievement of the goals of the programs.

The curriculum is designed to suit a particular group of people and their unique situation. Every society has a unique culture that it cherishes, and which makes them stand out among other societies. For example, Ghanaians in general like their traditional songs and dance and therefore drumming and dancing are some of the extra-curricular activities organized annually at the basic schools in Ghana and it is a way of passing on this beautiful culture to posterity. Aside from this, the curriculum is constructed to cater for the aspirations, interests of people, needs or identified problems in the society so as to use education as a way of addressing such problems. In this respect, instructional programs are usually designed to cater for all these areas of interest of the larger society. For example, considering the problem of high unemployment rate in Ghana and in Africa, it is generally agreed among African leaders that our educational system needs a review to ensure that young people who enroll are equipped with certain skills that can provide them employment later in life. It was in line with this philosophy that, Ghana in 1987 had to embark on a new education concept (Junior Secondary School [JSS]) that aimed at equipping learners with vocational and technical skills to enable learners engage themselves in trades that can guarantee their livelihood after leaving school (Antwi, 1992). This was an excellent idea, but the implementation was poorly done because there was no proper planning that proceeded the implementation.

In addition, the curriculum is designed to respond to the changing needs of society. Society, they say, is dynamic just as culture is also dynamic; because of this, some cultural practices that are not helpful need to be changed for the better. Changes that come may affect all aspects of life such as economic, social, political, religious and technological. In a situation, where the entire society is affected by such a change which may be positive or negative, the surest way to ensure that the change brings hope to the people is through the educational system by designing or redesigning the curriculum to suit the changing needs of the society. For example, presently, we are in a technological era and therefore technology is an important factor that determines a society's rate of development. According to the new Standards-Based Curriculum, the Education Strategic Plan of 2018–2030 outlines three priority areas and the second priority area highlights the need to "improve quality of teaching and learning and STEM at all levels" (Ministry of Education, 2018, p. 8). This suggests that the trend now is STEM and ICT, and no serious country can afford to be left behind.

Relationship Between Education, Culture and Curriculum

It is worth noting that society and education are interconnected in such a way that each influences the other in a way. This stems from the fact that education of the people is based on the culture, aspirations of the people, goals and values of the society. This implies that every community that wants to educate its members must first consider their problems or needs. In effect, the educational activities must be tailored toward solving the problems of that society (Yakubu, 2000). Yakubu is of the opinion that "importing, curriculum that has been successful in foreign countries into Ghana will never help us to solve our problems of survival" (Yakubu, 2000, p. 20). He further notes that "to transplant a curriculum from one culture into another culture is to do an injustice to the recipient culture" (Yakubu, 2000, p. 22). This means that education, culture and the curriculum are interwoven or inseparable because education takes place in a society and therefore is influenced by the society's culture which is an important aspect of the people.

Yakubu stressed that, we should learn from others but we "should not be gullible to their ideas" (Yakubu, 2000, p. 20). Therefore, for the school curriculum to be relevant to the people in the society it must be based on the culture, their needs or identified problems and their goals and aspirations. For instance, Ghana has an agricultural economy, we have rich land and good climate to do agriculture that provides food to feed the growing population of the country and its neighbors. And therefore, agriculture as a subject must be taught and practiced in all basic schools in Ghana, so that every youth leaving the basic school level should have the basic knowledge and skills in farming. The concept of operation feed yourself which was introduced by General Ignatius Kutu Acheampong in the 1970s should be re-introduced in schools and schools should encouraged to practice what they learn in Agricultural

Science classes. At least, secondary schools in Ghana should be able to grow vegetables for their own consumption. By so doing, students who may develop basic knowledge, skills and interest in farming may embark on a small to medium scale farming as an occupation after school.

Again, Ghanaians by nature love their traditional dresses or clothes, especially kente and smock which have also become the toss of tourists who visit Ghana. Since these traditional clothes have become so popular among Ghanaians and even among foreigners, why is the educational system not integrating the teaching and learning of such vocational skills in the school curriculum as life skills for the youth and ensure that these traditional wears are passed onto future generations.

Education in its general sense is an ongoing process that occurs in almost every place (home, church, community centers, schools, etc.) in the society with the sole aim of providing knowledge, skills, attitudes, values and norms that are cherished by the people. It is in this respect, that various scholars are of the view that education performs two main functions through the process of socialization and acculturation (Agyeman, 1992; Antwi, 1992; Jean-Francois, 2015). This is because education enables the transfer of the culture of a society from one generation to another. The school curriculum on the other hand, can be regarded as the wheel that carries education. As a result, the curriculum is designed to reflect the needs of that society or country to translate the society's goals, aspirations and philosophy of education into practice as it reflects in the program of instructions. These positions really indicate that there is a relationship between education, culture and the school curriculum which cannot be overlooked.

Standards-Based Curriculum for Basic 1–9 and Its Relevance to Ghana

According to the Ministry of Education of Ghana the "pre-tertiary education curriculum, which is officially defined by the subject syllabuses, is based largely on objective model of curriculum development which was used in many developed countries in the last half of the 20th Century" (Ministry of Education, 2018, p. 16). It is noted that the use of the objective model of the curriculum focused so much on.

> Knowing basic facts, principles, skills, and procedures at the expense of the processes of learning which involves higher cognitive competences such as applying, thinking

critically, creativity and practical; and personal qualities and social skills needed to become competent, engaging and contributing citizens. (Ministry of Education, 2018, pp. 16–17)

The main reason for the review of the existing curriculum is that it was outmoded and not in tune with the Ghanaian situation and modern trends of education. There are other challenges such as influence of globalization and the challenges of a sustainable future, and the adoption of standards-based curriculum that brought with it a "dual demand for increased educational accountability and rigor" (Ministry of Education, 2018, p. 17). These challenges necessitated the review. However, one of the key reasons for this paper is to highlight the need for the Ghanaian basic school to,

Provide flexible education pathways for identifying and nurturing the talents and interests of learners early enough to prepare them for the world of work, career progression and sustainable development. (Ministry of Education, 2018, p. 16)

And more to the point, the education system in Ghana is still more elitist or bookish and much focused on subject content with very little emphasis on the cross-cutting essential learning that can equip the learners with the knowledge and skills required to bring about sustainable development as expected.

In view of these challenges raised, one would expect that the curriculum designers of Ghana's education system would consider the societal needs, culture, values, aspirations, interests and abilities of learners in their selection of subject contents to be taught in our schools, how they should be taught, materials to be used in teaching and how beneficial it will be to the society even as Ghana try to be globally competitive. The Standards-Based Curriculum (SBC) is implemented across the country at the basic school level (in this write-up refers to KG1–2, lower and upper primary and junior high school). The reason is that, as at the time this chapter was being written senior high school curriculum was still being written. The subjects are presented according to the levels in the preceding paragraph.

Kindergarten (KG) 1–2

Creative Arts is made up of visual arts, performing arts, life skills, music, dance, and drama. Children are taught these areas of arts according to their developmental stages.

Religious and Moral Education is also about the belief systems practiced by the people of Ghana, and this includes traditional religion, Christianity religion, and Islamic religion among others. In the previous curriculum, there were seven subjects for KG which seem to be loaded for children at the age of four and five. However, the Standards-Based Curriculum has reduced it to only two subjects.

Basic 1 to 9

At the basic one to nine, Mathematics is taught from lower primary, upper primary, and junior high school. At the KG and lower primary level, it emphasizes numeracy (i.e., ability to understand and work with numbers). Mathematics is a core subject at the Basic Education Certificate Examination (BECE) and at the West African Senior Secondary Certificate Examination (WASSCE).

English Language is one of the core subjects taught from basic one to nine, that is lower and upper primary and junior high school. At the Kindergarten, and lower primary level the emphasis is usually on literacy (ability to read and write) and as they progress to upper primary and junior high it is taught as a subject.

Science is taught as a subject from lower and upper primary and junior high school as integrated science (i.e., Biology, Physics, Chemistry and Agricultural Science). The curriculum places emphasis on general knowledge in science, usually things in the child's environment (living and non-living things). French is taught at the lower and upper primary level and at the junior high school to provide basic knowledge in French which could be built upon at the senior high school level as a subject.

Computing is a subject taught to equip children with skills and knowledge to enable them to fit in this era of Information and Communication Technology (ICT) which drives almost everything in the world today. The basic knowledge and skills acquired in ICT will enable the youth to navigate their way through this era of competitive job market.

Ghanaian Language is also taught to provide literacy to children so that they can read texts in their local language (mother tongue). It is also a medium of instruction at the lower primary level alongside the English Language. It is taught as a subject from the upper primary onwards.

History is taught as a subject from basic one to nine to enable children to learn about the past events of their forebears and through that inculcate in them a sense of patriotism for them to contribute to the development of Ghana.

Physical Education as a subject that aims to ensure that all children or learners lead healthy and active lifestyles and develop competence to excel in a broad range of physical activities, such as athletics, games, and physical activities that provide career opportunities (Ministry of Education, 2019). It is taught as a subject but not examinable at both BECE and WASSCE. Our-World-Our-People (OWOP) is an integrated subject that combines Religious and Moral Education, Agricultural Science, Civics, Geography, and Computing among others. This helps school children to learn more about their environment.

The structure of the pre-tertiary education of Ghana starts with kindergarten which has two years. The curriculum of KG focuses on the 4Rs, which consists of reading, writing, arithmetic and Creativity and Religious and Moral Education. At this stage the designers of the curriculum placed much emphasis on literacy, numeracy, creativity and religious and moral education as a way of introducing the child to learning. Children at this stage are provided a lot of learning materials to play with as part of the learning process. This helps teachers to unearth their creative potential as they grow. Religious and Moral Education also introduces children at this stage to the spiritual aspect of man, that is the belief system of the society. All these helps lay the needed foundation for schooling at the lower primary level.

At the lower and upper primary levels pupils are taught mathematics, science, ICT which provides "fundamental building blocks for success in the era of technological advancement" (Ministry of Education, 2018, p. 1). The introduction of these subject areas will enable a child at this stage to develop interest, knowledge and skills that will spur him or her on to take more interest in these areas of study. It is therefore crucial for government to ensure that all the necessary textbooks and equipment needed to ensure a successful implementation are provided. The availability of such equipment and textbooks will arouse pupils' interest in learning these subjects.

English Language is the official language of Ghana and so it is very appropriate and well in place that pupils are taught English Language at their early ages so as to equip them with the ability to speak confidently wherever they find themselves. A working knowledge in English Language, and ICT will enhance children's confidence and ability of becoming global citizens and competitive in the labor market in future. However, to ensure that our curriculum is in line with our environment and culture, it is appropriate to ensure that the content of all our readers is contextualized. In other words, all our content should reflect our culture which the child can easily relate to. Just as in the same way, the learning of French Language will also make Ghanaian children grow to become international citizens and competitive. More importantly, Ghana is geographically located in West Africa which is dominated by Francophone countries. The knowledge of French Language will enhance peaceful co-existence and trade among industry players within the sub-region.

The inclusion of Ghanaian Languages in the curriculum is a good decision, because as a people we need to prioritize the learning of our mother tongue which gives us our identity as a group of people. It is also good to note that at the lower primary level the policy is that the child should be taught in the native language, because that is the language they know (entry behavior). Therefore, the teaching and learning of Ghanaian Languages in the classroom is well considered in the new curriculum and emphasized in our schools. It is sad to note that some schools forbid school pupils from speaking their native language on the school compound. It is shameful when one is unable to speak his/her own native language well, but the same cannot be said when one is unable to speak a foreign language (English or French) well.

History is an important aspect in the life of every group of people. Past events teach us to learn lessons from our forebears and help us to plan for the present and the future. No nation can forge ahead with its developmental planning well when the people do not know their history well. Therefore, it is our duty as a nation to teach our children our history from their early ages about our heroes and heroines such as Kwame Nkrumah, Emmanuel Obetsebi-Lamptey, Edward Akufo-Addo, Ebenezer Ako Adjei, Joseph Boakye Danquah, and William Ofori-Atta, Yaa Asantewaa among others who laid down their lives for our motherland, so that our children will know where we have come from as a people. This will inspire them to develop love for the nation and the desire to become good citizens and contribute their quota to the development of their country. As spelled out by designers of the Standards-Based Curriculum, "The study of the History of Ghana, will enable learners to reconnect to the past, appreciate Ghana's heritage and values and develop into responsible citizens" (Ministry of Education, 2018, p. 2). And as they progress to higher classes such as JHS the history of other nations can be taught to equip them with the history of our neighbors and distant countries.

Physical Education is a subject area that is critical for growing children to make them physically fit and strong as they are growing up to become adults. Aside from that, Physical Education enhances mental alertness and the physical well-being of people and therefore guarantees healthy working people and thereby reduce medical cost for the nation. In addition, it also provides an opportunity for recreation and entertainment for people. Today, sports are one of the biggest industries in the world and a source of livelihood for many young men and women. Through Physical Education more young talents are identified and groomed to become national stars such as Abedi Pele, Asamoah Gyan, Azumah Nelson, Vida Anim, Vida Nsiah, Mavis Akoto, Emmanuel Tuffour, among others who raised the flag of Ghana high in international competitions.

The subject, "Our-World and Our-People" in the curriculum focuses on the development of our attitude, values and skills. This aims at helping learners to acquire:

- *commitment, that is the determination to contribute to national development.*
- *tolerance, that is the willingness to respect the views of other people* (GES, 2019).

This subject will help children understand and behave well towards different people from different cultures and respect their cultural values. The subject will shape our perception in relation to the rest of the world and how it influences a peaceful co-existence among us as a people in the world. It provides detailed information about our world and environment and how to live comfortable lives by making judicious use of our resources available in the localities.

The writer is disappointed that the Standards-Based Curriculum is, however, silent on technical and vocational component of the Junior Secondary School (JSS) concept introduced in 1987 to equip learners with some basic life skills after school. This needs to be reconsidered in order to help unearth and nurture talents in the area. Besides, the exposure will help learners to make informed decisions in respect of career pathways; that is either to pursue TVET or SHS. Again, Agricultural Science should be taught as a subject on its own and not be subsumed under other subjects.

The Way Forward

Considering the nature of the contextualized curriculum and its emphasis on blending liberal education and TVET to equip learners with basic life skills to enable them to be employable after basic school, there will be the need to equip the schools with the necessary teaching and learning resources and tools, and train teachers who will be teaching at the basic level to make this concept work effectively. This suggests that this type of educational system will be capital intensive and will need a strong political will to undertake such a move. Most governments in African know that the surest way to develop is through science, technology and TVET. This understanding should be the impetus to spur those who have the will to chart this worthy course. The move by the government of Ghana to establish a TVET directorate that is fully in charge of TVET is a clear demonstration of the desire to embark on this pathway. In light of these, the following are suggested as the way forward to ensure that a remarkable progress is made.

The current high rate of unemployment in the country requires the government to seriously consider a blend of liberal, vocational and technical education as the focus of our educational system. The Standards-Based Curriculum should broaden the curriculum to include knowledge and skills acquisition for the world of work.

There is the need to establish a non-partisan commission to chart an educational policy direction for the country that can only be amended by two-thirds of the majority of parliament. This will forestall all tendencies of politicians to change the curriculum to suit their political agenda as has been the case over the years.

The government should always consider a roadmap for the implementation of the new educational system so that it is not rushed as previous ones. This will allow the government enough time to put all the important structures and inputs in place.

There is also the need for government to review the fee-free policy of basic education because quality education requires all the inputs needed to guarantee quality and central government alone cannot do it. So, all other stakeholders of education such parents, churches/missions, NGOs, philanthropists, among others, should be allowed to contribute towards educational development and delivery of quality teaching and learning.

Conclusion

The government's desire to prioritize the fundamental building blocks for success at the basic school level is in line with the global thinking in respect of quality education, socio-economic development, skills requirement, and the focus of Africa Union (Ministry of Education, 2018, p. 1). If this is the basis of the introduction of the Standards-Based Curriculum, then it is in the right direction. However, contextualization of the basic school curriculum will be a significant move to ensure that the ambitions and aspirations of Ghana in respect of what learners should know and be able to do in order to realize their potentials and contribute to the development of the country. Again, contextualization of the school curriculum will make room for the consideration of societal needs first. Therefore, the needs of the society will inform the planning of the school curriculum in order to ensure some of basic needs of society are addressed through the educational system. For instance, conscious steps need to be taken to ensure that the subject content to be taught is worthwhile and relevant to society, considering, socio-economic, cultural values, aspirations, interests and capabilities of the learners. This implies that the contextualized curriculum will be a problem-solving curriculum in which case formal education becomes a tool for solving societal problems. In other words, formal education will train problem solvers in society to take up the challenge of solving problems that confront the society.

The adoption of a contextualized curriculum will guarantee flexible educational pathways to identify and nurture young talents and interests of learners at an early age to groom them for national development. There are cases of young talents in Ghana who have made model cars from scrap metals who need support to develop their talents for the benefit of the larger society. The contextualized curriculum will enable the educational system raise literates who are confident and engaged citizens who can stand the test of all times. This type of curriculum will help in building character and nurture values that are in sync with the Ghanaian culture and value systems. This implies that the Ghanaian identity will always stand out wherever s/he is found.

In our desire to contextualize the curriculum, it is necessary to consider global standards and take steps to guarantee quality of teaching to turn out learners who are knowledgeable, skillful, confident and capable of contributing to the transformation of the country. In other words, as we train our youth to take up responsibilities in our societies and contribute to our transformation agenda, we should be mindful of their ability to compete in the global market. It is in light of this, that as Ghana consider contextualizing the curriculum we should as well be abreast with trends of the global world by considering seriously Science, ICT, Mathematics, and TVET as core areas in the curriculum.

References

Abroampa, W. K., & Addai-Mununkum, R. (2015). *Rudiments of curriculum construction.* Ducer Press.

Adentwi, K. I. (2005). *Curriculum development: An introduction.* Wilas Press.

Agyeman, D. K. (1986). *Sociology of education for African students.* Black Mask Limited.

Agyeman, D. K. (1992). *Sociology of education for African students* (2nd ed.). Black Mask Limited.

Antwi, M. K. (1992). *Education, society and development in Ghana.* Unimax Publishers Limited.

Freire, P. (2014). *Pedagogy of the oppressed.* Bloomsbury Academic.

Ghana Education Service [GES]. (2019). *Our-World-Our-People curriculum for primary schools (B1–3).* Republic of Ghana.

Jean-Francois, E. (2015). *Education and society.* Palgrave Macmillan.

Llego, M. A. (2022). *How to contextualize curriculum for improved academic achievement.* https://www.teacherph.com/contextualize-curriculum/

Ministry of Education. (2018). *National pre-tertiary curriculum Framework.* Republic of Ghana.

Ministry of Education. (2019). *Physical education curriculum for primary schools (Basic 1–6).* Republic of Ghana.

National Council for Curriculum Assessment [NaCCA]. (2023). *Standards-Based Curriculum.* https://nacca.gov.ghs

Su, S. (2012). *The various concepts of curriculum and the factors involved in curricula-making.* ResearchGate.

Sweetland, R. (n.d.). *Curriculum definition collection.*

Yakubu, J. M. (2000). *Principles of curriculum design.* Ghana Universities Press.

· 7 ·

MAKING ENDOGENOUS SCIENCE IN AND FOR EVERYDAY LIFE: A CONCEPTUAL CONNECTION FOR ENDOGENOUS SCIENCE IN LOW-INCOME EVERYDAY LIFE—A KENYAN EXPLORATION OF MAKERSPACE

Wanja Gitari

Introduction

Relevant (endogenous) science may promote current and future socio-economic development (Thisen, 1993), so African countries should strive for auspicious science education systems. This chapter attempts to contribute to the discourse on relevant science while engaging with the decolonial project in the context of global influences on science education. One can see the purpose of the chapter is admittedly a praxis balancing act for a decolonizing project, and it could be mistaken for seeking "legitimation and validation from the dominant," as cautioned by Dei and Cacciavillani, A. (Forthcoming). In outlining pivotal principles of decolonization, they warn that ". . . a genuinely decolonial project cannot seek legitimation and validation from the dominant!". They also posit that "decolonization goes beyond an intellectual act; it is an act of praxis, a practical activity of thinking and doing, that challenges academic and Western modern thought" (p. 2). Therein lies the praxis balancing act for this chapter whereby I claim, based on academic science epistemologies (Ford & Forman, 2006) and knowing so from my local knowledge, nature is the final arbiter.

I am grappling with how to engage with the decolonization of science education[1] in Africa, a traditional academic discipline, and willing to endure some of the contradictions and tensions uncovered in global projects. For instance, Carter (2017) illustrates this point using the incompleteness of anti-capitalist ventures in the fashion industry involving Kibera (slum) residents in Nairobi, Kenya. The British business entrepreneurial and global worker in ethical fashion, Vivienne Westwood, made several project decisions "contrary to her business interests" in "anti-consumption campaigns and anti-capitalistic stance" (p. 1070). Additionally, I invoke knowledge diffusion as a necessary concept to cite scholars from anti-colonial discourses; some might seem off the anti-colonial vision because they mention a postcolonial theoretical framework. In these instances, contradictions (scholarly tensions, maybe) are inescapable. Ultimately, all the theoretical concepts applied to the study support the production of endogenous science—an anti-colonial strategy in science/STEM education.

I also need to note here that the generalized reference to Africa is cognizance of the vast diversity of countries, peoples (Blacks, Arabs, Whites, Chinese, and others), colonial histories depicted in linguistic blocks (e.g., Anglophone, francophone, Lusophone), religions, Spiritualities, etc. Given the singular colonial origin of science education in the continent initiated by European colonists in the latter nineteenth century, I, therefore, use the term Africa for simplicity to engage with the arguments in the context of diversity.

As alluded to earlier, there are ongoing global influences on Africa's science education policies and programs (including curricula structures, contents, and teaching approaches) in contemporary times. These are continually influenced and sourced from countries that are directly linked to the colonizing of Africa (e.g., Britain) or indirectly through global governing institutions such as UNESCO (United Nations Educational, Scientific and Cultural Organization) and OECD (Organization for Economic Cooperation and Development). Jegede (1997) posited this scenario several years ago:

> If current developments occurring around the world are anything to go by, globalization with its attendant economic, political, social and other spin-offs, together with the phenomenal development in telecommunications, communications technology and computer technology will affect every person living on the globe in the twenty-first century. (p. 1)

Over the years, and because of persistent undesirable socio-economic situations in most of Africa, scholars have investigated and debated the efficacy of

Africa's science education. The concerns have spurred periodic modifications to curricula and countries' national policies and priorities for science education (see, for instance, the edited book by Otulaja & Ogunniyi, 2017).

African scholars who are based in Africa (e.g., Jegede, 1997; Ogunniyi, 1986, 2011) and those working in the Western world (Africans and non-Africans) point to an unsatisfactory reality and the need for change in how Africans conceptualize and implement their science education. I should point out that the distinction between working in and outside Africa is crucial in my decolonizing analysis. It concerns positionality and the likely nuanced differences in perspectives by scholars in their different contexts. It also honors those in the continent who labor in proximity to the problematic science education issues by distinguishing them from those who work from a distance away, benefitting from the modern conveniences of the Western worlds, the worlds they criticize. I fall under the latter category and dedicate this chapter to my colleagues in the African continent. I will not expand on this observation to avoid going off limits in the aim of the chapter.

Regarding the status of science education in Africa, nearly four decades ago, Ogunniyi (1986) delineated impediments and inconsistencies that, I should add, are still current as I write this in 2023. These include the focus on standardized exams, teacher training and development, resource scarcity, and the "consumer mindset" cited by Nachuha (n.p.). In this regard, Nachuha welcomes the new global initiative in science-related subject areas, STEM (i.e., integrating science, technology, engineering, and mathematics). The new global wave of STEM initiatives reached the shores of Africa not too long after scholars in the United States introduced STEM in the early 2000s. So, it seems like *a luta continua* in this as well. Like science education, the STEM idea is appealing to national development planning because it promises to equip STEM graduates with relevant skills to meet the demands for applicable workers in the economies of African countries. By extension, policymakers and economic development visionaries see a correlation between STEM education and socio-economic development. However, the correlation is debatable because of the complexity of the involved variables. See Schofer et al. (2000) and Sooryamoorthy (2020) for a discussion of the envisioned correlations.

Given the preceding background, this chapter will employ learning concepts in educational literature that support the decolonization agenda in Africa to focus on a practical matter in science/STEM education, the praxis posited by Dei and Cacciavillani (Forthcoming). In focusing on the practical matter, I invoke Martin Bernal's (1987) exposition of knowledge diffusion, Kwasi Wiredu's (1996) concept of particulars and universals, and Michael Young's (2008) observation that curriculum is a global institution, and Dei's and Cacciavillani's (Forthcoming) pointer that the curriculum is a powerful political entity. The implications are that curriculum developers, policymakers, activists, and others cannot easily do away with the curriculum institution. Wiredu, while recognizing that cultural particulars from the Western world have been severally imposed as universals in formal education, convincingly argues that it is conceptually consistent to adopt cultural particulars, for instance, "the Akan notion of free will and responsibility," that is, the two are practically inseparable, and at the same time accept the United Nations idea of free will devoid of responsibility in deviations such as acting under the influence of a physiologically "unsound mind" (see pp. 6–7).

Accordingly, the argument "illustrates a potentially fruitful interplay of conceptual universals with semantical particulars in intercultural dialogue." Sandra Harding (1997, 1998) discusses similar views in her work, separating science's core concepts (i.e., universals from European cultural particulars masquerading as universals). The core concepts are, for instance, that nature is the final arbiter in scientific propositions (Ford & Forman, 2006). Suppose a claim is made that water running at a certain speed can erode a certain amount of soil of a known soil type, with the tested hypothesis citing the relevant parameters. Eventually, the experimenters see the outcome and either validate or invalidate the scientific proposition. But, assessing many scientific propositions, especially in the social, environmental, and health arena, is not always straightforward. Yet even for these, scientists are expected to appeal to precautionary principles, the weight of evidence, and such analytical parameters, with the subject of study being the final arbiter.

The pilot study used the notion of a makerspace (do-it-yourself (DIY) impetus) to allow nature to judge the efficacy of the proposed ideas. The study participants enacted knowledge (i.e., demonstrated how they learned by appropriating and applying concepts) in the larger context of scientific literacy and focused on endogenous science. According to the learning literature, people acquire new ideas by evaluating sensory input based on prior knowledge (Bransford et al., 2000). Sensory input comes from the physical environment and local and global human interactions leading to universal knowledge diffusion (Bernal, 1987; Mazrui, 1986). Bernal exemplifies universal knowledge diffusion (the "invisible" or unacknowledged co-construction of ideas in society and culture) in etymological discourses among ancient

Africans, ancient Greeks, and beyond. Scientific discourses are no exemption to knowledge diffusion. Bernal's findings make it possible to envision makerspace phenomena in education as a context to integrate idea types, thereby building locally relevant scientific knowledge (endogenous science).

Makerspace phenomenon is a formalized do-it-yourself (DIY) approach traditionally associated with high technological equipment. For instance, fab labs for startup entrepreneurship have high-end technological gadgets like laser cutters, and hackerspaces have advanced computers and software for computer reprogramming. The technology-focused maker spaces are distinguishable from the educational kind based on goals, processes, and materials, with the educational kind being open-ended and focused on learning (ASEE, 2017; de Beer & Baarbe', 2017; Forest et al., 2014; Mersand, 2021; Pereira, n.d.) and operating in after-school programs (Barton et al., 2017; Blikstein & Worsley, 2016; Bullock & Sator, 2015). Some educational makerspace ventures, akin to the science education makerspace activity reported in this chapter, identify with "frugal innovation (work with what you have)" (Magoro, 2022). Regardless of how scholars conceptualize the structures and processes of science educational makerspace, the ultimate goal is to foster creativity, invention, and innovation as envisioned by Hurd (1991, 1997) for scientific literacy. Subsequently, Roffey et al. (2016) assert, in the context of formal education, that

> [t]he Maker Movement ... is a movement that will allow students to be creative, innovative, independent, and technologically literate; not an "alternative" way to learn. But what modern learning should really look like. (p. 3)

Roffey regards makerspace phenomena as a practical pedagogical situation for learning, a place to mobilize "boundary objects" (Barton et al., 2017; Young, 2008). This view is especially instructive when situating an inquiry in everyday life and provokes a critical analysis of the associated knowledge construction process by considering self-determination or agency (Barton & Tan, 2010; Freire, 1970; Hira & Hynes, 2018).

Arguably, makerspace phenomena would support the goals of science education in Kenya (and elsewhere in Africa). For instance, in 2016 Kenya began implementing a STEM curriculum that would require senior high school students to complete service hours in their communities and render school science/STEM (science education) meaningful to themselves and their communities (Kabita & Ji, 2017). Among other objectives, the policymakers wanted students' community service to entail knowledge-making with adults and appraising low-income realities. My study focused on the latter and explored knowledge-making in a staged setting because, when designing the study, the format of students' community service was unknown. As theorized in this chapter, building knowledge should show conceptual connections between scientific literacy, endogenous science, and making practices in a low-income situation in Kenya. I was unaware of other empirical work on knowledge appropriation and application concerning the makerspace phenomena in science education in low-income settings when writing this chapter. Therefore, the study findings fill a gap in the science education literature on knowledge-making in low-income situations and inform Kenya's 2016 STEM curriculum mandate.

I interpret the reported knowledge construction as endogenous science. I also view it as purposeful scientific literacy or knowing and doing from "with/in" the local community that consists of processes and products to transform scientific information (from school and non-school domains) to fulfill purposes in everyday life. The transformation occurs through reciprocal informing when one knowledge domain fills a gap between knowing-that and knowing-how in another knowledge domain (Sillitoe, 2007) to create relevant processes and products. Whenever such processes and products result from the needs in a local context and establish as relevant know-that and know-how, they take on regional characteristics and form endogenous science (Gitari et al., 2020). As explained later, the knowing and doing from "with/in" is pursued through creating and critiquing claims. Constructing and critiquing claims (Ford & Forman, 2006) occurred simultaneously during the making activity as actors (the participants) considered one of the 17 SDGs, SDG #6 on water and sanitation nested in the Kenya's 2030 Agenda (GoK-Vision; UN, n.d.) that aim to improve the living conditions of humanity.

As clarified later in the paper, water, as an aspect of SDG #6, was not the object of the study. Instead, water and sanitation (components of SDG #6) were used as research instruments, as was the makerspace setting. The object of the study was the making (through makerspace) that exemplified knowledge appropriation and application, as is expected when people interact with their environments and facilitate knowledge diffusion consciously or unconsciously. Harding (1998) discussed this aspect of cognition, indicating how different cultures have constructed ways of knowing and produced tools and systems that continue to reflect on the affordances of their environments. Brown (1995) and Schmidt (1997) illustrate such sociocultural cognition using iron (metalwork) technology in Kenya and the rest of East Africa.

The sociocultural cognition perspective and the three concepts cited earlier (i.e., cultural particulars and universals, knowledge diffusion, and curriculum as an institution) inspired two research questions: what affordances (i.e., ideas, tools, etc., recognized as opportunities) of knowledge appropriation and application would result in endogenous science? What are the implications of endogenous science to science education in Kenya and similar contexts? Consequently, the study was set in a qualitative research paradigm as explicated in Creswell (2013), and the fieldwork was undertaken as an educational makerspace activity between May 2019 and October 2019 in partnership with a community-based development organization known as [community partner][2]. To address the research questions, the study (i) analyzed idea types (e.g., local knowledge, school scientific knowledge, and integrated/other type) in a specified sociocultural context as people grappled with a community concern that required the use of school scientific knowledge and (ii) documented the physical tools (e.g., charcoal, sand, bottle, support stand) that residents chose to use, along with the purpose of the tools. Additionally, the study's approach prompted the involvement of research assistants (RAs) from the community and guided the recruitment of participants, data collection, and analysis. The involvement of local RAs inducted them into social inquiry and served a self-determination purpose in the pursuit of endogenous science.

Theoretical Background

The chapter employs diverse theoretical constructs to adequately explain how youths and adults, as a community of learners, created knowledge, in a specified context, through appropriating and applying ideas in everyday life. I articulate the theoretical propositions for learning in a community (Billet, 1996; Moore, 1998; Roth & McGinn, 1997) through socially situated cognition (Smith & Semin, 2004); grasp of practice involving knowledge authoring through constructor and critiquer roles (Ford & Forman, 2006); legitimate peripheral participation (Lave & Wenger, 1991); cultural-historical theory (Hedegaard, 2014); boundary objects (Young, 2008); and scientific literacy (Roth & Barton, 2004). I explain these propositions sequentially as follows.

Socially situated cognition (Smith & Semin, 2004) posits know-that and know-how when people collaborate to address a communal problem through a shared pool of meaning and assume the communal aspect in the co-construction of knowledge. In this case, Smith and Semin employ the term socially situated cognition to highlight the social component of learning.

Their argument is convincing and rendered the term socially situated cognition suitable for my study compared to the related term situated cognition because situated cognition does not privilege sociocultural input in analysis. Furthermore, socially situated cognition credits social aspects and diffusion of ideas (in all life domains: see Bernal, 1987) to scientific knowledge-making processes. This is necessary because in applying scientific knowledge people use ideas from other domains such as history, economics, politics, and Indigenous knowledge (Resnick et al., 1997; Roth & Barton, 2004; Roth & Lee, 2004; Sengul, 2019), and so forth. Certain youths have already demonstrated such intentional knowledge-making, mentioned later in the paper, by gathering information and equipment to innovate a gadget through DIY approach. The materials (physical or epistemological) used by them did not necessarily originate, in an ontological sense, in the local setting.

Socially situated cognition notion for makerspace in science education, therefore, supports interpretations of undertakings by people (or actors) regarding the "grasp of practice" inherent in the authorization of disciplinary knowledge (Ford, 2008; Ford & Forman, 2006). Authorization of knowledge considers individuals' roles in validating what counts as knowledge in science. The validation is done in a "learning community" and involves constructors and critiquers of claims. In this sense, constructors and critiquers externalize the internal community learning processes and shared ideas. The constructors are the individuals who initially spell out ideas for the community. Participants might regard ideas as original, but like most ideas, the individuals likely uniquely synthesized existing information using affordances in their environments (Billett, 1996), exemplifying knowledge diffusion. Ultimately, critiquers will be responsible for testing proposed ideas for trustworthiness. Therefore, the proposed ideas are tested against the material aspects of nature because nature is the "final arbiter," in the case of one of the youths' innovations: can the device scare lions at night?

Legitimate peripheral participation (LPP) refers to coaching when a less experienced learner (novice) is gradually guided into mastery by a more experienced learner or an expert. LLP occurs, for instance, when a master tailor assigns a peripheral task, such as sewing on buttons, to a novice tailor (Lave & Wenger, 1991). The novice tailor works on peripheral tasks while being inducted into more central tasks like garment patterning. Bonnette's and Crowley's (2020) study extends Lave's and Wenger's idea of learning by emancipated adults in a Makerspace. This paper approximates their use of LPP.

Cultural-historical theory is a strand of thought that accounts for histories and cultures of learners (Hedegaard, 2014). For instance, in observing young children grapple with mathematical concepts, the ethnographic researcher documents the learner's environment based on relevant past experiences of the community in which the learner is learning. The ethnographer also takes note of the applicable cultural systems in the learner's society, for example, a child doing mathematics homework while visiting their school friend. In this case, the visiting child gets coaching from a school friend and her family (Hedegaard, 2014).

The concept of boundary objects is adapted from Young (2008) to help express the local knowledge practices that align with ideas in school science (e.g., one can use local plants to filter water). The study references boundary objects as the non-school science materials appropriated and applied for water filtration, especially the local vegetation. Such broad framing of the paper includes discourses on messiness, for instance, that pertain to knowing in everyday life as demonstrated by Highmore (2002) and Steiner (1999) and consistent with transformative perspectives (Tikly & Barrett, 2011). The range of theoretical propositions explained above supports the general idea of scientific literacy and this chapter's specified form of literacy named endogenous science.

As posited by DeBoer (2011), Hurd (1997), and Young (1976), theorizing scientific literacy considers applicable characteristics to align with knowing in everyday life. That is because, for instance, scientific literacy that impacts the living conditions in a low-income context such as [area] is acquired in everyday life within the context of prevailing sociocultural needs. Concerning daily life, Highmore (2002) and Steiner (1999) show that, although everyday life cannot be fully represented through academic methodologies, its study is a valued component of how humans acquire knowledge. As such, qualitative researchers acknowledge the lack of tidy theoretical apprehensions (i.e., messiness) even as they seek to understand discourses in everyday life. The pilot study was mindful of such theoretical nuances. Consequently, the data analysis looked for aspects of scientific literacy, such as planned interventions for nature to judge the efficacy of ideas (i.e., the use of evidence in decision-making).

Hence, scientific literacy is not a standardized measure of know-that and know-how. Granted, standardized measures, such as in the school curricula's science competency, help decide on the match between individuals and fields of study in STEM fields. Instead, scientific literacy is a subjective description of what is within cognitive, and material reach for people (as learners) within notable time and space and for a given purpose (i.e., purposeful/ intentional appropriation and application of knowledge). Thus, learners make demands on their environment using their learning goals, and in turn, the environment imposes demands on learners through possibilities, affordances, and obstacles (Billet, 1996; Hedegaard, 2014). Many of the possibilities and obstacles are cultural and historical. In other words, the context is expressed by and through people in those settings and the affordances in their social, cultural, and natural environments. In the end, "[h]ow these [people's] motives and demands become coordinated may lead to changes in both the person's activities and the setting..." (Hedegaard, p. 194) through problem-solving processes. That means articulating scientific literacy through cultural-historical and socially situated cognitive lenses fosters an import of social, cultural, and historical cultural elements, like that performed in this study. Ultimately, the selected constructs help to advance transformation discourses in science education.

Contextual Background

Self-determination is known to lead people to purposefully appraise their daily living situations to the various degrees of aggregation and complex interdependencies among individuals, organizations, institutions, and global inputs that significantly impact attempts to appraise living conditions (Brinkerhoff, 2010; Lee & Kuzhabekova, 2019). Many of the issues in everyday life constitute realities in [area]. Such realities in [area] motivated the founding of [community partner's name—the community-based organization that partnered with me to conduct the study, and ultimately necessitated collaboration with the community organization to lessen some of the complexities associated with social inquiry in everyday life.

Explaining self-determination reminds me of the Kenyan nine-year-old boy, Stephen, who was featured in May 2020 on the British Broadcasting Corporation (BBC) for his invention of a hygienic hand-washing device to mitigate the spread of the COVID-19 virus (Wamukota, 2020); and of two high school girls- Esther and Salome- who innovated a device "that helps visually and hearing impaired individuals to accurately measure distances and angles" (Anderton, 2019, n.p.); and of the "solar-powered light system" invented by an 11-year-old Kenyan boy, Richard, to keep lions away from his family's livestock at night (Kermelotis, 2013). His invention became popular and was patented four years later. There is also the 14-year-old boy in Malawi,

William Kamkwamba, who built a wind turbine primarily to pump water for irrigation during a severe famine in Malawi (Kamkwamba & Mealer, 2009); and of the establishment of an African School for Inventors in Tanzania (BBC, n.d.). BBC also documents these episodic self-determination ventures in Africa and other financially strapped geo-political regions. All the youths mentioned here used locally available materials to actualize their innovations, aligning with *jua kali* innovators featured in Nashon and Anderson (2013) and the makerspace movement in Africa (see Thomas, 2018 on the Agbobloshie Makerspace Platform (AMP) in Accra, Ghana, for instance).

The determinations to appraise living conditions in the African continent concerning the broad theme of science education and makerspace phenomena are documented by Bilsel and Oral (1995); Good (2012); Lee and Kuzhabekova (2019); Magoro (2022); Marjanovic et al. (2013); Nathaly (2015); Okpala (2016); Thisen (1993); and UN (1991), among others. Furthermore, Good cites the acquisition of construction techniques and entrepreneurship as a favorable outcome of the Tanzania project and observes that community-based organizations (CBOs) serve as "learning platforms" because of the exchange of ideas and experiences that occurs. One may therefore consider these types of CBOs as expanded makerspaces, with the potential to promote scientific literacy while developing endogenous science. Additionally, UNIDO's (n.d.) report on the Third Industrial Development Decade for Africa 2016–2025 highlights the possibility of adding economic value to existing resources for competitiveness (i.e., diversifying the economies), and reports on gaps in endogeneity concerning STEM disciplines.

Integrating the Priorities of School Science with Making in Everyday Life

One priority of school science is the role of evidence in authoring experiences as knowledge (Ford & Forman, 2006). Thus, expectations for the part of evidence imply that people who study science in school should consider evidence when solving problems in everyday life, even if they are not inclined to pursue science as a career. Knowledge appropriation and application (making) entail this (Bransford & Schwartz, 1999; Roth & McGinn, 1997). Of course, even when people are mindful of evidence in everyday life, it does not mean they cannot switch from that mode as warranted by the situations in everyday life. Horton (1971) clarifies this by thoroughly explaining theoretical predispositions and commonsense use. As such, this paper refers to the term scientific literacy synonymously with science competency in analyzing and reporting the knowledge-making that was observed during the makerspace activity of the village pilot project because the activity involved youths who were studying science and adults who were likely applying, more actively and broadly than the youths, their knowledge(s) in everyday life.

Making in everyday life is conceptualized in the context of scientific literacy's multifaceted and multilayered dimensions (Jenkins 2009; Levinson, 2018; Roth & Barton, 2004) and evokes socially situated cognition. Therefore, the inventions by the youths mentioned earlier are good examples of socially situated cognition, involving scientific knowledge without noticeable modification (application) and with some modifications using local ideas and tools, or otherwise, of scientific knowledge (appropriation). The inventions also illustrate universal knowledge diffusion, as Bernal (1987) explained.

Self-determination Linked to Science Education

Hira and Haynes (2018) discuss purposefulness and self-determination as encapsulations of meaning and agency. Subsequently, meaning and agency are assumed in the design of the study reported here. Although scientific literacy generally highlights the expectation for knowledge users as individuals and communities to make evidence-based decisions in response to manifestations of natural phenomena in everyday life, likely, knowledge users may not have studied the natural phenomenon or its manifestations for first-hand evidence or primary data. However, in the absence of primary data, knowledge users are expected to know how to use the information that accrues from inquiries conducted by others (Bransford & Schwartz, 1999; Bransford et al., 2000; Roth & Barton, 2004). Such information is accessible through knowledge media, including school textbooks, scientific magazines, television, and the Internet, as evidenced by the documented youths who engage with DIY when addressing problems in their communities. The data analysis for this study therefore identified ideas outside the school curriculum and ideas in the school curriculum.

Methodology

The study utilized qualitative research methods through observations involving a field journal, focus group discussions, making and conversations, reflection forms, and interviews. The qualitative research paradigm (Creswell, 2013; Geertz, 1973; Gubrium & Holstein, 2014; Willig, 2014) facilitated the application of pertinent theoretical constructs for the transformation of science education in Kenya. It permitted the researchers to proceed critically and intentionally with the planned research agenda and to incorporate member checks. It also required cognizance of "trade-offs and dilemmas" (Brinkerhoff, 2010; Thisen, 1993) consistent with self-determination literature. Subsequently, the methodology prompted the engagement of schooled young adults in the community as research assistants and the freedom to use the language that afforded in the moment during the study because, as posited by Lodge (2019) and Okhee (2005), the words people choose from their sociocultural milieu to discuss scientific phenomena illuminate the nature of their scientific discourse.

Research Assistants, Site Advisor, and Participants

There were two research assistants (RAs). One of the initial[3] RAs was a primary school teacher, whereas the other RA was an administrative member of [community partner]. An additional project member was the site advisor in his capacity as the founding member and a leader of [community partner]. The involvement of local research assistants and research site advisor furthered the consciousness-raising agenda for the pilot project by granting them the opportunity to grapple with social inquiry.

Six Form Three (Grade 11 North American equivalent) students (youths) and seven adults (men[4] from the local community and two science teachers from the youths' high school) volunteered to participate in the study following institutionally approved ethical protocol. The recruitment of the volunteer participants was purposeful and followed the snowball sampling technique described by Bogdan and Bilken (2007) to ensure meaningful data collection in the short time available for fieldwork. The six students were invited to an information session by their science teacher based on her understanding of their interests in science and capacities to participate in research activity. I conducted an information session with the six students in mid-May

2019 in the school's science laboratory. I then explained the ethical protocol for study's participants and handed out the information and consent forms. Moreover, after considering the fieldwork expectations, I allowed the students reasonable time (one day) to decide if they wished to participate in the study. The six students signed their consent forms to support their role as youth participants and their rights as research participants. I also recruited two science teachers (one woman and one man as adult participants).

I trained the two research assistants (RAs) from the village community by explaining the purpose of the study and discussing the eligibility of adult participants. They apportioned the prospective list of adult participants, and each approached the eligible adults with the information letter and consent form. They recruited five adults. Some adults who volunteered to participate gave verbal consent instead of written signatures. The ethical protocol had a provision for verbal consent. The following is the participant list by pseudonyms in alphabetic order with female (F) and male (M) identifiers and the names suggested by participants[5]. Youths included Brizzil (F), Daniella (F), Owen (M), Ramsey (M), Vinex (F), and Zeddy (F); adults included Burner (M), Dilware[6] (M, science teacher who later assumed the role of an RA and "activity expert"), Den (M), Kamusi (M, later changed roles from RA to participant), Ken (M) Phares (M), and Verah (F, science teacher). Ken withdrew his consent after the focus group discussions. He did not explain. Notably, there is only one female participant on the adult list; she was recruited through the school and not from the community.

Data Collection and the Data

All the data collection tools incorporated member-checking (Creswell, 2013) as I liaised with the RAs during fieldwork and data analysis. Table 1 presents a summary of the data collection process.

Field Journal

Fieldwork observations were noted in a journal by the principal investigator and the RAs. The notes in the journal, amounting to three pages of a 9" × 6" notebook, were handwritten from what was observed or said, in person or through phone. Other notes were in emails.

Table 1 Summary of Data Collection Process

Data collection tool	Data collection focus	Data collection Timeframe in 2019	Data collection product
Field journal	Observations, emails, phone calls	June–October	Descriptions of fieldwork; 3 single space sheets[7]
Focus group discussion	Research team formation brainstorming on makerspace activity	June	Audio recordings, 7 MP3 audio segments of two FDGS; 90 minutes and 75 minutes respectively; transcripts amounted to 7 pages
Making and conversations	Assembling of water filtration trials	June-August	Audio recordings of 3 making activities 40–60 min each; 4 separate segments of recording ranging between 35 seconds to 40 minutes; transcripts amounted to 5 pages
Reflection form	Demographic data and reflections	September-October	Handwritten submissions by 6 youths and one adult
Interviews	Interviews to fill out reflections form	August; September; October	Audio recording, 2–4 minutes each, of reflections through interview for 3 adults; transcripts amounted to 2.5 pages

Focus Group Discussions (FGDs)

The participants met initially for 90 minutes in the school laboratory (designated makerspace room) as a team to deliberate on the study's objectives, expectations, and reasonable actions. In that meeting, they chose to work on SDG #6, the water purity aspect, providing reasons why. They also brainstormed the methods they would use for water purification, and they suggested their pseudonyms. They met for a second time for 75 minutes to assign roles: those who would look up information from textbooks and the local community, collect water from the local river, and find water filtration materials like bottles and sand. The proceedings of the FGDs were handwritten and audio recorded in seven MP3 audio segments ranging from three minutes to 45 minutes. The RA set it up similarly for all recordings to ensure unproblematic storage and transmission of files from the limited-storage size electronic gadgets available for data collection. The FGDs transcripts comprised seven handwritten pages of a 9" × 6" notebook.

Making and Conversations

Following the FGDs, the participants collected water from the local river, [river name], using an 11-liter recycled plastic bottle and stored the water in the makerspace room. They muddied the water to enhance the clarity of the filtration outcome. They then cut the bottoms of 200 ml water bottles and systematically assembled the bottles with various filtration materials: charcoal, coarse sand, fine sand, sieves, debris [fragments of porous sedimentary rock], herbs (i.e., *Molinga oleifera* leaves) pebbles, cotton wool, funnel-shaped container cut out from an 11-liter plastic bottle, and accessories (e.g., beaker, chair, clamper) to achieve the envisioned water filtration setup based on knowledge sharing during FGD. For instance, they had agreed that *M. oleifera* leaves may remove microorganisms from water, and debris can sieve large particles.

The general procedure consisted of layering the filtration materials in the 200 ml plastic bottles and clamping the bottles to a laboratory stand[8] last/third trial, further below. During three meetings, they attempted to filter the water using the same general procedure through trial and error. Each session lasted from 40 min to 60 min. In the first trial, they layered the materials in ascending order from the broader end of the bottle: pebbles, herbs, coarse sand, charcoal, and cotton wool. They poured muddy water into the inverted bottle; the outcome was more transparent (Figure 1). During the first trial, the participants observed that cotton wool trapped more refuse than other materials.

Subsequently, they used more cotton layers for the second trial. The arrangement for the second trial imitated the first trial in form and aimed to improve the clarity of the visually clear water from the first trial. The materials in the inverted 200 ml were in the following order: gravel, cotton wool, charcoal, herbs, cotton wool, sand, and cotton wool, as in Figure 2.

MAKING ENDOGENOUS SCIENCE IN AND FOR EVERYDAY LIFE

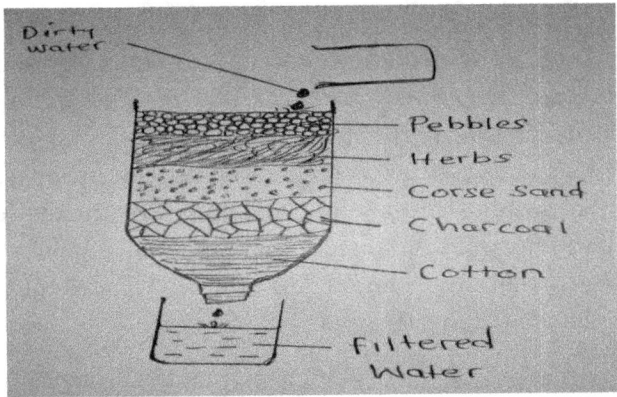

Figure 7.1 Representation of the First Filtration Trial

They poured out the translucent water from the first trial. The product was more transparent water. Therefore, the participants decided to layer the material differently for the third trial to clear the water from the remaining refuse. The material layering in trial three was in the following order: cotton wool, fine charcoal, herbs, fine sand, coarse sand, charcoal, and debris. The resulting water was not visibly clearer than the result of trial three, and they agreed that, although the water looked clean, the extent of "purification" could not be ascertained through the procedure they had used that far. This led the participants to discuss how they might determine that the water was clear and free of harmful microorganisms and other toxins.

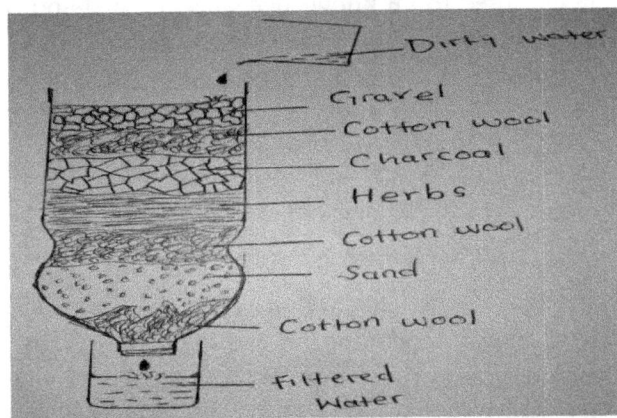

Figure 7.2 Representation of the Second Filtration Trial

Following, Dilware used an elaborate illustration based on the emergent common pool of meaning to depict a water filtration and disinfecting system that included measured layers, glass tubing, a heating device, a storage tank, an aeration nozzle, taps, and other features.

The entire making process was characterized by unstructured conversations, as when people share a pool of meaning in situated learning. The making conversations were audio recorded and produced four pieces of MP3 recordings ranging from 35 seconds to 15 minutes—the resultant transcripts comprised five handwritten pages of a 9" × 6" notebook.

Reflection Form

The three-page questionnaire forms were completed toward the end of fieldwork (see Table 1). The form had three main sections and five sub-sections for the third question. The forms provided information to collaborate and augment the data from other data collection tools. For example, it helped establish a link between Dilware's drawings and his experience as a chemistry teacher. The information sought in the form included (i) demographic data such as the category of participant, level of schooling, and occupation (for adults); (ii) prompt questions/statements on experiences with and knowledge of school science (including laboratory skills), experiences with, and knowledge of, the local knowledge, experiences with, and knowledge of "other" forms of knowledge, (iii) the participants' experiences and thoughts concerning (a) the goals of the project, (b) the sharing of ideas between youths and adults during the making activity, (c) the materials used for the making activity, (d) the strategies used to fill knowledge gaps, and (e) and the suggestion to set up a village innovation center run by [community partner], in [area] village. All the youths and two adults, Burner and Dilware, filled out eight forms by hand.

Interviews

The RAs conducted Interviews with the adults (Dennis, Faris, and Vera) who preferred oral responses to the reflection questionnaire form. Their interviews ranged from 2–4 minutes depending on the details provided by the interviewee, and associated transcripts covered two and a half-handwritten pages of a 9" × 6" notebook.

Data Processing and Analysis

The data processing and analysis were patterned on the inductive approach, also known as thematic analysis in the qualitative paradigm (Creswell, 2013; Reichertz, 2014; Willig, 2014). First, to familiarize myself with the data, I listened to audio recordings of FGDs, making activities, and interviews; and I then read through the written reflections on the reflection forms. During this initial step and subsequent steps, I paid attention to specific points in participants' utterances concerning the research objective and the literature. Specifically, I wrote down relevant impressions on situations of knowledge appropriation and application and idea types.

Second, when listening to audio data for a second time, I flagged segments on the digital recording for transcription and transcribed the flagged segments; while reading the reflection forms, I marked and jotted recurring ideas beside the participants' responses. Third, I typed out the flagged segments and my corresponding thoughts; for instance, on Dilaware's write-up concerning the goals of the project, I scribbled "awareness of local community on two levels …," and on Brizill's write-up on experiences and knowledge of school science, I noted, "she contributed ideas from her science class." I typed out the reflection segments in the order in which they appeared in the reflection form as listed above. Typing out the text helped me gain further insight into the data through additional handling because I continued to link participants' utterances with the study objectives and the literature. Fourth, I read through the selected write-ups of reflections and transcripts and generated analytical segments, for example, "we can purify water using a chemical." Finally, I narrowed down the analytic segments into analytic codes, for example, "find evidence."

The inherent meaning of the codes was enhanced by rereading field notes while looking for observations that were consistent or inconsistent with the generated codes. For example, while continuing with the data processing, I checked field notes based on a previous conversation with the research assistant (RA), and I found she wanted to know if it was acceptable for the participants to obtain information (evidence) on the Internet to verify the ideas being shared (e.g., if the chemical anhydrous copper sulfate can be used for water purification). The cross-checking verified the quality of the codes and led to the grouping of codes into categories. An example of a category associated with the transcript segment referred to earlier, is "finding evidence." Consequently, codes that were not supported by substantial transcript segments and/or field notes were discarded. Sixth, I developed themes from similar categories and associated transcript segments, for instance, "finding evidence" and codes that pointed to knowing-that and knowing-how were grouped under sub-themes and later into one theme, that is, expansion of the pool of meaning through self-determination and affordances in the sociocultural environments. After performing steps one to six, I reread the not-flagged responses for additional insight to complete the data processing and analysis.

The entire data processing and analysis also separated the adult participants' utterances from youth participants to compare for deeper thematic insights consistent with the inductive data analysis (Bogdan & Bilken, 2007; Creswell, 2013; Willig, 2014). It helped me to position the data from the participants' experience of the making and other fieldwork aspects, through member-checks (e.g., by asking the RA to explain why M. *oleifera* leaves were used for water filtration setup), and by sharing the first draft of this paper with the participants for input. Eventually enriching the outcome of the data analysis. Member-check (Bogdan & Bilken, 2007; Willig, 2014) was necessary to enhance the trustworthiness of the qualitative data-collecting tools.

Findings

The findings illuminate possibilities for endogenous science in four areas revolving around the human resource that is central to the enhancement of knowledge: (i) interactions on congenial knowledge co-construction between the youths and adults; (ii) expansion of the pool of meaning through self-determination and affordances in the sociocultural environment; (iii) exemplifying situated "universal knowledge diffusion" with accessible information sources; and (iv) expressions of the need to know or continued learning.

Interactions on Congenial Knowledge Co-construction Between the Youths and the Adults

The prevailing sociocultural norms in [area] for interactions between adults and youths in everyday life denote conversational and physical distancing and may not support the intentional co-construction of knowledge by youths and adults. That is, youths and adults do not typically interact within intentional knowledge-building social spaces to share meaning in everyday life. Instead, youths tend to share meaning with youths and adults with adults because the age groups operate in somewhat different social spheres. For instance, a young person is instructed by her father to tend the sheep. If her effort is unsatisfactory, she is reprimanded and told how to improve on her duty. There is often no social knowledge construction space for the girl to inform her father that the sheep show interest in the pasture in the early morning and not late afternoons and would benefit from only morning pasturing. Instead, in this case, the father assumes he is older and more mature than his daughter and does not require any idea exploration with her. She, too, might wish to keep the peace by doing what she is told without questioning her father's wisdom. As in most sociocultural scenarios, there are exceptions to the rule about the youths and adults' interactions, and the preceding example is only general; this is evident in Daniella's case. She spoke up confidently, compared to her peers, for the first time and continued to assert herself as the discussions and conversations progressed.

The making activity brought adults and youths in proximity, both conversationally and physically, and they interacted respectfully and productively throughout the project, which was an encouraging possibility for endogenous science. The youths did not talk much during the first focus group meeting except for one youth, Daniella. However, the RA moderating the FGDs prompted each youth to speak up. As they spoke, each expressed the reason for selecting water purification instead of sanitation (for SDG #6). After a long deliberation that lasted more than 1 hour, all the youths expressed their views on SDG #6, showing keen interest in the water problem in the community. By the end of the project, many youths were speaking up by simply monitoring the flow of conversation and then introducing their comments as appropriate.

The quotes provided below are extracted from the reflection questionnaire filled out by youths toward the end of the project, showing how the youths interacted with the adults. The comments point to the confidence that the youths gradually gained, through coaching by the RAs and the adults, as they felt they were contributing helpful ideas. Additionally, other comments show the adults' observations of the youths' engagement. Each type of participant (youths, adults), for instance, Vinex and Dilware, reflected on prior knowledge of sociocultural norms of interaction and eventually revised some preconceived ideas about the other type of participant. Whenever necessary, the identifier Y is used for youth, and A for adult. M and F are used for male and female, respectively.

The ideas were ... interesting and the youth ... exchange[d] their ideas with the adults. Whenever there was [need for] assistance ... we were able to communicate confidently. We as youths we learned more from the adults especially "I." (Ramsey, M)

I had no idea that even adults out there can think beyond their capacity, but it was surprising that I learnt even them know a lot than even us. (Vinex, F)

[S]haring ideas between youth and adults was a positive impact to the project. (Zeddy, F)

This has improved our thinking capacity. Our brains if I may say so my mind in particular has opened up. I think beyond my own expectation. For days now I have turned to become more courageous and confident. The adults also have a great impact to us cause sitting together and discussing ideas have led to gaining more intellectually. (Daniella, F)

The appreciation of working together was mutual. Burner (A, M) wrote in his reflections form that "sharing was free and there was no subordination. All talk was sincere ... not forced from every participant that took part in the research." Dilware (A, M) summed it up well for the adults: "[T]he project intermingle[s] both students, teachers, and people from the community. The interaction help[ed] in gathering information from all angles[s] and stages of life, current and ancient." He then added that working with the youth helped improve their "underdeveloped ideas."

The adults dominated the floor in all interactions by sharing their knowledge. Although sociocultural norms allow adults to speak demandingly with the youth, the manner of speaking by the adult participants was mostly educative, as if to set a learning context for the youths. Den, for instance, referred to the exposure he had gained by traveling abroad to a high-income country and living in a disenfranchised neighborhood in Nairobi, Kenya's capital city. He also made instructive references to how the people of [area] obtain the water used in their homes. He was keen on educating his listeners. For example, during one of the focus group discussions, he prefaced a point on water purification with "let's start educating people ...; that's educate people in the community ... in our region and throughout the country." The context he set helped inform other participants about the significance of water and the corresponding lack of the provision of clean water for domestic use in [area].

Subsequently, other participants began to offer insightful rejoinders. For example, another adult Verah (F), a science teacher, stated her reason accompanied by a larger vision: "... we are going to minimize the cost of living by reducing the cost of buying clean water; you have seen people buying clean water to consume at their houses." Additionally, Daniella (Y, F) supported the views on providing clean water, by saying that "mine is very simple: clean water will spread easily. . . . because our focus is human welfare." The way she prefaced her point is interesting, given the "educating," by Den, which preceded her point. She needed to alert everyone to her limited understanding, with "mine is very simple," of the broader and complex context highlighted by the adults.

In another instance, Kamusi (an adult) sought to educate about water purification by prompting the youths, as a coach would do. He did this by prefacing his invitation with a mention of relevant chemical compounds, including anhydrous copper sulfate, copper II chloride, and chlorine solution; materials such as litmus paper; concepts such as boiling point and freezing point of water; and technical practices concerned with the waiting time required by users of chlorine-treated water to ingest the water after treatment. Overall, the adults seemed to appreciate the opportunities derived from respectful dialogue with the youths, an essential setting for endogenous science. Den summed up this appreciation in his reflection form as follows:

> Youths have little experience about life because they have just lived briefly but when we come to adults the adults have a lot of experience for life so when two comes together sharing knowledge it means that sometimes most of the youth, they have the most current knowledge all that and what is going on around and also the elders also have knowledge about life and what has been going on through in line with the project. So, I can say that there was that open sharing of knowledge between the two groups and my experience is that it exhausted all the areas needed to come up with the most efficient [means] for the problem.

The participants also had light moments during the activity. Both the youths and the adults exhibited relaxed demeanor as one would hope for endogenous science in everyday life, rather than a formalized environment as was prevalent in the initial FGD. There were laughter, the use of multiple languages, and code-switching. For example, "utakuwa ume-separate [laughter]"; "hatutaweka radioactive something?" This code-switching in [language name] translates as "will you have separated"; "will we not put a radioactive something?" I have reported further details on the language and code-switching aspect in another finding.

Expansion of the Pool of Meaning through Self-determination and Affordances in the Sociocultural Environment

The participants were keen to delve into the pilot project and involve knowledgeable community members as much as possible. They all exhibited a determination that underscored their perspective of water as a basic human need consistent with SDG #6. Beyond that, they illustrated socially situated cognitive learning by evoking connections with various affordances in their sociocultural environment. A dialogue on the significance and impact of water was started by several adults during the first FGD when they provided a context for the related SDG. Speaking with urgency and agreeing with the decision to work on water activity, Verah introduced the economic aspects of clean water:

> Go for clean water, purification of water because it has a direct impact on the residents: one, it is going to provide safe water for consumption, for domestic use, that is the livestock and having in mind that this area most likely, livelihood of most people here is livestock keeping, dairy cows and so forth.

Additionally, Den (A, M) added his action points that also included care for the environment:

> We will involve community; use existing water project; revive water projects if there are any; set up water points; explore the method we can use to make sure they have access; get the people organized; clean the [area] Water Project; ... plant trees in water shed areas because we have wells ... involve the administration to plant trees, that can be a source of clean water.

Concerning the significance of water, Burner wrote in the reflective questionnaire:

> Clean water ... will help reduce mortality rate by reducing the percentage that die through water borne diseases. It will also help in raising standards of the poor who cannot afford to buy mineral water from shops.

Den also raised an issue on equity and access to water as he clarified the situation of water in the [area] area:

> [Area] Water Project was [meant] for irrigation and domestic use [but we can] use the [area] water tanks because [when] they put up the project purity [of water] was

MAKING ENDOGENOUS SCIENCE IN AND FOR EVERYDAY LIFE   145

not on their minds ... [also] look for a way for those people who do not have piped water their homes.

Dilware (A, M) agreed with Den's equity and access concern by pointing out that "by the end of the project we will be able to have [inaudible segment] hoping to have water for everyone, so we don't use water which is meant for irrigation for consumption." Although the objective of the making was not to supply clean water, this participant's comment shows, that opinions were swayed as the participants interacted, the kind of swaying that occurs during knowledge co-construction. Such interactions between the adults and the youths were reported in an earlier finding. The emergent vision to supply water to households continued to broaden the perspectives of the participants by raising logistics as well as a safety concerns as follows:

> How are we going to make sure that this pure water, this clean water is going to reach each and every resident of [area]? ... purifying water for every person within our area that we are dealing with because we already know that apart from the tap water that we are having from maybe the Ministry of Water, we still have some households where they are fetching water from the rivers. What are some of the ways in which you are going to incorporate so that we can ensure this water is clean both for the consumers who are using maybe rainwater, tap water, or water from the river or even the lakes or whatever we are going to have? (Kamusi, A, M)

Brizill (Y, F) reiterated the points raised by the adults by highlighting the need to purify any water under consideration. She contributed her views on the need for pure water and offered additional information by naming water sources in [area]. She pointed to a nearby river that could supply the water for the project activity because, according to her, the river is comparatively large and is not seasonal, unlike other rivers with significantly low volumes of water in dry seasons. The seasonality of the rivers was explained further by an adult as the conversation progressed. To further support her proposition, Brizill stated: "... we get clean water from [river name], it is the best to use. So, after we get the product then we test the impurity of the water."

Kamusi (A, M) followed the lead from others by providing insights and evoking a systems approach that emphasized the economic and political logistics of the envisioned distribution of purified water. He posed a question, suggested a solution, and mentioned a security concern, as given below:

> How shall we know the amount of water we will be distributing to each and every family gauging their consumption which we don't know? ... have a very big storage tank, the other tanks placed strategically—eight tanks or so in every village ...

because if we are talking about giving people the basics on water purification, some of them will not compute molarity [molality].... and have some people guard on it [the water tanks] so it's not tampered with.

Offering the most pointers to the sociocultural pool of meaning thus far, Den engaged with this dilemma in an educational style. He suggested to

visit every household to create awareness; give them basic concepts, give those [chemical] reagents ... because if we involve the other people who are providing water they may think we want to take their project ... create awareness, maybe we have a chief *baraza* [public meeting with the chief], in the church, all those things; we speak to them and show them how water is treated before using it ... it is going to be more effective before we go to further parts involving project managers in the surrounding area.

During the interview, Phares (A, M) reflected on the water provision discussions by offering a health and wellness viewpoint and supporting it with scientific ideas:

The project is of great help in improving community health and preventing some of the water borne diseases [inaudible]; if more of emphasis is put on creating awareness on the causes, effects, and control of water related diseases this will lead to a healthy society that we expect to work more effectively.

He supported these claims by emphasizing the hope that was prevalent among the members of the [area] community: "The community fully backed up the suggestion and is looking forward.... People are aware, because it [the reality of water bourne disease] is a problem that is running through the village..."

Exemplifying Situated "Universal Knowledge Diffusion" with Accessible Information Sources

The previous two findings highlight the socially situated cognition of a common pool of meaning. The current finding further describes the tapestry of the pool of meaning. At the start of making, each participant's prior knowledge informed their decision to participate. For instance, Owen's (Y, M) choice was informed by daily observations in his environment. As a topic for investigation, he had suggested poverty related to another SDG: "because in Kenya people live in poverty"; Brizill (Y, F) explained her reason for not choosing poverty, as "[poverty] will only cater [to] adults, but [SDG on water and sanitation] will cater to the whole community." Another youth (Zeddy, F) observed that water and poverty are closely linked. Finally, Kamusi (A, M) chose poverty and when probed by the research assistant for supportive information, he quipped, "that is why it's . . . research, we think through it together." Kamusi, a primary school teacher, wanted to include many perspectives before selecting one option. His approach was based on his prior knowledge from his upbringing, schooling, work environment, or everyday life.

Owen, a youth, supported his choice with reason: "because the process is easier." Possibly, he had imagined a straightforward creativity process based on his prior experiences with laboratory work at school, or he had imagined the makerspace activity as a process that would not involve deliberations or the delicate manipulation of the water filtration contraption. However, in the FGDs, he had heard ideas about the complexities of the [area] Water Project, the use of different types of paper bags, and other ideas that may have gradually unsettled the imagination of an easy makerspace phenomena. Evidently, such knowledge was acquired during movements in everyday life, including travel, school, job, home, entertainment, and other human interactions in and outside the [area] community.

For instance, Den acquired some of his ideas abroad: "I had an opportunity to visit [name of country withheld for confidentiality]. You cannot see a [trash] paper anywhere." He was pointing toward the cleanness of the environment in the country he visited. Den's point was a trail off from the first FGD on the decision to work on a water activity and to leave out the sanitation aspect of SDG #6. The point included information sharing directed at the youths with remarks such as "we used paper [paper bags made from wood pulp] back then; back in the 1970s" (Den). He also explained what plastic material recycling entails and then posed a check-in question for the youths, "How do you do it here at the school? Do you have [waste designated garbage and recycling] bins?" He added that pulp-based paper "disintegrates" when discarded to educate his listeners. Den's information sharing and apparent authoring of recycling knowledge had piqued Zeddy's and Owen's (Y, M) curiosities prompting Owen to ask, "the plastic and nylon paper, can they be recycled?" Vinex also penned a related insight in the reflection questionnaire. Her reflection was on the "positive effect" of the project: ". . . and because there is . . . use of local [material] (stones, charcoal and others), this will help [the people] in utilizing them [the materials] instead of disposing of them."

The participants eventually agreed, through consensus, that water activity was most relevant because water could impact community welfare in many ways, including poverty, and moved on to exemplify universal knowledge diffusion during the assembling of the water purification contraptions. Multiple chats were happening, with code-switching between English (the language of instruction and international business transactions in Kenya), Kiswahili, and [local language name]. An example of code-switching was "uta-boil?" meaning "will you boil"? And that of a chat-phrase in Kiswahili was "sadhana kama haitakuwa na hizo germs" translated to "I'm not sure it won't have those germs." The choice of the spoken language may have prompted access to certain information. The source of the information in this case may be based in academic science because other comments included "it's a long time since I saw a book of science"; "the last time I saw a science book was in Form Three" [Grade 11 North American equivalent].

The information sources mentioned by the youths in the reflection forms included the two high school science teachers, biology and chemistry subject matter, adults, and research on the Internet. The participants exchanged ideas on academic science, including "irradiation; fractional distillation; liquids that are close to boiling point; microorganisms; doing research." Acknowledging the role of school, Kamusi (A, M) suggested, "Maybe Brizill (Y, F) can help us because she is fresh in class." Following this prompting, the youth accessed information on water filtration on the Internet and read aloud the recommended procedure as it appeared online. She then helped to clarify the chemical compounds used for softening water (sodium bicarbonate, soda ash, and aluminum citrate), upon prompting by Kamusi, who pondered aloud, "if I remember correctly . . . ." In this regard, the youths also served as sources of information. Brizill was referred to as "the expert" by Kamusi during this exchange. Like Brizzil and other youths, Vinex appreciated the opportunity to apply the knowledge she had acquired in school. In her reflection, she wrote as follows:

> After going through the study of science in school, I got a lot of knowledge on how to use it in practical science. Due to this, I was able to give and share ideas with others so as to come up with a naturally and locally method of [purifying the] dirty water used at our homes.

She added her appreciation of the approach to use local materials for making:

> Engaging in the project has made me to know even locally undermined materials can also be used . . . . As stones can clean up dirty water, charcoal can remove colour

of dirty water making it safe. Through this I have an experience ... using [these] materials.

The local community contributed to knowledge diffusion by sharing information on the materials that were used in the activity: 200 ml and 11L plastic water containers, sieves, sand from a nearby construction site, gravel, charcoal, cotton wool, herbs, and others. As Phares (A, M) explained in writing his reflection, "we had challenges especially collecting the materials. They [community members] provided several suggestions from which we made the best choice in the course of the project. They helped, and their contribution made it a success in this project." One of these contributions refers to a local vegetation known as *nthanje*. This vegetation was acknowledged locally as a "water purifier." However, none of the participants could find it, and the project time limitation did not accommodate the further search for *nthanje*.

Expressions of the Need to Know or Continued Learning

This category implicates cultural-historical theory (Hedeegard, 2014). The category reports on the participants and community intimations that would further enhance the making of endogenous science in prevailing environments. One of these issues is sanitation, the item that is coupled with water in SDG Goal Six. The participants devoted considerable time discussing sanitation in terms of outer houses, that is, toilets that do not use a water flushing system and are located at a considerable distance from houses. Den (A, M) started the conversation by raising his concern regarding the students' health at the local secondary school where the youths were attending. He explained that students' health might be compromised because "students don't use toilets properly." The dialogue on toilets moved beyond the concern for students to the suggestion to ask local leaders "to investigate who doesn't have toilets" in the [area] community. This was followed by considerable curiosity by youths and adults about the health code (i.e., depth and width of the toilet hole, the ratio of persons per toilet) for such toilets. Other adult participants mentioned the prevalence of toilets (i.e., shallow holes) that are not dug according to the building code. Den then expressed his concern regarding where the waste from the school was deposited: "all the waste from this school should not be released into [name] river." [Name] is the seasonal river, less than three kilometers from the school.

Conversations concerning incinerators were also notable as participants sought to gain further information. There was curiosity regarding their appearance, functioning, costs, whether they produce harmful chemicals (e.g., Sulphur gases) as a by-product of the working mechanism, and whether it would be necessary and cost-effective to have several incinerators strategically positioned throughout the village, among others. Brizill (Y, F) expressed concern about incinerators concerning the destruction of the ozone layer.

Other need-to-know view was shared by Brizill in her statement that "it would be nice for us as a group to visit a developed country then we can come back with ideas to develop our area"; and Dilware (A, M) who observed in the written reflections, "I have been in this locality for three months [and] gathered information ... about the place, but I cannot say I know so much about the place". Notably, none of the participants expressed concern over the likelihood of contaminants being introduced by water purification materials used in the water filtration activity (e.g., plastic bottle, cotton wool, charcoal, and debris from nearby construction sites). However, the participants discussed the idea of pure water versus clear water. They tried to work out a process to test the water they filtered—clear water—tested for purity at a laboratory in Nairobi, the capital city of Kenya. Nairobi is about a six-hour drive from the [area]. However, the logistics were prohibitive, and time was limited. Burner's (A, M) views on the idea of a village innovation center (VIC) summed up the unanimous support by the participants for structured, purposeful, and continued learning: "[t]he suggestion to set VIC will help enlighten [area] residents on the SDGs [and] make them understand the importance of team work as well as the need for their safety health-wise and in other aspects of individually oriented safety."

Discussion and Implications

Intentional deliberations by the individual and community around sociocultural issues aligned with school science, in the context of science education, are crucial for constructing endogenous science and, by extension, local human capacity building. Therefore, the following discussion is structured around sociocultural deliberations and signals purposeful and sustained knowledge appropriation and application in everyday life. It represents a possible road map to a local form of scientific literacy—endogenous science.

Socially Situated Construction of Endogenous Science

The making of endogenous science would be unrealistic without relaxing certain sociocultural norms respectfully, as exemplified in the first finding. Respectful relaxing requires anyone posing their ideas to be aware that their propositions are open to criticism by critiquers, and the necessity to allow nature (arbiter) to decide (Ford & Forman, 2006) and hold the experts' ideas loosely. For instance, in Lave and Wenger's (1991) learning situations, the term expert is used for the more knowledgeable, whereas novice is used for the less knowledgeable. However, Bransford et al. (2000) suggested rethinking the use of the term experts in the context of a community of learners because role reversals inevitably occur as socially situated learning progresses. By extension, the conceptualized role reversals indicate an aspect of the rich tapestry that is likely when humans interact in everyday life, as occurred when one of the youths had the skill to look up information in a subject area. The role reversal was also echoed, albeit in a different experiential realm, when one of the study's research assistants switched to a participant role. Such eventualities are inescapable components of learning in everyday life (Highmore, 2002; Steiner, 1999). They resonate with Bransford et al. (2000) suggestion to regard the expert-novice divide loosely as a continuum within a community of learners.

Therefore, the findings show the importance of enhancing a community's pool of meaning through exploratory dialogues (Barton et al., 2017; Smith & Semin, 2004; Roth & Lee, 2004). In embracing trade-offs and dilemmas (Brinkerhoff, 2010), the adults and youths negated sociocultural norms in contributing to the pool of meaning. The adults further leveraged their relationship with the [community organization's name] and took the lead, respectfully, to share information at the start of the makerspace activity. On the other hand, the youths (e.g., Owen, Brizzil, and others), who were initially hesitant to enter dialogue with the adults, participated meaningfully by seeking clarification and sharing ideas and even reversed expert-novice roles as posited by Bransford et al. (2000). Such a reversal of functions would be conducive to the broad construction of endogenous science and specific situations involving the Kenyan science/STEM curriculum.

Specifically, the resultant dynamics in the group discussion evoked the notion of legitimate peripheral participation (LPP) as posited by Lave and Wanger (1991), in that the youths entered the making by exhibiting bits of peripheral information and seemed to contribute substantial suggestions as they built on what the adults were saying. The youths acknowledged the possibility of being in the peripheral (their trepidation), in FGDs, and in written responses. For instance, Daniella prefaced her input with "mine is very simple" when suggesting her preferred SDG. But the youths' legitimate participation was enhanced when the adults called upon them to provide know-that and know-how. In one of the exchanges, Kamusi even referred to Brizill as an expert. Such scenarios echoed self-determination by the youths or the asserting of agency as learners in the community. Furthermore, the exchanges between the adults and youths illustrate that sociocultural intentionality through knowledge appropriation and application is writ with "trade-offs and dilemmas" (Brinkerhoff, 2010).

The trade-offs and dilemmas were expressed mainly by the participants following Den's explanation of the local municipal water project, further demonstrating how information is exchanged in general in a community of learners during situated learning (Billett, 1996). When such information sharing is authorized through a grasp of practice (Ford & Forman, 2006), the appropriation and application as endogenous science gains relevance in the community's everyday life. This approach would help to operationalize the school science's transformation agenda (Barton et al., 2017; Barton & Tan, 2018; Freire, 1970; wa Thiong'o, 1986) through Kenya's science curriculum because the exemplification of agency is necessary in the context of influences and impacts of external forces (e.g., colonialism and poverty). However, an expanded discussion of agency would have required more time in the field than was available for the reported study.

Looking to the future, the community in [area] would benefit immensely from views that allow youths to be involved in purposeful knowledge appropriation and application. Reversed expertise (Bransford et al., 2000) in the community's building of endogenous science would welcome youths' (students') contributions to and from the science curriculum. When the participants shared ideas from the science curriculum, for example, the relevant chemical properties of copper anhydrous, the adults double-checked with the youths (students) to ascertain whether the adults' memory of the uses of copper anhydrous was consistent with the canons of school science.

Another example of role reversal is related to the proposition of the value of water by those presumed as more knowledgeable (adults) and was taken up by those who were supposed as less knowledgeable (youths). In acknowledging the adults know-that (from domains that included politics, economics, and history), the students positioned themselves as learners to be educated. In other words, they were eager to learn more about the cited municipal water project and how related to the provision of safe water for domestic use. In these interactions, one can see the possibility of a continual integration of ideas that adults and youths determined to bring to the pool of meaning, and, looking to the future, how the purposeful integration would fluctuate between a demonstration of scientific literacy, scientific competency, and the construction of endogenous science. This chapter, therefore, suggests that youths can be purposefully involved in making as part of their community service hours stipulated for Kenya's science/STEM curriculum (Kabita & Ji, 2017) because the literature supports the use of makerspace phenomenon for learning science (Barton et al., 2017; Blackley et al., 2017, 2018; Hira & Hynes, 2018).

Another aspect of the youths and adults' interactions with the potential for the purposeful and intentional construction of endogenous science through the Kenyan science curriculum is an attempt to validate what counts as knowledge. The findings show constructive arguments about the distinction between pure and clean water, with the most knowledgeable person attempting to clarify the differences. However, the participants did not have the opportunity to conduct laboratory tests to rule out microorganisms in clear water (i.e., nature as the judge) so that the water would be declared safe for domestic use. Furthermore, the participants did not have ample chance to explore the physical and chemical nature of filtration materials and the consequence of using the materials.

Representations of Scientific Possibilities

For knowledge-type representation, the making was designed as a socially situated learning model involving those actively engaged with schooled learning and those whose ongoing learning is entirely from everyday life. Two of the adults were high school science teachers, and they bridged the gap between those who engaged with learning entirely from everyday life (adults) and those who focused on schooled knowledge (youths). The science teacher-adults demonstrated relevant cognitive continuity by facilitating conversations on the border of science curriculum and everyday life. Such potentially cognition-bridging ideas involve boundary objects (Young, 2008) and are potential sites for the purposeful application and appropriation of ideas between local knowledge and school science. Dilware (a chemistry teacher) represented one such object as a diagram illustrating water purification

The diagram included a heating feature for water purification. The representation of water purification is a boundary object, as Young (2008) posited because it attempts to integrate idea types from a school science domain, such as metric system measurements, glass tubing, and others, into a non-scientific domain. In his illustration, Dilware shows heat using the symbol of a flame familiar to [area name] people. His reference point for disinfecting with heat is not electricity, as would be featured in a Western-based text, but the familiar (everyday life) heating system that used a wood fire. Additionally, the students were intrigued by the possibility of working with boundary objects (Young, 2008), especially the vegetation *nthanje*, to filter water. Notably, the participants integrated a range of ideas from the science curriculum because such knowledge was considered more reliable than ideas from everyday life.

Bransford et al. (2000) argue that considering prior knowledge can be a foundation for further learning. In this case, the consideration can be the impetus to investigate and build on boundary objects, repair actors' (i.e., peoples') agency (Barton and Tan, 2018), and create endogenous science. As mentioned earlier, socially situated learning circumstances allow for the posing of questions and the searching for information (from non-digital and digital sources) on what other sociocultural learning groups, including the scientific enterprise, have found about the issue under investigation. Actors then plan further interventions for suspected cause-and-effect relationships, and so on. All this is unlikely to develop in everyday life without intentionally and consistently working on scientific literacy (and competencies). The seeming lack of continuation results from the interruptions wrought by schooling. Schooling interrupted the continued organic development of socially situated cultural science-like literacies in Kenya and in other low-income cultural-historical contexts (Mazrui, 1986; Sillitoe, 2007), the mindset that would anchor self-determination efforts by an individual and/or a community at a sociocultural level.

Another pointer is the possibility of using a local plant (a grass-like aquatic vegetation known as *ithanje* in the local language) to filter water. As a follow-up to this study, if a community of learners was to investigate the efficacy of *ithanje*, as a boundary object, for water filtration using local knowledge and school science, the learners would likely find an affordable solution to address the SDG on clean water and sanitation. In the process of addressing the SDG, and as demonstrated in Dilware's drawing, the learners would develop tangential ideas, including a study of the nature of filtration materials, to benefit the growth of other ideas (i.e., local knowledge) through universal knowledge diffusion within the community. The youths alluded to such cognitive continuity, with suggestions such as, "we can all go to a developed country to gain ideas." They suggested exploring boundary objects (Young, 2008) by pointing to the universal diffusion of ideas, as Bernal (1987) documented.

Leveraging the Kenyan Science Curriculum for the Ongoing Development of Endogenous Science

The second research question sought to comment on Kenya's new curriculum requirement for senior high school students to engage in community service. Community service is consistent with the renewed emphasis on science competency for self-determination in Kenya (Kabita & Ji, 2017). Science competency is the education system's equivalent of fostering self-determination through science education or the mass promotion of scientific literacy in everyday life. As mentioned earlier, the desire to know more through knowledge diffusion in the context of makerspace can be leveraged in the form of communities of learners throughout the country to support Kenya's curriculum's proposed community service hours for senior high school students. The Kenya policymakers can package the initiative as makerspace innovation centers for localized self-determination. Arguably this would be one of the most far-reaching ways to purposefully advance knowledge for self-determination (i.e., appraise situations and conditions in everyday life), leading to enhanced consciousness-raising ad demonstrated by Freire (1970).

Such purposefulness aligned with expressions by the participants in their verbal and written responses when they supported the idea of a village innovation center. Based on this support, organizations such as [community partner] can further the proposition by designating a makerspace village innovation center (see Author), and the Ministry of Education in Kenya can consider makerspace as a viable model for engaging high school youth with community service (Authors). These two recommendations would benefit from creative energies being documented among youths elsewhere (e.g., Stephen and others mentioned earlier in the chapter). Finally, future research can consider the effect of code-switching by designing investigations that study similar sociocultural communities of learners (as discussed in Lodge, 2019) who (i) use their national language(s) (e.g., Kiswahili) as the only languages for makerspace activity; (ii) use the language of instruction in school (e.g., the English language) as the only language; and (iii) who code-switch between available languages (e.g., [local language], Kiswahili, and English). The literature on "language and thought" and "language and possibility" would benefit from such investigations.

Notes

1. I'll use the terms science education and STEM education interchangeably because most education systems in Africa are in the process of implementing STEM programs and like in the rest of the world, it is not entirely consistent how STEM integration, vis-a-vis separate subject areas like science and mathematics, is being implemented in K-12 levels (Holmlund et al., 2018).
2. This is a startup organization with the vision to uplift the living conditions in the [area]. For the purposes of this paper, the area is considered as the part of lower [region] that lies within a 5-km radius of the shopping center known as [name].
3. This RA later switched roles from RA to participant.
4. The sex biased outcome may have to do with sociocultural norms whose discussion is beyond the scope of this paper.
5. The "sound" of the names echoes Ngugi wa Thiong'o's (1986) commentaries on the agency (and identity) of postcolonial Kenya.
6. Dilware switched roles with Kamusi mid-way in the project—from participant to RA and "activity expert." The other RA did not need a pseudonym because her data collection role remained the same.
7. The pages referenced in the table are handwritten sheets of a 9" × 6" notebook.
8. All the diagrams were drawn by Dilware, the chemistry teacher and "activity expert" who later stepped in as an RA when one of the initial RAs decided to continue with the research as a participant. Dilware took a photograph of the outcome of the first trial to provide an alternative visual representation of the water filtration.

References

Anderton, K. (2019, August 14). *Two teenage girls in Kenya have created something amazing.* https://www.forbes.com/sites/kevinanderton/2019/08/14/two-teenage-girls-in-kenya-have-creating-something-amazing-infographic/?sh=54b7f8e34018

American Society for Engineering Education (ASEE). (2017). *Advancing the maker movement: Making and makerspaces at engineering and engineering technology schools and departments and outside the engineering academic maker community.* https://ira.asee.org/wp-content/uploads/2017/12/2017-Advancing-the-Maker-Movement.pdf

Barton, A. C., & Tan, E. (2010). We be burnin! Agency, identity, and science learning. *Journal of the Learning Sciences, 2,* 187–229.

Barton, A. C., & Tan, E. (2018). A longitudinal study of equity-oriented STEM-rich making among youth from historically marginalized communities. *American Educational Research Journal, 55*(4), 761–800.

Barton, A. C., Tan, E., & Greenberg, D. (2017). The Makerspace movement: Sites of possibilities for equitable opportunities to engage underrepresented youth in STEM. *Teachers College Record (1970), 119*(6), 1–44.

Bernal, M. (1987). *Black Athena: The Afroasiatic roots of classical civilization.* Rutgers University Press.

Billet, S. (1996). Situated learning bridging sociocultural and cognitive theorizing. *Learning and Instruction, 6*(3), 263–280.

Bilsel, A., & Oral, O. (1995). Role of education, science and technology in developing countries. *Proceedings Frontiers in Education 1995 25th Annual Conference. Engineering Education for the 21st Century, 2,* 4c4.11–4c4.14. Corpus ID: 145589619. https://doi.org/10.1109/FIE.1995.483223

Blackley, S., Rahmawati, Y., Fitriani, E., Sheffield, R., & Koul, R. (2018). Using a Makerspace approach to engage Indonesian primary students with STEM. *Issues in Educational Research, 28*(1), 18–42. http://www.iier.org.au/iier28/blackley.pdf

Blackley, S., Sheffield, R., Maynard, N., Koul, R., & Walker, R. (2017). Makerspace and reflective practice: Advancing pre-service teachers in STEM education. *Australian Journal of Teacher Education, 42*(3), 22–37.

Blikstein, P., & Worsley, M. (2016). Children are not hackers: Building a culture of powerful ideas, deep learning, and equity in the maker movement. In *Makeology* (1st ed., Vol. 1, pp. 64–79). Routledge. https://doi.org/10.4324/9781315726519-5

Bogdan, R. C., & Bilken, S. K. (2007). *Qualitative research for education: an introduction to theories and methods* (5th ed.). Pearson Education.

Bonnette, R. N., & Crowley, K. (2020). Legitimate peripheral participation in a makerspace for emancipated emerging adults. *Emerging Adulthood (Thousand Oaks, CA), 8*(2), 144–158. https://doi.org/10.1177/2167696818785328

Bransford, J. D., & Schwartz, D. L. (1999). Rethinking transfer: A simple proposal with multiple implications. *Review of Research in Education, 24,* 61–100.

Bransford, J. D., Brown, A. L., Cocking, R. R., et al. (Eds.). (2000). *How people learn: Brain, mind, experience, and school.* Committee on Developments in the Science of Learning and Committee on Learning Research and Educational Practice, Commission on Behavioral and Social Sciences and Education. National Research Council, National Academy Press.

Brinkerhoff, D. W. (2010). Developing capacity in fragile states. *Public Administration and Development, 30,* 66–78.

British Broadcasting Corporation (BBC). (n.d.). *Africa's school for inventors.* https://www.bbc.com/news/av/business-2004

Brown, J. (1995). *Traditional metalworking in Kenya.* Oxbow Books.

Bullock, S. M., & Sator, A. J. (2015). Maker pedagogy and science teacher education. *Journal of the Canadian Association for Curriculum Studies, 13*(1), 60–87.

Carter, L. (2017). A decolonial moment in science education: Using a socio-scientific issue to explore the coloniality of power. *Revista Brasileira de Pesquisa em Educação em Ciências, 17*(3), 1061–1085.

Creswell, J. W. (2013). *Qualitative inquiry and research design: Choosing among five approaches* (3rd ed.). Sage.

De Beer, J., & Baarbe', J. (2017). *Africa's Maker movement: An overview of ongoing research*. https://openair.africa/africas-maker-movement-an-overview-of-ongoing-research/

DeBoer, G. E. (2011). The globalization of science education. *Journal of Research in Science Teaching, 48*(6), 567–591.

Ford, M. J. (2008). "Grasp of practice" as a reasoning resource for inquiry and nature of science understanding. *Science and Education, 17*, 147–177.

Ford, M. J., & Forman, E. A. (2006). Redefining disciplinary learning in classroom contexts. In J. Green & A. Luke (Eds.), *Rethinking learning: What counts as learning and what learning counts. Review of Research in Education* (Vol. 30, pp. 1–32). American Educational Research Association.

Forest, C. R., Moore, R. A., Jariwala, A. S., Fasse, B. B., Linsey, J., Newstetter, W., Ngo, P., & Quintero, C. (2014). *The invention studio: A university makerspace and culture*. https://files.eric.ed.gov/fulltext/EJ1076126.pdf

Freire, P. (1970). *Pedagogy of the oppressed* (M. B. Ramos, Trans.). Continuum.

Geertz, C. (1973). *The interpretation of cultures*. Basic Books.

Government of Kenya (GoK). (n.d.). *Explore data categories*. Retrieved August 17, 2020, from https://www.opendata.go.ke/

Good, J. (2012). *"Community" collaboration in Africa: Experiences from Northwest Cameroon*. UBIR. https://ubir.buffalo.edu/xmlui/handle/10477/38508

Gubrium, J. F., & Holstein, J. A. (2014). Analytic inspiration in field work. In U. Flick (Ed.), *The Sage handbook of qualitative data analysis* (pp. 35–48). Sage.

Harding, S. (1997). Is modern science an ethnoscience? Rethinking epistemological assumptions. In E. C. Eze (Ed.), *Postcolonial African philosophy: A critical reader* (pp. 1–29). Blackwell Publishers.

Harding, S. (1998). Gender, development, and post-enlightenment philosophies of science. *Hypatia, 13*(3), 146–167.

Hedegaard, M. (2014). The significance of demands and motives across practices in children's learning and development: an analysis of learning in home and school. *Learning, Culture and Social Interaction, 3*, 188–194.

Highmore, B. (2002). *Everyday life and cultural theory: An introduction*. Routledge.

Hira, A., & Hynes, M. M. (2018). People, means, and activities: A conceptual framework for realizing educational potential of makerspace. *Educational Research International*, Article ID 6923617, pp. 1–10.

Holmund, T. D., Lesseig, K., & Slavit, D. (2018). Making sense of "STEM education" in K-12 contexts. *International Journal of STEM Education, 5*(32).

Horton, R. (1971). African traditional thought and Western science. In M. F. Young (Ed.), *Knowledge and control* (pp. 208–266). Collier-MacMillan Publisher.

Hurd, P. D. (1991). Why we must transform science education. *Educational Leadership*, 49(2), 33–35.

Hurd, P. D. (1997). Scientific literacy: New minds for a changing world. *Science Education*, 82, 407–416.

Jegede, O. J. (1997). School science and the development of scientific culture: A review of contemporary science education in Africa. *International Journal of Science Education*, 19(1), 1–20.

Jenkins, E. W. (2009). Reforming school science education: A commentary on selected reports and policy documents. *Studies in Science Education*, 45(1), 65–92.

Kabita, D. N., & Ji, L. (2017). *The why, what and how of competency-based curriculum reforms: The Kenya experience.* IBE-UNESCO. In-Progress Reflection No. 11 on Current and Critical Issues in Curriculum, Learning and Assessment. Retrieved October 13, 2018, from https://unesdoc.unesco.org/ark:/48223/pf0000250431

Kamkwamba, W., & Mealer, B. (2009). *The boy who harnessed the wind: Creating currents of electricity and hope.* Harper Collins Publishers.

Kermelotis, T. (2013, February 26). *Boy scares off lions with flashy invention.* https://www.cnn.com/2013/02/26/tech/richard-turere-lion-lights/index.html#:~:text=Dubbed%20%22Lion%20Lights%2C%22%20the,moving%20around%20carrying%20a%20flashlight

Lave, J., & Wenger, E. (1991). *Situated learning: Legitimate peripheral participation.* Cambridge University Press.

Lee, J. T., & Kuzhabekova, A. (2019). Building local research capacity in higher education: A conceptual model. *Journal of Higher Education Policy and Management*, 41(3), 342–357.

Levinson, R. (2018). Realizing the school science curriculum. *The Curriculum Journal*, 29(4), 522–537.

Lodge, W. G. (2019). What's in a name? The power of the English language in secondary school science education. *Cultural Studies of Science Education*, 15(1), 287–301.

Magoro, K. D. (2022). https://openair.africa/digital-mandhwane/

Marjanovic, S., Hanlin, R., Diepeveen, S., & Chataway, J. (2013). Research capacity building in Africa: Networks, institutions, and local ownership. *Journal of International Development*, 25(7), 936–946.

Mazrui, A. A. (1986). *The Africans: A triple heritage.* BBC Publications.

Mersand, S. (2021). The state of makerspace research: A review of the literature. *TechTrends*, 65(2), 174–186. https://doi.org/10.1007/s11528-020-00566-5

Moore, B. J. (1998). Situated cognition versus traditional cognitive theories of learning. *Education*, 161–171; 119, 1; ProQuest.

Nashon, S., & Anderson, D. (2013). Interpreting student views of learning experiences in a contextualized science discourse in Kenya. *Journal of Research in Science Teaching*, 50(4), 381–407.

Nathaly, F. D. (2015). *Stakeholder collaboration in community-based organizations (CBOs): The case of a sanitation CBO working in Dar es Salaam, Tanzania.* https://aaltodoc.aalto.fi/handle/123456789/15901#files-section

Ogunniyi, M. B. (1986). Two decades of science education in Africa. *Science Education*, 70(2), 111–122.

Ogunniyi, M. B. (2011). The context of training teachers to implement a socially relevant science in Africa. *Africa Journal of Research in Mathematics, Science and Technology Education*, 15(3), 98–121.

Okhee, L. (2005). Science education with English language learners: Synthesis and research agenda. *Review of Educational Research*, 75(4), 491–530.

Okpala, H. N. (2016). Making the case for academic libraries in Nigeria. *New Library World*, 177(9/10), 568–586.

Otulaja, F. S., & Ogunniyi, M. B. (2017). Introduction. In F. S. Otulaja & M. B. Ogunniyi (Eds.), *The world of science education: Handbook of research in science education in Sub-Saharan Africa* (pp. 1–6). Sense Publishers.

Reichertz, J. (2014). Introduction, deduction, abduction. In U. Flick (Ed.), *The Sage handbook of qualitative data analysis* (pp. 123–135). Sage.

Resnick, L. B., Pontecorvo, C., & Säljö, R. (1997). Discourse, tools, and reasoning: Essays on situated cognition. In L. B. Resnick, R. Säljö, C. Pontecorvo, & B. Burge. (Eds.), *Discourse, tools and reasoning* (NATO ASI Series; Series F: Computer and Systems Sciences, Vol. 160, pp. 1–20). Springer. https://doi.org/10.1007/978-3-662-03362-3_1.

Roffey, T., Sverko, C., & Therien, J. (2016). *The making of a makerspace: Pedagogical and physical transformations of teaching and learning*. http://www.makerspaceforeducation.com/uploads/4/1/6/4/41640463/makerspace_for_education_curriculum_guide.pdf

Roth, W.-M., & McGinn, M. K. (1997). Deinstitutionalizing school science: Implications of a strong view of situated cognition. *Research in Science Education (Australasian Science Education Research Association)*, 27(4), 497–513.

Roth, W.-M., & Barton, A. C. (2004). *Rethinking scientific literacy*. Routledge Falmer.

Roth, W.-M., & Lee, S. (2004). Science education as/for participation in the community. *Science Education*, 88, 263–291.

Schmidt, P. R. (1997). *Iron, technology in East Africa: Symbolism, science, and archeology*. Indiana University Press.

Schofer, E., Ramirez, F., & Meyer, J. (2000). The effects of science on national economic development, 1970–1990. *American Sociological Review*, 65(6), 877–898.

Sengul, O. (2019). Linking scientific literacy, scientific arguments, and democratic citizenship. *Universal Journal of Educational Research*, 7(4), 1090–1098.

Sillitoe, P. (2007). Local science vs. global science: An overview. In P. Sillitoe (Ed.), *Local science vs. global science: Approaches to Indigenous knowledge in international development* (pp. 1–22). Berghahn Books.

Smith, E. R., & Semin, G, R. (2004). Socially situated cognition: Cognition in its social context. *Advances in Experimental Social Psychology*, 36, 53–117.

Sooryamoorthy, R. (2020). *Science, policy, and development in Africa*. Cambridge University Press.

Steiner, G. (1999). *Learning: Nineteen scenarios from everyday life* (J. A. Smith, Trans.). Cambridge University Press. (Original work published 1988)

Thisen, J. K. (1993). The development and utilization of science and technology in productive sectors: Case of developing Africa. *Africa Development*, XVIII(4), 5–35.

Thomas, S. S. (2018). *TED, Penn State and a makerspace in Ghana; DK Osseo-Asare and Ysamine Abbas design as research*. Retrieved on February 10, 2023, from https://www.psu.edu/news/research/story/ted-penn-state-and-makerspace-ghana/

Tikly, L., & Barrett, A. M. (2011). Social justice, capabilities, and the quality of education in low-income countries. *International Journal of Educational Development, 31*, 3–14.

United Nations (UN). (1991). Endogenous capacity building in science and technology in Africa. *United Nations Economic Commission for Africa: Intergovernmental Committee of Experts for Science and Technology Development (IGCESTD) Seventh Meeting, Addis Ababa, Ethiopia, 4–8 November 1991*. https://repository.uneca.org/ds2/stream/?#/documents/9f547d46-f309-5f6a-bf9d-4f0d825424e6/page/3

Wa Thiong'o. (1986). *Decolonizing the mind: The politics of language in African literature*. EAEP Nairobi.

Willig, C. (2014). Interpretation and analysis. In U. Flick (Ed.), *The Sage handbook of qualitative data analysis* (pp. 136–149). Sage.

Wiredu, K. (1996). *Cultural universals and particulars: An African perspective*. Indiana University Press.

World Bank. (n.d.). *The World Bank in Kenya*. Retrieved July 28, 2020, from https://www.worldbank.org/en/country/kenya/overview#3

Young, M. F. D. (1976). The schooling of science. In G. Whitty & D. Young (Eds.), *Explorations in the politics of school knowledge* (pp. 47–61). Naffuton Books.

Young, M. F. D. (2008). From constructivism to realism in the sociology of the curriculum. *Review of Research in Education, 32*(1), 1–28.

· 8 ·

LINGUISTIC SOCIAL INJUSTICE IN THE UPPER EAST REGION OF GHANA

Ephraim Avea Nsoh and Helen Atipoka Adongo

Introduction

Social justice has preoccupied mankind for several centuries. As the world becomes more and more globalized and complex, concerns about social justice and equity have become a cross-cutting issue and a requirement for bilateral and multilateral relations. The United Nations (UN), regional groupings, and Civil Society Organizations (CSOs) have compelled countries and national-level organizations to promote social justice. In most cases, the efforts in this respect have resulted in the inclusion of social justice issues into national constitutions and laws and regional charters and conventions. The domestication of social justice in national laws has formed the basis for local institutional and organizational operations.

The goal of all these efforts has been to promote the basic rights and freedoms of citizens. Unfortunately, linguistic and cultural rights have continued to suffer amid this social justice crusade (Owu-Ewie, 2006; Skutnabb-Kangas et al., 1995, 1994). This is despite the Universal Declaration of Human Rights by the UN in 1948, which was followed in 1966 by the International Covenant on Civil and Political Rights, the International Covenant on Economic, Social and Cultural Rights in 1976, and several other related international laws. Not even the UN's declaration of the Rights of the Indigenous Peoples could salvage the linguistic and cultural rights of the world's minority population especially those that concern the child in the classroom. Despite the long civil rights movement history of the United States and Canada, they remain two of the countries worldwide where Indigenous people and immigrant populations' linguistic rights have been grossly abused and continue unabated as documented in the literature (Sarah, 2006; Washington Post, 2021). One of the reasons for this linguistic human rights and language rights neglect is the failure of international and local laws to elaborate implementation clauses, especially in the educational system, and the inclusion of binding clauses on national and regional policies and laws.

Decolonizing the Ghanaian education system especially its curriculum is incomplete without a language-in-education policy that affirms the role of Indigenous languages in the school system. Until the 1870s, when indirect rule was adopted in British West African colonies, Ghana like its francophone and lusophone colonies, were under the assimilatory system of government where citizens were expected to adopt the governance, education, cultural and even a lifestyle that conformed to those of their colonial masters (Boampong, 2013; Heugh, 2006; Wolff, 2021). The political minority elite together with their neocolonial collaborators continue to "de-indigenise" (Wolff, 2021) and colonize the African mind through an education system that promotes English as the medium of instruction and superior language. This over-glorification of the importance of foreign languages and the minimization of Indigenous languages have resulted in a disorientation of pupils which makes the African child unable to participate fully in the development of their communities. It thus makes them believe in foreign solutions that hardly align with our culture and development needs. The ultimate result is the perpetuation of social injustice on innocent children.

Linguistic social injustice permeates every sector of every country. A distinction has usually been made between language rights and linguistic human rights. Our claim in this chapter is that a denial of these rights to the child in the school culminates in linguistic social injustice because they restrict her/his performance in education and ultimately in employment and community participation. As expected, the sector where it is most noticeable is the education sector as mentioned previously. This is arguably the sector that could ensure a more impactful linguistic social justice (Owu-Ewie, 2006; Skutnabb-Kangas & Phillipson, 2017) and eventual decolonization of the African mind.

Discussing linguistic legitimacy, Reagan (2021) observed that delegitimation of a child especially in the education domain renders the child ineffective,

> ... in the language of the school, on language attitudes and beliefs about students and student ability, on the acquisition of literacy, and for virtually all aspects of academic achievement. In addition, the rejection of the individual's language constitutes a violation of language rights. (p. 353)

In Ghana, the 1992 Constitution reflects the general character of linguistic and cultural rights as stipulated in international human rights laws. As a result, the clauses requiring compliance are non-binding on educational and cultural institutions such as the Ministry of Education, Ghana Education Service, and the National Commission on Culture. Whenever they appear to be binding, they have no strong legal backing. In most African countries especially in francophone and lusophone countries, foreign languages such as English, French, and Belgian are used as media of instruction (Bamgbose, 2004, 1999; Anderson, 2018; Golovko, 2018; Nsoh, 2007; Wolff, 2021).

The chapter therefore intends to look at Indigenous language use in schools in the Upper East region. The intention is to subject the language policy to a classroom situation in some private and public schools in the study area where the status of Ghanaian languages was assessed. The overall objective of this study is to determine the extent to which linguistic social injustice has permeated the school system through the marginalization of Indigenous languages in education, which results from the denial of linguistic human rights to pupils and students. The chapter also seeks to demonstrate the negative impact of colonization on language in education and the need to decolonize our education system through the Indigenization of the school system.

Thus, the overarching question was, to what extent has the denial of the linguistic rights of children in the classroom perpetuated linguistic social injustice against pupils and students in the Upper East region? The specific questions were (1) what motivates linguistic social injustice in the Upper East region? (2) how has the school system contributed to linguistic social injustice and "de-Indigenization" of pupils in the region? (3) what are the imprints of linguistic social injustice in the region? (4) what is being done to remedy the situation to make Indigenous communities and their languages co-exist with each other and with foreign languages?

In this chapter, we claim that pupils/students are denied linguistic human rights in spite of local, regional, and international laws. The result is that children are ineffective in the classroom while becoming mentally colonized.

The pupils thus endure linguistic social injustice throughout their school life. Ultimately, this affects their educational performance and reduces educational opportunities and community participation. We argue that educational authorities are not only helpless in the face of an English-Only threat but are complicit in the elite's conspiracy to create an English dominance in the education system at the expense of Indigenous language education. The situation frustrates our efforts to completely decolonize our educational system.

Theoretical Framework

Our proposed theory is *the elite-language policy theory*, which is an adaptation of the elite theory (Michels, 1962; Pareto, 1935). The elite theory was developed in its classical form in the late nineteenth century with its tenets being that most societies are categorized into the elite and non-elite groups. According to the elite theory, the elite is believed to possess certain qualities or properties such as wealth, power, knowledge, prestige, education, religious piety, artistic superiority, holiness, etc. (see Pareto, 1935); that enable them to lead; control; and manipulate the masses. This portion of the population is the strongest, most powerful, and most influential in a nation-state. This classical, political, and ideological position of the elite theory stood in opposition to two other theories: the democratic theory, which espoused the "government of the people, by the people and for the people," and the "Marxist vision of class conflict leading to revolution and egalitarian socialism" (Encyclopadia.com, 2023; also see Higley & Burton, 2006). According to Higley and Burton (2006, p. 3), liberal democracy is a creation of the political elite. They observed, "The bundle of political behaviours and institutions that constitute liberal democracy is primarily an elite creation to which mass publics gradually and slowly accede." Other tenets of the elite group include their ability to organize themselves into a force, their ability to build linkages between themselves and other social forces, their accessibility and succession routes as a group, and how they exercise their power (Encyclopedia.com, 2023; Pareto, 1935). All these constitute the cardinal elements of the elite group who exercise their influence and power over the non-elite masses. Because of the exceptional qualities and values possessed by this minority ruling group, it can manipulate or completely control the non-elite class. The elite group is a minority, but their membership cuts across all sectors of a country, including politics, business, finance, religion, the arts, and more.

In adapting the tenets of the elite theory to a theory of language policy, we made a few assumptions. First, the elite class has a vested interest in the language policy in education because their influence in society is rooted in their own education, and the education of their families, community, friends and relations. Therefore, a critical component of education is the role of language. Second, education is an important quality or property of the elite group and any policy that facilitates its progress is of great concern to the group. Since they are key formulators and determiners of language use in education, they will influence the policy direction to align with their interest. According to Golovko (2018, p. 101), "Cisse saw in the opposition of the elites to the introduction of national languages their desire, specifically to guarantee their positions for themselves and their families, thereby making language a vehicle for social stratification for society." In the case of language policy decisions, the group that is likely to influence the choice of language(s) includes the political class (the executive and legislative arms) and the ruling party in a democratic setting. Others are the technocrats at the ministries of education and affiliated agencies and educational authorities at the regional and district levels. The middle class, business leaders, and other respected community members also belong to this influential segment of the elite class.

The ideological orientation of the party in power or military rulers, manifesto promises, and technical advice from technocrats hugely inform decisions on language policy. Our third assumption is that English and some other foreign non-African languages are viewed as more prestigious with much greater opportunities than Indigenous languages, especially in education. Indigenous languages have a negative perceptual value both from their speakers and non-speakers. Even those in the lower social group aspire to speak or be educated in English. The tendency, therefore, is for the elite to skew the language policy to their taste. Fourthly, we assume that the interest of the elite group represents state interest. Fifth, we also assume that the lower class, which is the majority aspires to the same language education in school as the elite group. Finally, we believe that linguistic social injustice in school undermines efforts to decolonize our school system.

It is reasonable to assume that some sections of the population in Ghana prefer an English-Only education. This is due to two reasons. First, there have been protests against the use of Indigenous languages in schools by Ghanaians, which led to the removal of Indigenous languages as compulsory subjects in 1993 following the poor performance of students at the first-ever Senior Secondary School Certificate examinations (SSSCE). Second, many parents in the lower income group place their children in low-cost private schools, most of which promote an English-Only education in their schools (see Anderson, 2018; USAID, 2018).

In the planning and formulation of language policy, language practices, beliefs, and management are critical factors (Spolsky, 2007). Even though language policy management remains the preserve of the government in Ghana, private schools have operated outside the official prescription. The situation is not different in the Upper East region as language practices and beliefs vary. We observed that seven of the languages are Indigenous to the Upper East region, and the language situation is complicated by the presence of other Indigenous and non-Indigenous languages such as Akan, Ewe, Ga, Hausa, English, and Moore. Due to the colonial antecedent that promoted English and created a diglossic situation where Indigenous Ghanaian languages are considered lower varieties, coupled with the increasing global influence of English, the influence of the elite few on the language policy direction is evident.

This is particularly so when English education is considered a powerful controlling tool for the political class, who have the economic power to place their children in English-Only schools. The tendency is for the elite class, who have the best education, financial muscle, and political control, to promote a language education that best fits their aspirations and not those of the masses. The ruled or masses to mimic the power and influence of the elite, get their children into low-cost private schools (USAID, 2018) and, in doing so, buy into the argument of the elite who believe that an English-Only policy will provide better opportunities for children.

The preference for an English-Only language is facilitated by multilingual language practices that make it difficult for the local language to be used and for members of the elite group to set up low-cost private schools to attract children from the non-elite group. Since the non-elite aspires to an English education, elite proprietors who are aware of this, promote an English-Only education and justify this by citing the prevalence of multilingualism and the lack of teachers qualified to teach Indigenous languages, among other reasons.

Methodology

This is a case study of linguistic social injustice in school in which we used qualitative research methods namely, interviews and clustered sampling techniques. The data was collected in the last quarter of 2021 in the Upper East region by two service persons who worked as our assistants. Additional data were taken from the College of Languages Education of the University of Education, Winneba, two Colleges of Education. Fifty participants were involved: 14 University of Education, Winneba students studying Ghanaian languages, 13 students from the St. John Bosco and Gbewa Colleges of Education; three regional education officials, ten headteachers, one classroom teacher, one school secretary, and ten parents. The interviewers used semi-structured interview guides, each with six to 12 questions. While schools were purposefully selected, students were conveniently sampled to include only those that offered Indigenous language programs. Education officials selected for the study included individuals who were familiar with the school system in the Upper East region and were in positions to make policy decisions. Examples are the regional Directors or their representatives. Private or public basic schools located within a convenient range of the city center were selected due to limitations of resources and time. Interviews were recorded on the mobile phones of the research assistants and transcribed into exercise books. The data were typed into laptops and manually coded by the two researchers and a former MPhil student, who is doing part-time teaching at the University. We identified the main themes, compared them, and drew our conclusions.

Study Area

The Upper East region has a population of over 1, 294,000 comprising 15 administrative districts. It has 759 public basic schools and 314 private schools, totaling about 1,073 basic schools (Ministry of Education, 2019). Out of the 1,073 basic schools, the Bolgatanga Municipality has 383 basic schools of which 212 are public/government schools while 171 are private schools Ministry of Education (2019). The literacy rate for the region is 48.1% against a national average of 69.8%. The rate for females is 43.7% against a male rate of 52.8% (GSS, 2021). It is one of the most disadvantaged of Ghana's 16 regions with a rural poverty incidence of about 67% (GSS, 2018). There are six Indigenous Ghanaian languages in the Upper East region, namely, Bisa, Buli, Farefari (Gurenɛ), Kasem, Kusaal, Ligbi, and Mampruli. Five of these languages (Buli, Farefari, Kasem, Kusaal, and Mampruli) are Mabia (Gur) languages while Bisa is a Mande language. Non-Ghanaian languages such as Moore, Hausa, and English are commonly spoken, especially in the towns.

However, until July 2020, when the President of Ghana announced the proposed approval of Farefari (Gurenɛ) to be taught as one of the official Ghanaian languages in schools, Kasem was the only approved Indigenous Ghanaian language in the region. Three of the languages, Farefari (Gurenɛ), Kasem, and Kusaal, are currently studied at the University of Education, Winneba. The languages are mostly under-researched with very limited material. Farefari and Kasem are also taught at the two Colleges of Education in the region (St. John Bosco and Gbewa Colleges of Education), while only Farefari is taught outside the region in one College of Education in the Northern region (Bagabaga College of Education).

The Current State of Linguistic Social Injustice in The Region

As previously stated, there are six Indigenous languages in the Upper East region. Only five of them are broadcast on the government radio station in the region, URA-radio. Mampruli is not represented. At the national level, none of these languages are included in the Ghana Broadcasting Corporation's (GBC) radio and TV programs. In education, until 2020 (when Farefari (Gurenɛ) was approved), Kasem was the only government-approved language that was examinable by the West African Examination Council (WAEC). As will be established in the next section, there is a near exclusion of local languages from education in the region. English is the language for government business and even traditional institutions like the Houses of Chiefs conduct their business in the English language because of the multicultural and multilingual nature of the region.

There is no documentation in the history of the region of efforts to promote regional or district languages (lingua francas) (see Nsoh et al., 2001). Hausa could be seen as taking the role of a *lingua franca*, but its use is largely limited to selected city centers, for instance in Bawku and Bolgatanga. In addition, there has been little documentation of the Upper East region's six Indigenous languages. The only exceptions to this are Farefari, Kasem, and Kusaal due to their inclusion in the curriculum at the University of Education, Winneba and the use of Kasem as a medium of instruction and a subject of study in some basic schools, Senior High Schools, and Colleges of Education. Farefari and Kasem are taught as optional subjects at the Colleges of Education.

Preliminary observations and data collection suggest that Indigenous languages are under-represented at all levels of education in the Upper East region.

International Legal Framework on Linguistic and Cultural Rights

Linguistic human rights are mostly linked to minority cultures and languages. The concept of dominant languages is understood in the context of more widely spoken versus restricted use of languages usually in the same geographical and linguistic environment. This concept of dominant versus minority informed the promotion of Spanish in Spain, French in France, and English in Great Britain starting in the fifteenth century despite the existence of minority languages in these countries.

The one-state-one-language concept guided these three European countries, among others, as they expanded into Africa, South America, and elsewhere across the globe. It also informed the suppressive and assimilation approaches adopted in Spain and its colonies in the Americas, as well as France and its colonies in Africa. In North America, most Indigenous communities, their cultures, and Indigenous languages were completely wiped out through the boarding school system (Sarah, 2006; Skutnabb-Kangas & Phillipson, 2017; Washington Post, 2021). Thus, although Britain, France, and the United States were signatories to minorities' treaties, they refused to offer equivalent rights to their own minority group citizens and colonies in Africa and elsewhere (Skutnabb-Kangas & Phillipson, 2017). The attitude of these major powers toward the rights of minorities is reflected by the delay in adding explicit language protecting minority rights to the UN Declaration of Human Rights and by the perpetuation of injustices against minorities (see UN Meeting Coverage and Press Releases: https://press.un.org/en/2022/ga12 448.doc.htm).

When minority rights were finally included in international law, they were expressed in vague language that did not specifically address the promotion of Indigenous languages in education policy.

Africa's Legal Response to Linguistic Rights

Like all international charters on human rights, the UN Declaration of Human Rights includes only generic wording regarding culture and does not explicitly address minorities and minority rights. Worse still, there are separate clauses on education and culture, but these are not directly linked; this makes it difficult for educational institutions to fully implement the propositions. For example, clauses 1–3 of Article 17 in the African Charter on Human and People's Rights are captured in the following terms.

> 1) Every individual shall have the right to education 2) Every individual may freely take part in the cultural life of his community 3) The promotion and protection of morals and traditional values recognized by the community shall be the duty of the State. (p. 4)

The African Union (AU) Agenda 2063 follows a similar trend. According to Aspiration 5 of the agenda. An Africa with a strong cultural identity, common heritage, shared values and ethics

> Pan-Africanism and the common history, destiny, identity, heritage, respect for religious diversity, and consciousness of African people and their diaspora will be entrenched.

Other AU documents, such as the Charter for African Cultural Renaissance (2006), previously called the Cultural Charter for Africa (1986), the African Academy of Languages (ACALAN) (2006), and the Language Plan of Action for Africa (1986), explicitly link language and culture policies to classrooms and curriculum. In other words, these documents provide a link between policy and the curriculum or classroom. For instance, the Charter for African Cultural Renaissance provides two articles (18 & 19) on the use of African languages. Article 19 states.

> African States should prepare and implement reforms for the introduction of African languages into the education curriculum. To this end, each State should extend the use of African languages taking into consideration the requirements of social cohesion and technological progress, as well as regional and African integration. (p. 16)

The ACALAN lists among its main objectives the promotion of "functional multilingualism, especially in the education sector" and promises to specifically deliver its mandate by "technically assisting Member States of the

African Union in the formulation and implementation of national language policies."

The Language Plan of Action for Africa (2006) sought to give life to the various decisions and policies on language and culture including the Organisation of African Unity (OAU) Charter, the Charter for African Cultural Renaissance, the inter-governmental conference on cultural policies, and the Legos plan of Action. It aimed at ensuring that issues of language and culture were implemented at the national, continental, and regional levels. Unfortunately, evidence across the continent clearly shows that the implementation plan has not achieved most of its objectives. In addition, the plan tended to retain, accentuate, and further widen the minority-majority gap between African languages by requiring the selection and promotion of what it referred to as "viable, regional Indigenous languages as official or working languages, which resulted in the privileging of 'official languages' over languages deemed unworthy of selection and promotion."

To emphasize the importance of the choice of the language of instruction, the plan proposed that only languages that are familiar to the learner or population are used as media of instruction and in the national literacy campaign. Action (k) states,

> In recognition of the fact that, to impart formal or other types of knowledge, the vehicle of instruction or communication should be a language familiar to the learner, the absolute necessity that each Member State should as an essential part of its educational policy, prescribe as media or vehicles of instruction those Indigenous African languages that best and most effectively facilitate the learning process.

There is no doubt that the AU has the necessary legal and administrative documentation to ensure that member states put in place policies and practices that promote the thriving of languages and cultures. However, the main obstacle is the lack of political will and determination among member states. As is stated in the AU's Language Plan of Action for Africa, "the adoption and promotion of African languages as the official languages of the state is dependent primarily, and as a matter of absolute imperative, on the political will and determination of each sovereign state."

We have thus far focused on international documents and policies related to Africa-wide language and culture policies and have not yet delved into the implementation of such policies at a national or regional level among the AU member states. Apart from the establishment of regional agencies such as ACALAN, there is no evidence that the AU is collaborating with the

Ghana's national and regional institutions to ensure that its stated goals for language and education are realized.

National Level Legal Provisions

The earliest official mention of Indigenous language education is the twelfth principle of Sir Gordon Guggisberg's 16 principles of education. Guggisberg was a British governor of the Gold Coast (Ghana) from 1919 to 1928. According to this Principle "[w]hilst an English education must be given, it must be based solidly on the vernacular" (Williams 1964, p. 293). In line with this principle, European teachers were required to learn the local language before entering the classroom. The principle also obligated lower primary teachers to use the language most familiar to the child in teaching (Ansah, 2014; Atintono & Nsoh, 2012; Boampong, 2013; Dzameshie, 1988; Nsoh & Ababila, 2007; Owu-Ewie, 2006). The principle and its educational implications guided the Indigenous language-in-education policy and language planning in general to date.

The debate over the period has been whether Indigenous languages should be the only media of instruction in early grades. There have been four positions: (1) using Indigenous languages in only the first year, (2) permitting Indigenous language use up to basic 3, (3) adopting a bilingual or multilingual education policy in which Indigenous languages and English are used concurrently but with an early exit, and (4) implementing an Indigenous language as a medium of instruction throughout primary education (late exit). The fourth option has been the least popular position. An attempt to implement the Indigenous language as a medium of instruction and subject of study was met with agitations at various stages in educational development in Ghana. The elite population felt that it was a strategy to give Ghanaians an inferior education (Graham, 1971). English education has been considered superior and a window to opportunities as compared to an Indigenous language education (Adika, 2012; Anderson, 2018). The 1992 Constitution of Ghana guarantees equality, rights, and freedoms of all persons and proscribes discrimination against anyone in article 17 (1&2) which states that,

1. All persons shall be equal before the law.
2. A person shall not be discriminated against on grounds of gender, race, color, ethnic origin, religion, creed, or social or economic status.

The interpretation of discrimination is presented in Article 17(3).

> For the purposes of this article, "discriminate" means to give different treatment to different persons attributable only or mainly to their respective descriptions by law, place of origin, political opinions, color, gender, occupation, religion, or creed, whereby persons of one description are subjected to disabilities or restrictions to which persons of another description are not made subject or are granted privileges or advantages which are not granted to persons of another description.

The interpretation of Article 17(3), thus, implies that any decision to promote an English-Only policy in the classroom without regard to the first language(s) of the child would be discrimination against pupils, especially when they do not speak and write in any other language. The Constitution again upholds the cultural rights and practices of all citizens in Article 26 (1) as follows:

> Every person is entitled to enjoy, practice, profess, maintain, and promote any culture, language, tradition, or religion subject to the provisions of this Constitution.

The provisions in the 1992 Constitution uphold the rights of every Ghanaian, including children, and their language and linguistic human rights, which form part of their cultural rights.

Findings

Parents

The study focused on data from basic schools, college and university students, parents, and some education officials. In speaking with respondents, we sought to establish the status of Indigenous languages in schools. Parents had a positive attitude toward Indigenous language education. They felt strongly that their children should learn about their Indigenous cultures and languages in school. One parent made the following comments:

> As a parent, I would just like to advise my colleague parents that they should not always speak English to their children and that you want your child to be able to speak English and write English. Remember, your child is not from Britain or from Europe. It is of great importance to your child to be able to speak your own dialect and know a lot about your culture and tradition. So please, I would like all parents to support me and help our children to know much about the culture and heritage.

Other parents who made similar comments bemoaned the inability of schools to introduce Indigenous languages as subjects and use them as media of instruction. In confirmation of their belief in Indigenous language education. They also maintained that their children should be encouraged to use their mother tongues, believing that this would benefit them.

Although they insisted on the importance of Indigenous language instruction, parents believed their children should also learn and use English because they associated foreign language with academic success and access to professional opportunities. As one parent stated, "... it is the more educated that are in the formal sectors ..." For parents like this one, to be fully educated was to be educated in English.

Although parents expressed a desire for their children to learn in both Indigenous and English languages, they consistently prioritized English instruction in their decisions about school placements for their children. As predicted by our theory parents from the less privileged group want their children to learn English so they will have access to more employment opportunities.

Headteachers

Headteachers of both private and public basic schools agreed that the use of the mother tongue or first language (L1) was very beneficial in making children understand the subjects they were taught. One headteacher had this to say:

> Comparing the local language to English, the pupils understand better the Ghanaian language than in English. This is because they are already familiar with the local language than the English language.

The same head of school appeared to know and accept the current language policy and insisted on applying it. She said, "We use both L1 and L2 (second language) for them to understand well." There was a policy from above that we should use L1 in the lower primary, so we are using L1 for now.

However, some private school headteachers gave reasons why the language policy was not effective in their schools. Some attributed it to the lack of Ghanaian language teachers in their schools; some claimed it was because the languages had not been approved by the government as official Ghanaian languages; and others attributed it to pressure from parents to teach their children to speak English, as captured in the following comment:

> The language policy in my school is that the teachers enforce the use of the English language, both in speaking and writing, and emphasizing on French, since it is also

taught in this school for some time now. We have been struggling with how to integrate the local language into the schools in the municipality.

This headteacher went further to acknowledge the relevance of local language usage in the classroom by explaining the efforts they were making to apply the policy as he indicated:

> "To me, I think it will be good. We plan to introduce the local languages to be taught and used as a media of instruction. It will go a long way to help our children and the education system as well."
>
> The submission by the headteacher shows that although teachers are struggling to integrate multiple languages, they still value Indigenous language instruction.
>
> One private school headteacher in Bolgatanga spoke to the challenges of Indigenous language education in a multi-lingual setting:
>
> Sometimes, we are forced to use the local language as a medium of instruction, especially at the nursery and the lower primary. But sometimes we find some difficulties because Bolga is a multi-lingual society, and therefore, most of the children speak different languages. When this happens, it is not easy for the teachers to decide which language will benefit all the pupils in the class and use that language.

Some private schools employed an old-fashioned policy of teaching only in English and prohibiting the use of mother tongues in school. One headteacher said:

> The language policy in this school is that we instruct pupils to speak English both in the classroom and outside the classroom. Pupils are punished in the school for speaking the local language.

Some headteachers seemed to not know the current language policy. For instance, one headteacher said the following:

> The current language policy in education is that the English language be used as a medium of instruction throughout all levels even though at some levels teachers try to use the local language to supplement teaching.

Private school teachers and parents seemed determined to deny students Indigenous language instruction for reasons that served their interests without regard for the needs of the children. While parents seemed to be motivated by their egos, private school administrators and teachers seemed to be focused on monetary rewards. School administrators, teachers, and parents shared the elitist belief that an English-Only policy was the only way to ensure student success in the academic and professional realms (Pareto,

1935). Such motivations and beliefs played a key role in preventing the adoption of Indigenous language instruction in private schools.

Tertiary Students

We also interviewed Ghanaian language students from nine of the languages (out of 12) being taught at the Ajumako campus of the University of Education, Winneba. The languages included Akan, Dagaare, Dagbani, Dangme, Ewe, Farefari (Gurenɛ), Ga, Kasem and Nzema. Data from these sources helped to validate data on Indigenous languages and from the schools in the Upper East. Similarly, we interviewed students at the two Colleges of Education in the Upper East region. For most of them at the colleges, the Ghanaian languages were compulsory at the point of entry, so they chose the languages they either spoke or were familiar with. Students at the University were motivated to study Ghanaian languages by relations, friends, personal interests, and familiarity from previous language education.

Many of the participants intended to pursue languages beyond the first degree while others thought they were at the end of the road. Students were happy with the programs because they were studying their own languages, which were comparatively easy for them to learn. However, students also faced criticism from others who did not see the value in studying Ghanaian languages and did not believe there would be job opportunities for graduates of the program. One respondent explained; "They look down on us simply because we are studying our own languages." Another student added; "Some will say you are a Fante but why have you gone to study Fante again? Can't you speak Fante?" Some simply do not take the study of Ghanaian languages seriously. A respondent recalled, "Once I introduced myself to some friends of mine and it was like, ah, is Twi to a course that we do at the university? They started laughing at me, but I am determined." Students also were concerned about inadequate teachers, teaching and learning resources, and employment opportunities.

The two representatives of the Ghana Education Service (GES), who coincidentally were graduates of Ghanaian language study, were very conversant with the language policy in Education. They indicated that all teachers were expected to be conversant with the policy, which they learned about through training workshops (although there had not been any training in the recent past). However, they admitted it was difficult to enforce the policy in the classroom for various reasons, including deficiencies in both English and Ghanaian language instruction and the tendency for Indigenous language teachers to take non-classroom assignments. Adding to this, many graduates of Ghanaian language programs take jobs in teaching English or end up working in other areas of the education sector. The use of graduates of Ghanaian languages as English teachers in schools is further worsening the teacher gap in the Ghanaian language teacher space. This is due to factors such as the non-approval of most of the languages for teaching and learning in the region, the poor perception of and limited opportunities for Indigenous language instruction in the region. Aside from Kasem, none of the Indigenous languages in the Upper East region were examinable, making these languages undesirable to students, teachers, and educational authorities.

Ghana Education Service (GES) Officials

Despite obstacles to Indigenous language instruction and study, GES officials felt strongly that the emphasis on English-Only education was negatively impacting the performance of students. One of them explained, "Our children are affected because they had not gotten the opportunity to learn their mother tongue at the beginning of their studies." She added; "They are not even fluent in the L1 yet, and they have to learn the L2." Thus, there is a disconnect between speaking English and performance. That is, English-Only education negatively impacts student learning outcomes.

On the vexed question of why private schools do not use Indigenous languages in schools, the officers explained that even in many public schools, the policy was not respected, so it was not surprising if private schools were ignoring it with impunity. According to them, since the attitude toward English-language instruction was generally positive among parents, the tendency was for private schools to model their facilities along the lines of English grammar schools to attract students. They remarked; "because they grade their schools after grammar schools abroad like Britain, they wouldn't tolerate L1, and parents feel proud when their children are in such schools."

GES officials also explained that limitations in resources and facilities posed a challenge to Indigenous language instruction. Most schools were lacking in new textbooks, translation services, and Information and Communications Technologies (ICT) facilities that could be used for Indigenous language instruction.

Discussion

Decolonization and Language Education

The Ghanaian education system is still replete with vestiges of colonization, which negatively impacts student learning outcomes. This is obvious in language education, especially at the basic level where children are compelled to learn through English (Anyidoho & Anyidoho, 2009; Owu-Ewie, 2006). Even though the current language policy supports a bilingual language policy in the classroom, there appears to be a "conspiracy" among the major stakeholders in education, namely, educational authorities, parents, and school heads to promote an English-Only education in basic schools. The situation is worse in private schools which proscribe the use of Indigenous languages and maintain a grammar school type of education, perpetuating a colonial education system that defeats efforts to decolonize our education system. Decolonizing our education curriculum must be preceded by a language in education policy that trains children in their culture and environment.

The Multiplicity of the Local Language and the Choice of English Language

As observed earlier in this chapter, there are about 80 Indigenous Ghanaian languages in the country in addition to several non-Ghanaian languages such as Hausa, Moore, English, and French. The complaint by some headteachers about the multilingual nature of the classrooms, especially with increasing urbanization and multiculturalism in many Ghanaian towns and cities, is a confirmation that multilingualism is one key reason why Indigenous languages are losing a grip on the classroom and on education in general (Dakubu, 1996; Dorvlo, 2011; GSS, 2021). English remains the official language used in education and for government business. The debate for a national language has long been forgotten. Language use and particularly, the choice of an official and national language(s) are informed by several factors, including historical considerations, as is the case with many African, Latin American, and Caribbean countries (Golovko, 2018; Wolff, 2021); status, which in our case is interwoven with the history of the language and also relates to the relative sizes of language-speaking groups, with Akan being the largest in Ghana, Hausa in Nigeria, and Niger and Moore in Burkina Faso; the majority-minority divide; and language usage norms in areas such as education and commerce.

Categorization of Indigenous Languages

Viewed from the perspectives in the previous section, languages of instruction and study in Ghana may be classified into the following groups: dominant/non-dominant, government-approved/non-approved, Indigenous/non-Indigenous, majority/minority, and northern/southern languages. Sometimes it is an outright political decision; this can be seen, for instance, in the approval of smaller languages like Kasem and Nzema as government-approved languages despite their smaller population size vis-a-vis other languages. Another example is the announcement of the approval of the Farefari language by the President of Ghana at a political function in the Upper East region, which was a political move. In most cases, language classifications and terminologies are interwoven with power relations and reflected in language education (Atintono & Nsoh, 2012; Bamgbose, 2004, 1999).

Thus, English is considered a prestigious world language and seen as affording the greatest potential for education and employment opportunities and is therefore preferred not just by parents but also by the political and administrative class. What is more, the erroneous claim that using Indigenous African languages, such as Akan, Hausa, Ibo, Wolof, or KwaZulu as modes of instruction and languages of study could result in conflict has led to the predominance of foreign languages like English, French, Spanish, or Belgian in African schools (Anyidoho & Anyidoho, 2009; Atintono & Nsoh, 2012; Graham, 1975; Wolff 2021).

The Role of Politics in the Choice of Language in Education

Thus, despite the existence of strong cultural and language institutions and their reflection in the statute documents of the country, such as the national constitution and the cultural policy, English remains the dominant and most preferred language of the Ghanaian classroom and school system, as can be observed in the Upper East region. First, the region has seven Indigenous languages. Interestingly, Kasem, the approved language has fewer speakers as compared to Farefari and Kusaal according to the 2010 population census and the colonial government-approved Nankani (a dialect of Farefari) as one of the eight regional languages in the 1920s (Boampong, 2013). This suggests that the choice of Kasem as an approved language was politically motivated.

Even though Farefari and Kusaal languages are taught at the University of Education, Winneba, where teachers are trained, and Farefari was approved as a government-sponsored language, and despite the existence of a language policy requiring the use of Indigenous languages either solely or along with English, the data from our study suggests a preference for English-language education in both public and private schools. This was corroborated by the responses of parents and the education officials who were interviewed. Even though parents expressed a desire for their children to learn their mother tongues, many preferred English-Only grammar-type private schools to public schools where Indigenous language instruction was more prevalent. Indeed, they often chose private schools based, at least in part, on their English-Only policies.

The decision to insist on English-Only instruction was informed by surveys of parents' preferences. With the elite group setting up low-cost private schools for less privileged parents who also believe in the supremacy of English, policies requiring Indigenous language instruction will continue to be breached. Parents' perceptions of the supremacy of English and its job opportunities (cf. Anderson, 2018; Funk, 2015) will also continue to influence language policies. The situation frustrates educational authorities, who look ineffectual in the face of public and private schools' blatant disregard of the language policy. We are left with a language policy that is hardly implemented and enforced at the schools; and the failure of educational authorities to take action against non-compliant schools implies their complicity in the situation (Anderson, 2018; Golovko, 2018).

Inability of GES Officials to Implement Indigenous Language Policy

The data from our study supports the idea that education officials and heads of schools were ineffective in enforcing the implementation of the language policy in classrooms. The GES officials, for their part, listed numerous factors that made it impossible for them to enforce the law. In addition, apart from a lack of ICT, translation, and textbook resources for instruction in the language, the GES did not have a policy that requires reference to teachers' local language background in job postings (Nsoh & Ababila, 2007; Owu-Ewie, 2006).

Heads of schools and education officials also highlighted related problems, such as the non-examinable status of the Indigenous languages, inadequate teachers and textbooks, and in particular the unattractiveness of the languages to parents, school heads, and proprietors. These challenges have culminated in the institutionalization of English as a medium of instruction and the subject of study while Indigenous languages are heckled out of the classroom. It is unbelievable that in this age of educational development, a child will still be punished for speaking her/his language in school. It appears intellectuals and educators are losing the fight for Indigenous language education. It is not therefore surprising that there is a gradual shift in phrasing, away from the use of the "mother tongue" and toward the "familiar" language of the child, in literature (Kapenda, 2020). In due course, government and school authorities will argue that English is the most familiar language of the child if the current situation does not improve.

The Approved/Non-Approved Distinction and Impact on Indigenous Languages

The approved/non-approved distinction by the Ministry of Education (MoE) and the Ghana Education Service (GES) could also account for the marginalization of the other Indigenous languages in the classroom, despite their ability to improve learning outcomes (Owu-Ewie, 2006), as was suggested by the educational authorities, some parents, and particularly most of the school heads interviewed.

The Influence of Monetary Gains on The Choice of School Language

The data suggests that the preference for English among private schools is partly informed by monetary interest. Parents prefer schools with an English-Only tradition and often assess their children's outcomes based on their English-language abilities (see USAID, 2018). Parents are therefore not likely to accept instruction in the child's local language. Heads of private schools are likely to respond to the needs of parents in the interest of attracting more students and greater financial gain. A proprietor is less likely to hire a local language teacher, especially given the combined factors of parental preferences and the cost of remuneration.

Negative Attitude Toward the Study of Indigenous Language

At the Colleges of Education and universities, Indigenous language programs are marginalized and, as a result, are lacking in adequate and appropriate materials and facilities; students in these programs are disrespected by fellow students, among others, and limited in their employment opportunities due to this marginalization. For instance, students spoke of numerous factors discouraging them from continuing their Indigenous language studies.

Indeed, student respondents from the University of Education (UEW) and the Colleges of Education (CoE) reported that they learned better in Ghanaian language programs since they were learning in their mother tongues; even one Buli student who offered Dagbani believed she learned better (cf. Adika, 2012; Chomsky, 1965). Also, in one of the private schools that adopted the English-Only policy, the headteacher of the school explained that, in spite of the multilingual situation in their classroom, which partly motivated their choice of English, they recommend the use of Indigenous languages in the nursery and lower primary to facilitate learning. As one headteacher said, "Sometimes we are forced to use the local language as a medium of instruction, especially at the nursery and the lower primary."

Unfortunately, the decision-making minority, which is composed of elite groups such as the educational authorities, proprietors of private schools, and the political class, does not favor Indigenous language instruction and is therefore unlikely to support a policy that promotes such languages which do not inure to their benefit.

Conclusion

The marginalization of Indigenous languages in the classroom is mostly motivated by five main factors: (1) perceptions about their prospects vis-à-vis those of the English language; (2) poor knowledge about the language policy; (3) inability (or rather the helplessness) of educational authorities in enforcing the language policy; (4) increasing multilingual classrooms; and (5) in the case of private schools, monetary influence. To sustain mother tongue education, advocates must concentrate on finding solutions to these challenges. Until these issues are dealt with comprehensively, Indigenous languages and their speakers, especially the pupils/students in the Upper East, will continue to suffer linguistic social injustices. One way to deal with these challenges is to pass an act of parliament with an elaborate implementation program and an advocacy plan.

Thus, the data suggest that the current classroom situation denies the child his/her linguistic right. In most cases, the child's home language and the classroom language do not match. Unfortunately, the choice of which language to use for their instruction lies outside their power. In spite of the existence of the language of instruction policy, school authorities and other government officials are unable to enforce this policy in both public and private schools. The situation is made worse by the preference of parents and school proprietors for the use of English as a medium of instruction at the expense of Indigenous languages. This situation coupled with government's decision to sponsor only two Indigenous languages in the Upper East region (Kasem and Gurenɛ) for classroom instruction continues to perpetuate linguistic injustice to the child.

A major implication of the current language situation in the classroom in Ghana and the Upper East region, in particular, is the recolonization of the education curriculum, and consequently, the minds of pupils and students. Exposing our children at that early age to a language education that ultimately exposes them to foreign cultures and beliefs through an inappropriate language policy, is to uproot them mentally from their societies and cultural environment. The situation frustrates efforts to decolonize our schools and communities.

Recommendations

Two main strategies may be adopted to promote linguistic human rights in the classroom and ultimately reduce linguistic social injustice, in the Upper East region in particular and in the country as a whole. First, in the processes leading to the crafting of the 2017 language-in-education draft policy, attempts were made to expand and extend consultations to prominent individuals, stakeholders, and interest groups. For instance, linguistic, language, and education experts and authorities as well as local and international institutions such as National Council for Curriculum and Assessment (NaCCA), Ministry of Education, Ghana Institute of Linguistics, Literacy and Bible Translation (GILLBT), representatives of the universities, and USAID Learning were involved at various stages of the process. However, as we sought to argue from the Elite-language policy theoretical perspective, the consultations failed to reach much of the elite class which could influence the direction of the language policy in favor of Indigenous languages. The process largely turned out to be an exercise dominated by a group of intellectual elites with limited involvement of the political class and elite groups from other sectors of the economy, such as industry and ethnic/traditional leadership.

The involvement of the Minister of Education and a few technocrats around him was not enough to convince the influential elite of the need to promote Indigenous language education. Any future attempt to draft or review the existing policy must not target only the Minister of Education but also the Ministries of Education, Tourism, Culture and the Creative Arts, Local Government, and Rural Development, and of Chieftaincy Affairs and all agencies under them. In particular, the program should target as many elite groups from as many sectors as possible. Until we touch the most influential elite groups and stakeholders across the sectors, it will be almost impossible to craft an acceptable language policy that takes the Indigenous language background of pupils and students into consideration.

The second approach is to establish an advocacy program that targets influential groups and individuals in the mass population. As we predicted, many members of the middle class and some members of the lower class have tried to place their children in schools with English education because they perceive this type of education as providing better opportunities for them. In addition, there is a generally positive perception of English education and a negative one for Indigenous language education. Coupled with the increasing influence of English across the globe, the desire for English-language instruction continues to rise by the day. The advocacy should target multiple layers of middle- and lower-class groups and the general population by generating public awareness of and sensitivity to this issue.

In adopting these two strategies, care should be taken to develop clear pathways for the Indigenous languages and English in education. The elite must be convinced that the introduction of Indigenous languages in education would not in any way interfere with English education. Alongside the effort to convince the elite that Indigenous languages in education would not interfere with an English education, they must also be convinced that local languages would not only help in their children's education but, indeed, make them better citizens of their communities and Ghana.

Ultimately, our strategy should be to decolonize our curriculum and the minds of pupils and students, whose choice of the language of instruction depends on the choices of parents, educational authorities, proprietors of schools, teachers, and the government. We cannot afford to make choices that disadvantage the young ones in the classroom and make them aliens in their culture and environment.

Appendix: Coding Abbreviations

PA	→Parent
Q	→Question
HT1DOA	→Headteacher 1, Doayin Academy basic school
HT2MOS	→Headteacher 2, Mount Sinai Educational Center
HT3STPP	→Headteacher 3, St Peter and Paul Academy Junior High School (JHS)
AHT4STPP	→Assistant headteacher 4, St Peter and Paul Academy JHS
HT5STPP	→Headteacher 3, St Peter and Paul Academy, JHS
HT6ABIL2	→Headteacher 6, Abiliba No2 JHS
HT7AKAN	→Headteacher 7, Akantome JHS
HT8AWOGE	→Headteacher 8, Awogeya JHS
HT9BASE	→Headteacher 9, Baseego Primary School
HT10DOROJ	→Headteacher 10, Dorongo JHS
HT11DOROP	→Headteacher 11, Dorongo Primary School
HT12KAL-T	→Headteacher 12, Kalboe-Tindinsobelego JHS
HT13 OLA	→Headteacher 13, Ola School Complex
HT14STJON	→Headteacher 14, ST John JHS
SEC1DOA	→Secretary 1, Doayin Academy basic school

References

Adika, G. S. K. (2012). English in Ghana: Growth, tensions, and trends. *International Journal of Language*, 1(1), 151–166.

Anderson, M. (2018). Literacy education in northern Nigeria: Issues, resources and training. In B. Anneke & J. Janson (Eds.), *Education for life in Africa* (Vol. 119). African Studies Center.

Ansah, G. (2014). Re-examining the fluctuations in language-in-education policies in post-independence Ghana. *Multilingual Education*, 4(12), 1–15. http://www.multilingual-education.com/content/4/1/12

Anyidoho, A., & Anyidoho, N. A. (2009). Political considerations in the choice of medium of instruction. *Institute of African Studies Research Review*, 2009 (supra-9), 9–34.

Atintono, A. S., & Nsoh, E. A. (2012). Local language use as a strategy for rural communities to shape their own development agenda: The role of higher education institutions in Ghana. In A. A. Apusiga & D. Millar (Eds.), *Endogenous knowledge and African development: Issues, challenges and options*, (Captured Africa Project). KNUST Press.

Bamgboşe, A. (1999). *Language and exclusion: The consequences of language policies in Africa* (Vol. 12). LIT Verlag Münster.

Bamgbose, A. (2004). *Language of Instruction Policy and Practice in Africa*. www.unesco.org/education//languages_2004/languageinstruction_africa.

Boampong, C. A. (2013). Rethinking British colonial policy in the Gold Coast: The language factor. *Transactions of the Historical Society of Ghana, New Series, 15*, 137–157.

Council on Curriculum and Assessment (NaCCA). (2017). *Draft Ghana language-in-education policy*.

Chomsky, N. (1965). *Aspects of the theory of syntax*. MIT Press.

Dakubu, K. M. E. (1996). *Language and community*. Ghana Universities Press.

Dorvlo, K. (2011). Language use in education in minority language areas: The case of Logba. In H. Lauer, N. A. A. Appiah, & J. A. Andersen (Eds.), *Identity meets nationality: Voices from the humanities* (pp. 100–110). Sub-Saharan Publishers.

Dzameshie, A. K. (1988). Language policy and the common language controversy in Ghana. *Institute of African Studies Research Review, 4*(2), 16–27.

Encyclopedia.com. (2023). Elite theory. https://www.encyclopedia.com/social-sciences/applied-and-social-sciences-magazines/elite-theory

Funk, A. (2015). Internationalization, international competencies and employability. In J. H. C. Walenkamp (Ed.), *The world's mine oyster: Studies in support of internationalization in Higher education*. University of Applied Sciences.

Graham, C. K. (1971). *The history of education in Ghana from the earliest times to the Declaration of Independence* (No. 108). Psychology Press.

Golovko, E. (2018). Literacy and development in Senegal: From colonial roots to modernization efforts. In B. Anneke & J. Jansen (Eds.), *Education for life in Africa* (pp. 100–118). African Studies Center.

GSS. Ghana. (2021). *Population and housing census: Ghana Report-Literacy & Education*, 3D. GSS.

Ghana Statistical Service. (2018). *Education statistics: Tracking progress in Ghana's basic level education across districts, 2010–2016* (1st ed.).

Haraway, D. J. (1997). The Virtual Speculum in the New World Order. *Feminist Review, 55*(1), 22–72. https://doi.org/10.1057/fr.1997.3

Higley, J., & Burton, M. (2006). *Elite foundations of liberal democracy*. Rowman & Littlefield Publishers.

Ministry of Education. (2019). *Education Sector Performance Report [ESPR], Ghana*. Planning, Budgeting, Monitoring, and Evaluation Unit [PBME]. https://assets.globalpartnership.org/s3fs-public/document/file/2020-16-Ghana%20-%20ESP-IR.pdf?VersionId=foXJ6Zqb.K1lSYmnT.c4EtcxpliHRs3c

Nsoh, A. E., Logugye, R. B., & Atintono, S. A. (2001). Facing the multilingual situation squarely: A practical approach. In D. D. Kuupole (Ed.), *New trends in languages in contact in West Africa* (pp. 49–60). St Francis Press.

Nsoh, E. A., & Ababila, J. A. (2007). Indigenous language policy and language planning in Ghana: the role of politics. In H. Weber, S. Beckmann, A. P. Cate Ten, et al. (Eds.), *Language diversity and language learning: new paths to literacy* (pp. 441–449). Linguistik International.

Michels, R. (1962). *Political parties: A sociological study of the oligarchical tendencies of modern democracy*. The Free Press.

Owu-Ewie, C. (2006). The language policy of education in Ghana in perspective: The past, the present, and the future. *Languages and Linguistics, 32*, 39–58.

Pareto, V. (1935). *A treatise on general sociology*. Dover Publications.

Reagan, T. (2021). Linguistic legitimacy, language rights and social justice: "No one is free when others are oppressed." In *Linguistic legitimacy and social justice*. Palgrave Macmillan. https://doi.org/10.1007/978-3-030-10967-7_11

Sarah, G. T. (2006). *Endangered languages: An introduction*. Cambridge University Press.

Skutnabb-Kangas, T., & Phillipson, R. (1995, reprinted 2017). Linguistic human rights, past and present. *Language Rights*, 1, 28–67.

Smith, Linda B. & Sheya, Adam (2010). Is Cognition Enough to Explain Cognitive Development? Topics in Cognitive Science 2 (4):725–735.

Spolsky, B. (2007). Towards a theory of language policy. *Working Papers in Educational Linguistics*, 22(1), 1–14.

USAID. (2018). *Language mapping study: Analysis report*. Partnership for Education. Learning.

Washington Post. (2021). *Hundreds of graves found at former residential school for Indigenous children in Canada*.

Williams, D. (1964). Comparative education. *Review*, 8(3), 290–306. https://www.jstor.org/stable/1187059

Wolff, E. (2021). The "de-Indigenization" of African languages. *Academia Letters*, Article 2702. https://doi.org/10.20935/AL2702

· 9 ·

EMBODIED COGNITION AND ANTI-COLONIAL EDUCATION IN HIGHER EDUCATION

Elmarie Costandius and Shelley Pryde

Introduction

I start by acknowledging the Land where we find ourselves; by reflecting on Indigenous histories and what we can learn from the Land, humans and non-humans. Alison Norman (2022) at Trent University argues that acknowledgment helps us to understand our place within history and its relation to our ongoing, active participation in society. Acknowledgment is an important step towards thinking about the changes necessary for reconciliation and redress. With a Land acknowledgment, we are reminded that Indigenous teaching creates communities of collaborative learning that aim to subvert colonial knowledge hierarchies and enable new futurities (Dei et al., in press). As such, acknowledging who currently benefits from the Land of Indigenous peoples is important.

As white Euro-Western academics (and settlers) in South Africa, there is no denying that we benefit from the Land forcibly taken from Indigenous South Africans, who are still today abused by capitalist-colonial drives, but this acknowledgment should not lead to apathy. At the same time, Tuck and Yang (2012) argue that for settlers, the pursuit of critical consciousness and social justice can become moves to "innocence," which could release the settler of feelings of guilt or responsibility, and obfuscate the need to give up Land, power or privilege. Land is acknowledged as the continued site of both decolonial projects and neo-coloniality, and as such, must be considered in relation to the continued being of Indigenous peoples and knowledges, as well as persisting settler colonialisms (Garba & Sorentino, 2020, p. 768). This also means that critique of settler colonialism cannot simply "include" Indigenous people and ideas in the settler—colonial state, but rather must examine the state itself and how it governs social order and understandings of the Land (Garba & Sorentino, 2020, p. 778).

It is such complexities that we continue to grapple with in our teaching praxis at Stellenbosch University (SU). As educators in the Department of Visual Arts, we have often employed art-based methodologies such as working with sound, body sculpture and paint. We have come to realize through working with these and similar embodied practices that learning through participation, using the senses and taking into consideration the environment could be more effective than traditional learning theories and practices. This does not mean that learning theories such as constructivism and experiential learning are not relevant, but adding contextual and active embodied learning could deepen understanding of issues related to social justice. Effective learning requires doing and thinking in action, and knowledge and understanding are enhanced through embodied contextual experiences.

When Land acknowledgment moves beyond the discursive and becomes embodied, we become aware of the space and place that we occupy and tune in to our sensory awareness and what affects us as we move through and experience spaces. In my work on embodied learning, I have often included a standing practice together with Land acknowledgment, where participants stand still and think about shared and relational responsibilities towards the Land, humans and non-humans. This inclusion is indebted to similar embodied practices such as the walking practices of Springgay and Truman (2017). My engagement with methodologies such as Indigenous enquiry (Somerville et al., 2010), walking interviews (Jones & Evans, 2012), pedestrianism (Middleton, 2011), mapping (O'Rourke, 2013) and sonic art performance (Springgay & Truman, 2017) have also supplied useful blueprints for how to become aware of space and place.

In light of these experiences and considerations, we use this chapter to argue for embodied cognition as a strategy towards anti-colonial education in higher education teaching and learning places and spaces. We begin by discussing the Western case for embodied cognition, linking anti-dualist philosophies to teaching and learning in the arts. Second, we relate these ideas to Indigenous knowledge and new materialist perspectives. Thirdly, we use the Visual Redress project at SU to engage with the concepts of space and place, examining the importance of space and place to pedagogies that create welcoming experiences for students. Finally, we use the embodied workshops in the Shared Humanity co-curriculum course as an example of how embodied learning could contribute to anti-colonial education on the SU campus.

Embodied Learning and Cognition

Aristotle, and after him Descartes, argued for the separation of the mind and body, constructing a hierarchy with the body positioned as unreliable, and the mind as rational. This idea came to underly much Western thought, influencing academic research, and educational theory and practices. Accordingly, much previous educational theory is based on behaviorism, which does not recognize the contributions of the body and senses to cognition and gives little attention to the affective domain of learning.

Problematizing such mind—body dualisms, Spinoza's (1992) theories of affect suggest that the power of the mind to think is equivalent to the power of the body to act, and that there is a relation between the power to act and the power to be affected. Spinoza (1992) argues that affect functions autonomously to cognition and that a body can be affected in many ways that can increase or decrease the ability of a person to act. Humans are driven by actions of the mind and reasoning, but also by actions or passions of the body that is always connected to the mind (Hardt, 2007, p. x). Affects can be actions resulting from internal and external causes. Spinoza (1992) asks, what can a body do? Deleuze (1992) reacts to Spinoza's question by arguing that while we are concerned about the soul and the mind, we do not know what the body is capable of until the body autonomously reacts. Deleuze (1992) says, "What a body can do corresponds to the nature and limits of its capacity to be affected" (p. 218). The ability to be affected means that one is influenced by experiences created by engagements with the environment, humans and non-humans. Although Spinoza's perspective overall remains within the rationalism of European enlightenment philosophy, his notions of different types of knowledge offer a useful frame through which to consider art and embodied learning as modes of cognition (Kerr, 2020).

Dewey and Merleau-Ponty's works have contributed much to discussions of embodied cognition, specifically in educational theory. The work of Dewey

(1938) tells us that learning is a body—mind experience. Dewey (1938) argues that considering physical and social surroundings could further contribute to learning experiences. According to Dewey (1938), sensation emerges from the engagements of minds, bodies and their environments. Dewey (1938) also criticized dualist thinking and the polarisation of the body/mind, nature/culture, reason/emotion and self/other. Merleau-Ponty (1962) similarly rejects Cartesian dualism, stressing that the mind is inseparable from our situated, bodily nature. It is through the body that we have access to the world, and as such, cognition cannot be comprehended without the body's engagement with the environment (Merleau-Ponty, 1962). Merleau-Ponty (1962) argues that there are stresses between what is given (our bodies) in terms of what we can do and what we think we can do (in our mind).

More recently, Macrine and Fugate (2022, p. 15) problematize constructivist learning theories, pointing out that while doing away with the simplistic idea of learners as only knowledge receivers, they still describe learning as a product of the individual's intellectual activity. Constructing one's own individual knowledge is divorced from the complexities or reality of one's own learning space, resulting in a vision of "education" that consists only of sitting in a class with workbooks, rote memorization and drills for standardized testing (Newman et al., 1989, as cited in Macrine & Fugate, 2022). Embodied cognition, conversely, is embedded (in certain goals and concerns), extended (engaged in socialization, routines and societal norms) and enacted (the body is self-producing and adaptive to different environments) (Macrine & Fugate, 2022, p. 18). Citing Smith and Sheya (2010), Macrine and Fugate (2022) discuss how cognitive psychology has gone through a theoretical shift to "acknowledge that sensorimotor processing is fundamental to understanding information" (p. 16). Manning (2014, as cited in Springgay & Zaliwska, 2015) says that we should find ways of activating ideas and thoughts that are "experienced rather than known, that [are] material and affective" (p. 136).

Embodied learning is also different from traditional cognitive learning because it considers the personal in learning processes (Kolb, 2015). With a focus on personal experience through embodied experiences, the learner is more present. However, this does not mean that learning is simply "experience" divorced from cognition: Kolb (2015) outlines experiential learning as a process beginning with experience but followed by reflection on the experience. Even as something is experienced, such experience must also be conceptualized and internalized to result in effective learning. Fugate et al. (2018, as cited in Macrine & Fugate, 2022) relatedly suggest that in a teaching and learning environment, the learner "needs to be seen and taught as a whole being" and that learners should be permitted "to experience themselves as an integrated whole" (p. 20). For this reason, they argue that embodied learning can be used as an alternative methodology that mitigates the reestablishment of human and non-human dualisms.

Such notions of learning value the potential of experiencing things in the moment, but also of deploying repeated embodied efforts towards adjusting neural highways formed over many years. Kontra et al. (2012) refers to accepted research that shows how movement and action help to form our awareness and learning in early life, and that there is reason to believe that it continues to do so later in life. This embodied cognition also includes the use of physical objects, materials or "manipulatives" (Donovan & Alibali, 2022) that can be used during learning processes. Materials and objects are used as a medium for learning through experimentation, discovery and exploration. Bennett (2010, p. 10) suggests that non-human things and forces possess "thing-power" and are able to exchange properties. This links comfortably to art-based methodologies, as the art process is based on experimentation with materials in relation to the self.

Bourdieu (1989) talks about the theory of art-in-action to describe how ideas are realized through practice, but whether this suggests that art is simply a method for thinking or can produce new knowledge is debated. According to Barrett (2007), art-based practice is a different form of creating knowledge. It is a valid alternative mode of inquiry to traditional learning and research. St. Pierre (2015) calls art practices the "physicality of theorising" (p. 92). Golanska (2020) offers a more mixed account, describing the artistic process as an "integration of different modes of thinking/knowing—intuitive-rational, bodily-intellectual and material-semiotic" (p. 6). Rousell (2019) says "art is real and not a representation," "art is a composition of sensations" and "art creates new forms and potentials of life within ecologies of relation" (p. 31). What remains relevant is that embodied/material/discursive engagements are important in a teaching environment, and that the turn to include material alongside discursive dimensions is welcomed.

Embodied and experiential learning as tools also offer the possibility of cultivating new ideas. Hofstadter (1985) argues that making variations on a theme is the crux of creativity. He argues that fluid thought depends on ideas constantly slipping from one into another without us noticing it. When ideas are connected, they start migrating and developing in unexpected ways. Each new idea could open up new ideas and build new connections, and often when unusual connections are made, new perspectives can result. In fact, each new idea builds on a previous idea, described by Hofstadter (1985) as non-deliberate yet non-accidental slippage. The more we are exposed to different ideas, the more opportunities there are for new connections, working with materials and including movement of the body, which open up the possibilities for new connections even more. As Hofstadter (1985) argues, our chances of serendipitous breakthrough are maximized by this kind of process.

These briefly outlined perspectives culminate in a conception of cognition grounded in sensory and motor activity. Our experiences of the world are always relational—mediated through the body and situated in an environment—and therefore, learning should take this into account. I have traced a through-line from theories of mind–body, through educational theory that recognizes the primacy of learning through experience, ending in arguments for art-based, embodied cognition. Art is affective, and affect is a driving force, meaning we can use our ability to feel and experience as a driving force in teaching and learning in art. The implications of these ideas for anti-colonial education are that we cannot ignore the body and the sensory in learning situations if we are to undo the symbolic order embedded through colonial and Eurocentric pasts in higher education. This is an idea to which Indigenous epistemologies have offered important contributions, not just for considering how learning takes place, but also for expanding notions of what types of knowledge can be learned and produced.

Embodied Learning, Indigenous Thinking and New Materialism

Defining Indigenous Epistemologies

Indigenous knowledge practices are experiential and are context specific. Indigenous knowledges stem from people who lived in a relational manner with nature, animals, and humans; from people who lived in a place for a long time; from knowledges transferred orally through generations (Dei, 2000). According to Dei (2000), Indigenous epistemologies are grounded in a deep appreciation of the Land and "how the self/selves, spiritual, known and unknown worlds are interconnected. ... grounded in a people, a place and a history" (p. 115). Indeed, for the Khoi, the first people of southern Africa, the Land has both a material and a spiritual significance and the self is integral to nature and the other. The other is not seen as "lifeless objects but as organisms

... the other forms and is formed by the interplay of agency" (Klaasen, 2018, p. 9). For Indigenous thinkers, the experience of the world is relational.

Importantly, Indigenous perspectives challenge colonial discourses of dominion over Land: Land is more than simply a surface on which people move, meaning that people should neither be removed from Land, nor should Land be controlled or exploited. Indigenous theories operate from an ontological comprehension that takes non-human agency as a given (Rosiek et al., 2019). The objects of our research do not wait passively to be uncovered and described. Rosiek et al. (2019) say that this changes the relationship between the subject and other agents (human, non-human, objects) from a spectator and investigator to a participant in the ethical association with others—human and non-human. Sousa and Pessoa (2019, p. 522) say that Indigenous peoples engage with the world in a holistic way and see the world in a non-binarist way when it comes to human and non-human relations, mind and spirit, or what is tangible and intangible. They argue that Indigenous knowledges present the worldview that "all materiality (alongside spirituality) plays a role in the processes we experience" (Sousa & Pessoa, 2019, p. 522). Massey (2013) claims that how we imagine space can influence our worldview and has consequences. Therefore, if we imagine space and the human—nature encounter as relational, ethical aspects of how to engage with nature change (Rosiek et al., 2019). Relationality offers more environmentally sustainable futures.

Despite the potentialities of Indigenous epistemologies, there are also challenges involved in engaging with them in scholarship. Watts (2013) suggests that it is often difficult to engage with or respect Indigenous theories from a Eurocentric perspective because of different ways of viewing the world. Watts (2013) says that a person with an Indigenous perspective may struggle to assimilate in an environment where binaries and dualist thinking are the norm. Rosiek et al. (2019) argue that Indigenous peoples integrating into a settler cultural environment can result in a loss of relational capacity.

Examining New Materialism

Like Indigenous theory, new materialism is based on an integrated way of seeing the world. From a new materialist perspective, things and matter, and human and non-human, can be social agents and possess agency. In humanist traditions, the human is put into a binary opposition, in specific hierarchies, ignoring the complexities of the in-between. The concept of Other becomes a dualist concept, instead of thinking of others as a part of ourselves and being interlinked. Authors such as Barad (2007) put forward the idea that we should understand our place in the world as engaged in interrelated networks, and that we should use the concept of entanglement. New materialism is based on non-dualist perspectives (following the work of Spinoza), such as body–mind, human–nature and object–subject. This means that things are not separate or in a binary opposition, but rather interweaved.

New materialism is a turn to materiality and a turn to ontology—how the world is—above a sole focus on epistemology—how we understand or theorize about the world. Barad (2007), in her book *Meeting the universe halfway*, says that people emerge through and as part of their entangled intra-relating. We are entangled with what is around us: self, others, body, mind, political, social, historical, the spaces that we are in, buildings, signs, what you read or do, family, etc. The relations between the components in an entanglement are also relevant, as they also affect one another. Phenomena emerge from a relation between things, not from a single element in the relation.

The Power of Embodied Cognition

Using embodied experiences also relates to apprenticeship-based learning, which has been practiced in Africa as an educational methodology long before colonialism. Apprenticeship-based learning is based on learning through participation, actively taking part and learning in a real-life social setting. This produces collaborative learning in a community linked by a shared goal (Lave, 1977). McLaughlin (2000) says that an apprenticeship learning environment could create spaces for a feeling of community and enhance feelings of safety, especially when interacting with peers from different racial, gender, class or cultural groups. Downey et al. (2015) argue that individuals gain apprenticeship-based expertise through "incessant active learning processes of re-discovery, variation, innovation, inspiration, disciplining—even failure" (p. 185). From an Indigenous knowledge perspective, engaging with local pedagogies and community techniques could naturally be integrated into apprenticeship-based learning. In addition, apprenticeship-based learning goes beyond Cartesian dualism to promote an "ubuntu perspective of—I am because we are—to better reflect the democratic and inclusive ways of being, seeing and thinking" (Le Grange, 2019, as cited in Hlatshwayo et al., 2020, p. 104). Relationality between humans and nature as practiced by Indigenous practitioners through apprenticeship-based learning could assist in decolonizing curricula and teaching and learning practices.

Braidotti (2013), from a new materialist perspective, also argues for apprenticeship-based learning. An emphasis on process, experimentation and adaptability is part of Braidiotti's (2013) theory on nomadic subjectivity. She suggests that actual embodied practices might assist in engaging with anti-colonial consciences.

Decentring the human therefore also means decentring Western knowledge in relation to Indigenous thinking. Mbembe (2016) argues that an Africa centrality is important for all who live here. Sibiya and Ndaba (2023) draw on Freire's concept of praxis and argue that we should go beyond debates on decolonization to explore "possibilities of undoing the colonial project in terms of systems and structure through praxis" (p. 215). They argue that the concept of decolonization has been investigated mainly at a theoretical level, without translating it into practice/praxis (Sibiya & Ndaba, 2023, p. 216). Decolonizing the mind is crucial, as Wa Thiong'o (1986) argues, but learning and unlearning in praxis through the body are also of crucial importance, especially in relation to social justice work.

Implications for an Embodied, Anti-colonial Pedagogy

Bozalek and Zembylas (2017) put forward "response-able pedagogies" that create "relational processes through which social, political, and material entanglements ... [such as students, facilitators, discourses, texts] are rendered capable through each other to bring about social transformation" (p. 64). Bozalek and Zembylas (2017) argue that "response-able pedagogies" incorporate collective knowing, being, doing and making—and this could involve "how to flourish together in a complex world," and "being and becoming and making-with" (ontological) and "knowing-with" (epistemological) (p. 69). Another concept in new materialist thinking is diffraction. Bozalek and Zembylas (2017) refer to Haraway (1997), who considers diffraction to bring in the self in relation to knowledge that is situated. By this she means a critical interrogation and embodied perspective of the effects of one's own place in the production of knowledge.

Zavala (2016) argues that anti-colonial education comes alive when engaging in dialogue and reflection by naming people's social worlds. This enables terminology to critique and understand the complexities involved in colonized worlds. Apart from developing a language, healing and reclaiming identities and spaces are crucial aspects that Zavala (2016) emphasizes. Reclaiming involves "recovering who people are (their cultural identities), their practices, and their relation to place (Land, cosmos)" (Zavala, 2016, p. 5).

Considering these frameworks, our use of embodied learning strategies in the visual arts have sought to explore how such strategies can facilitate more relational, Indigenous knowledge-informed, and African-centric cognitions. The need to rethink how we do higher education is clear if we consider the deeply entrenched dualism of much Western thought, but I have found that we cannot simply rely on old tools to uncover new ideas and solutions. The perspectives offered by Indigenous knowledges and new materialisms, plugged into arguments for embodied cognition, can help us explore the possibilities of art-based and embodied learning for anti-colonial education. It is from this potentiality that I undertake my discussion of Visual Redress and the Shared Humanity practice-based workshops at SU.

Visual Redress Project: Changing Learning Spaces and Places

A space becomes a place when it is associated with experience. Certain meaning is connected to a place through experience. To change the meaning of a place, the experience of the place needs to be adjusted. Thinking or reading about a place could have an effect, but an embodied experience could have a greater effect. Experiential learning should therefore be considered when decolonization of spaces and places is the outcome.

Lefebvre (1991) argues that spaces are socially constructed and that places are infiltrated with politics. Lefebvre's (1991) theory on the production of space explores in which manner space is perceived, conceived, and lived ("spatial triad"). The perceived space concerns how people think about space. The conceived space relates to the symbols, codifications and abstract representations in the space, while the lived space is about the bodily engagements/enactments within the space, and how it is used and inhabited. Lefebvre (1991) says that space is a mental and material construct, and that spaces shape those who inhabit and move through them. It can naturalise behavior and favor certain modes of being over others. Merrifield (2002) argues that spaces can be changed or redefined through experience. Merrifield (2002) describes space not as a dead, motionless object, but as fluid and alive. Experiences of spaces can therefore be recreated and re-described all over again.

Considering what happened culturally, socially, politically, and economically in Africa during colonialism and specifically in South Africa, we should consider the spaces on many campuses, which largely represent a colonial history. Taking into deliberation the material aspects of living include, for example, how architecture or physical objects such as statues, shape our daily existence, making visible "socioeconomic structures that produce and reproduce the conditions of our everyday lives" (Coole & Frost, 2016, p. 1). Things or matter, human and non-human, can be social agents and possess agency.

Decolonizing the university therefore also requires addressing the "economy of symbols" that have normalized segregation and racism, such as statues, artworks, names of buildings and spaces, and other lasting tokens of apartheid and colonialism (Mbembe, 2015, p. 6). Mbembe (2016) argues that educational spaces should allow "everyone the possibility to inhabit a space to the extent that one can say, "This is my home. I am not a foreigner. I belong here." This is not hospitality. It is not charity" (p. 30). How do we practically engage in the ongoing production of space to reconstruct and redefine spaces? One strategy I have explored in my own work is to engage with one another in embodied practices in those spaces, so that we associate the sensitive spaces with something new and make room for everyone to feel ownership over the space and place.

How do we navigate anger and sadness, or healing and belonging, related to learning spaces on campuses? Ndlovu-Gatsheni (2018) argues that students attacking the Rhodes statue was emblematic of attacking colonialism.[1] Long-pent-up frustrations in societies can erupt when people feel misrecognized, misrepresented or marginalized. Noble (2012, p. 4) in his book on iconoclasm talks about "stresses and tears in the social fabric," saying that the destruction of public statues has been a by-product of other kinds of social, political, or religious issues in society.

The current SU Visual Redress project aims to redress spaces and remove hurtful symbols such as plaques and statues, but also to contextualize those symbols that remain on campus. SU (2021, p. 6) describes visual redress as follows: ... an attempt to right the wrongs of former and current powers by removing hurtful symbols (e.g., of apartheid), social injustice and misrecognition and by remedying the harm that has been caused by these visual symbols through compensation with new visual symbols that allow for the inclusion of a variety of expressions, stories, identities, and histories.

The Visual Redress project is based on the master's course in critical citizenship, as well as on student projects aimed at creating a welcoming learning space all students. In 2013, I decided to move projects outside the studio to engage students and communities on and around campus in social justice-related projects, which led to the Visual Redress project. The concept of visual redress spontaneously developed when a group of students did a project on Women's Day in 2013 called *Eva*, which addressed the absence of women statues on campus. After this project, the term "visual redress" became a concept that was used in various projects that aimed to decolonize spaces and make the campus a welcoming space for all students. The Visual Redress project is not only focused on physically transforming the space but also on encouraging critical dialogue and awareness (SU, 2021).

During the 2015/2016 student protests, a tyre was set alight in front of the Jan Marais statue on the main square on SU campus, called the Rooiplein (translated as the Red Square), by some protesters, while other students tried to clean it up. This demonstrates the contrasting perspectives on campus: Marais as a generous donor versus Marais as an imperialist exploiter. The Rooiplein is often used as a gathering place for student activism, such as the #RhodesMustFall and #FeesMustFall movements and, more recently, #RacismMustFall. The Rooiplein is therefore a space where much anger, frustration and fear had been experienced.

In 2017, I wrote a Visual Redress plan that was presented to the University management, and institutional funding was made available for the project. During the student protests in 2015/2016, I asked a master's student, with fellow students from the Open Stellenbosch movement, to conceptualize new artworks for campus. *The Circle* of women resulted from that request and was implemented in 2019 with institutional funding. Benches with welcoming messages in 16 South African languages and dialects were also added to the Rooiplein.

We realized through the Visual Redress project that working with visual aspects (such as artworks and welcoming messages on benches) was insufficient, and that I have to go further to start working with embodied practices and materials in art-based learning, especially when it comes to social justice learning. Social justice issues are not for rote learning—they require deep body–mind experiences. Visually decolonizing learning spaces and places is crucial and could be conducive to having experiences to enhance learning but are not sufficient. Listening to a lecturer or engaging in conversations about anti-colonial education could be an experience, but involving the body in a more active manner could be more conducive to learning. Embodied learning is not new, and working with materials and including the senses is also not new—the problem is that we are not making use of the immense possibilities of embodied learning.

In the work that followed the Visual Redress project, I implemented embodied experiences instead of only addressing visual spaces on campus and worked with many students and staff in various workshops at different faculties. The workshops would start with a standing practice, becoming aware of the historical and current environment where we are, and working with materials such as clay and/or a creative concept development process (Costandius, 2019). Physically standing together is different from imagining standing together. Feelings sit in the body; for instance, the body might start to sweat uncontrollably when in a discomforting situation. The body could be affected or could react before the mind has time to think about the action. The body is therefore also a source of knowledge. Information given to us by the body can reveal what still need to learn or unlearn.

One example of an embodied learning workshop was at the Faculty of Law at SU, where we worked with what was already in the lecturer room: framed photos of former high court judges in South Africa, mostly from the apartheid years. The participants decided to work with the photos, as they felt that it affected their feeling of belonging in a learning space associated with white men from a previous era in South Africa. The participants could use any materials to engage with the photos, but cloth in different colors was made available to them. A female student, for instance, spontaneously wrapped the face of one of the judges in the shape of a *hijab* (a scarf used by Muslim women to cover their face and neck). This opened up many new possibilities of engaging with the colonial history and gender relations. This is a typical example of slippage (one idea slips into another and opens up new linkages) to which Hofstadter (1985) refers.

Another workshop with students and staff at the Faculty of Theology focused on the place where the faculty was situated. Before the settlers came, the place currently occupied by the Theology building was a sacred gathering place for Indigenous Khoi people of southern Africa. The participants were asked to use their bodies to reimagine the building, taking those historical facts into consideration. Participants were asked to spontaneously form sculptures in small groups using their bodies. The image of the students and staff sitting in a circle opened discussions on the gathering place of the Khoi and how that should be remembered and honored when moving through the current building.

Participants in these types of workshops have consistently expressed the awareness that cognitive engagements are not the only way to generate new ideas and understandings. Two students remarked after the workshop: "It was very enlightening and has introduced me to a new way of critical thinking and solution development" and *"The visual arts one allowed me to understand more of what is happening in everyday life and what we can do to build community especially the workshop."* Another student reflected on her own learning journey related to social justice:

> On my social justice journey I recognise that I am nowhere near done. I will continue to be open to growth and learning and recognizing the impact that I can make. I need to appreciate my physical experience and realise how it can impact my life. I need to embrace the embodiment perspective in social justice advocacy to deepen my understanding of the complex interplay between physical experience and social injustices.

This experience became a kind of embodied learning experience for me too, in my own teaching praxis, as I realized first-hand how embodied practices can facilitate spontaneous and critical engagements with spaces and materials.

Shared Humanity Practices and Workshops

The Shared Humanity course consists of seven sessions taught by various lecturers from different faculties at SU (see Table 1). The Khampepe Report that was commissioned by Judge Sisi Khampepe (2022) in reaction to a racist incident on the SU campus suggests that the current Shared Humanity co-curriculum course should become compulsory for all students. In reaction to the report, workstreams were established to implement the suggestions. Some of the workstreams are Institutional culture; Student experiences; Race, human categorization and science; Structures, policies, regulations and transformation; and Curriculum offerings embedded in the process of teaching and learning renewal.

Session 5 is the Visual Arts session (see Table 2), in which we have been experimenting with embodied learning for the last three years. The Visual Arts session consists of six parts: knowledge, values, social structures, resilience, cultural sensitivity, and design thinking and diffraction. With each of the parts I invited a speaker, but also very importantly, included embodied practice such as working with clay and mixing skin color with spices. The students engage with the six concepts individually, but thereafter also engage in collaborative workshops where they paint, draw with light or record sounds

Table 1: Shared Humanity Course Outline

Sessions	Discipline	Subject Matter Experts	Critical Question
Introduction	Anthropology	Prof. Jess Auerbach	Is it possible for people to change?
Session 1	Education	Prof. Jonathan Stephanus Coetzee	How is racism learned and unlearned?
Session 2	Science and Technology	Dr. Mpho Tshivhase	For who do chatbots pose a threat?
Session 3	Engineering	Prof. Wikus van Niekerk	Why exactly can South Africa not produce enough electricity for its citizens?
Session 4	Health Sciences	Prof. Tulio de Oliveira	Will climate change fuel the next pandemics?
Session 5	Visual Arts	Prof. Elmarie Costandius	How do I find my space and place in a changing world?
Session 6	Law	Prof. Thuli Madonsela	Is the law a reliable instrument for the delivery of social justice?
Session 7	Economics	Mr. Lorenzo Davids	What explains the rise in homelessness in urban settings?

when walking in different directions from the Rooiplein. The sound practice encourages students to notice how sounds change depending on where you are in the town of Stellenbosch. Stellenbosch is still mainly a segregated town because of the laws that were implemented during the colonial and apartheid eras. The senses are involved and often also challenged, which enable more affective body–mind entanglements (Massumi, 2015).

After the embodied learning workshops, students were asked, "Which session developed your critical thinking capabilities?" Examples of the students' feedback is provided:

> The Session 5 [Visual Arts] workshops had the greatest impact on me because it was the most engaging session with in-person workshops and activities that encouraged creative critical thinking and idea generation. It was very enlightening and has introduced me to a new way of critical thinking and solution development.
>
> I've come to realise that values have always seemed quite abstract to me, and I find myself struggling to list values, not being sure what is considered valuable, but with these practices and reflections I have come to understand the term much deeper.
>
> I found that I looked forward to the sessions [Visual Arts] more so than in the previous modules. I loved to learn about different concepts and reflecting on what was said and how I could apply that to my practical life. I consider myself a sensitive, open-minded and tolerant person and I enjoyed the sessions on cultural sensitivity and social structures. In studying medicine, it is not often that one is faced with

Table 2: Visual Arts, session 5 outline 2023

Date	Concepts	Duration	Presentations	Venue	Practices
Wednesday, 19 July 2023	1. *Knowledge* Knowledge production, whose knowledge, who speaks, Indigenous knowledge, decolonizing knowledge, Land acknowledgment	30–60 minutes	Prof. George Sefa Dei	SUNLearn (online) and Padlet	Grounding ourselves practice linked with theme, Prof. Elmarie Costandius
Thursday, 20 July 2023	2. *Values* Respect, empathy and tolerance	30–60 minutes	Prof. Nico Koopman	SUNLearn (online) and Padlet	Blind drawing practice linked with theme, Prof. Elmarie Costandius
Friday, 21 July 2023	3. *Social structures* Hegemony, hierarchy and equality	30–60 minutes	Prof. Aslam Fataar	SUNLearn (online) and Padlet	Clay exercise practice linked with theme, Prof. Elmarie Costandius
Monday, 24 July 2023	4. *Resilience* Social cohesion, self-efficacy, self-esteem, optimism, cognitive reappraisal, active coping and mindfulness	30–60 minutes	Prof. Ashraf Kagee	SUNLearn (online) and Padlet	Mindfulness practice linked with theme, Prof. Elmarie Costandius
Tuesday, 25 July 2023	5. *Cultural sensitivity* Stereotyping, diversity, bias, shame, social identities	30–60 minutes	Ms. Qaqamba Mdaka and Dr Jill Ryan	SUNLearn (online) and Padlet	Tasting and mixing spices practice linked with theme, Prof. Elmarie Costandius

Table 2: *Continued*

Date	Concepts	Duration	Presentations	Venue	Practices
Wednesday, 26 July 2023	6. *Design thinking and diffraction* Binary opposition thinking	30–60 minutes	Prof. Vivienne Bozalek	SUNLearn (online) and Padlet	Diffractive reflexivity, Prof. Elmarie Costandius

reflecting on your own attitudes and cultural sensitivities. I enjoyed changing the focus from "hard skills" to "soft skills". Ultimately, I truly believe this Visual Arts session will have a lasting impact on my attitude and life outlook. I think everyone needs to go through a module like this at some point in their lives.

It remains a challenge to pinpoint exactly how embodied learning influences participants, but reading the reflections of students can provide some insight into their experiences. Different experiences emerged from the individual versus group practices.

Some students felt that the individual learning space helped them to reflect on real issues in their life, saying for example: "The visual arts one allowed me to understand more of what is happening in everyday life and what we can do to build community, especially the workshop." Students commented that they enjoyed the individual practices and felt that they achieved something: "… I loved this part, because it made me really proud of what I could achieve … all on my own." Group engagements focused on social justice issues tend to be more stressful, and students are often not willing to engage as freely. The individual practices therefore allowed students to engage with sensitive and often uncomfortable issues in which they would normally not engage in group sessions.

Simultaneously, it is not helpful to focus solely on individual practices and avoid group engagement. Carrying insights through from individual practices to group sessions has proved to be an important strategy. The spices, for instance (used in some of the practices), stain the skin, and one would be reminded of the engagement long after the practice was started. In the practice, students were asked to follow an individual process, but they also discussed afterward in group reflections how they now look at spices connected to history and sociopolitical issues instead of only an everyday ingredient used in the kitchen. Playful group activities such as the painting of values on a big piece of paper also allowed students to collaboratively address serious issues.

Conclusion: Embodied Learning and Anti-colonial Education

Embodied learning is not new. Many theorists who engage in perspectives on learning, Indigenous and new materialist thinking, as well as perspectives on apprenticeship-based learning, argue for embodied, relational and contextual teaching and learning pedagogies. We can learn from Indigenous practitioners when it comes to relational mind—body practices, and more recently from new materialist perspectives that trouble non-relational and dualist thinking. Immersive embodied practices have the potential to assist in decolonizing the body—mind, which could enhance teaching and learning practices.

Theoretical knowledge is often disconnected from the body (especially if one cannot relate to what is being learned). In academia we mostly deal with theory over practice, allowing theory to stand in for reality, or become a representation of reality. Practice can facilitate learning in real time and in reality. Although receiving theoretical information often helps us to classify and cognitively understand concepts, it might not help us to fully internalize new ideas or change our perceptions. However, internalizing learning through embodied practices could result in a more transformative effect. Embodied experiences can challenge dominant knowledge systems by asking us not to map theory onto disparate realities, but rather to consider how affect, the body, the sensory and the material sit in relation with reality. In the project of decolonizing theory and the body—mind, situated and embodied practices provide important insights and methods.

Art-based practices allow new possibilities because they are exploratory and often unpredictable (Manning, 2015). Art-based practices specifically encourage connections of ideas that are normally not put or seen together, and that is what Hofstadter (1985) sees as the crux of creativity, which is necessary in moving educational thinking forward. In my work, I have noticed how engaging with concepts such as knowledge production, values and social structures while experiencing them in an embodied way enables participants to "stay longer" with issues, and work through them within themselves and in collaborative ways. This relates to Haraway's (2016) concept of "staying with the trouble." In my work I argue for experimenting and exploring and therefore also staying longer with the trouble; engaging with concepts in an embodied way, including materials and becoming aware of the environment where the practices take place.

In teaching praxis, I have engaged with many students and staff who felt disconnected from their environment (e.g., a university campus, residence or town) and struggled to find their place and space in a complex world. It is as if the participants (and I) live in an unrelated world of constantly aspiring for something that is not perceived as attainable, because learning is not grounded in local context. Embedded and embodied practices could assist in learning, especially in the postcolonial and post-apartheid context in South Africa.

The embodied practices with which I have been experimenting are premised on a basis of Land acknowledgment and the agency of the material and the non-human. While this work remains in progress, my experience thus far has produced interesting and unexpected slippages and ideas that have helped students connect theory with real life, and produced critical dialogues between humans, spaces and places. Combining individual and group practices has also proved to be a strategy with potential to allow students to engage with uncomfortable topics in a less intimidating way, while learning from one another and becoming open to difficult realities. This can be explored further in future praxis.

As in the Visual Redress projects and workshops and the Shared Humanity course practices, research can be done while engaging in the projects, so learning in action also becomes research in action. This engages participants in the knowledge production process, creating a collaborative learning environment and a shared sense of ownership that could enhance social justice and anti-colonial education. The learner, the environment and the content are related and should be treated in a relational manner. Engaging in the environment where we find ourselves enables context-specific knowledge creation. Social justice education does not only happen through theoretical or rote learning, and alternative educational practices need to be explored to further learning processes.

What remains salient is that if we are to work towards decolonizing our body—mind and implementing anti-colonial education strategies, we must take seriously insights from Indigenous knowledge and emerging perspectives such as new materialism. Informed by these perspectives, a relational embodied approach where we engage deeper with our historical, current and possible future contexts could assist in decolonizing the body—mind.

Note

1 Between 2014 and 2016, students participating in the #RhodesMustFall movement at the University of Cape Town demanded the removal of a statue of Cecil John Rhodes from campus. This spurred much discussion on colonial symbols and spaces on university campuses across the country.

References

Barad, K. (2007). *Meeting the universe halfway: Quantum physics and the entanglement of matter and meaning.* Duke University Press.
Barrett, E. (2007). Experiential learning in practice as research: Context, method, knowledge. *Journal of Visual Art Practice,* 6(2), 115–124.
Bennett, J. (2010). *Vibrant matter: A political ecology of things.* Duke University Press.
Bourdieu, P. (1989). Social space and symbolic power. *Sociological Theory,* 7(1), 14–25.
Bozalek, V., & Zembylas, M. (2017). Diffraction or reflection? Sketching the contours of two methodologies in educational research. *International Journal of Qualitative Studies in Education,* 30(2), 111–127.
Braidotti, R. (2013). Nomadic ethics. *Deleuze Studies,* 7(3), 342–359.
Coole, D., & Frost, S. (2016). Introducing the new materialisms. In D. Coole & S. Frost (Eds.), *New materialisms: Ontology, agency & politics* (pp. 154–164). Duke University Press.
Costandius, E. (2019). Fostering the conditions for creative concept development. *Cogent Education,* 6(1), Article 1700737.
Dei, G. J. S. (2000). Rethinking the role of Indigenous knowledges in the academy. *International Journal of Inclusive Education,* 4(2), 111–132.
Dei, G. J. S., Costandius, E., Odiboh, F., & Heumen, H. (2024, in press). Social justice and inclusion in African higher education in the era of COVID-19: Lessons for educational transformation. *Journal of Higher Education in Africa,* 21(2).
Deleuze, G. (1992). *Expressionism in philosophy: Spinoza.* Zone Books.
Dewey, J. (1938). The philosophy of the arts. In J. Boydston (Ed.), *The later works of John Dewey 1938–1939: Experience and education, freedom and culture, theory of evaluation, and essays* (Vol. 13, pp. 357–368). Southern Illinois University Press.
Donovan, A. M., & Alibali, M. W. (2022). Manipulatives and mathematics learning: The roles of perceptual and interactive features. In S. L. Macrine & J. M. B. Fugate (Eds.), *Movement matters: How embodied cognition informs teaching and learning* (pp. 147–161). The MIT Press.
Downey, G., Dalidowicz, M., & Mason, P. H. (2015). Apprenticeship as method: Embodied learning in ethnographic practice. *Qualitative Research,* 15(2), 183–200.
Fugate, J. M. B., Macrine, S. L., & Cipriano, C. (2018). The role of embodied cognition for transforming learning. *International Journal of School & Educational Psychology,* 7(4), 274–288.

Garba, T., & Sorentino, S. (2020). Slavery is a metaphor: A critical commentary on Eve Tuck and K. Wang's "Decolonization is not a metaphor." *Antipode, 52*(3), 764–782.

Golanska, D. (2020). Creative practice for sustainability: A new materialist perspective on activist production of eco-sensitive knowledges. *International Journal of Education through Art, 16*(3), 1–26.

Haraway, D. J. (2016). *Staying with the trouble: Making kin in the Chthulucene*. Duke University Press.

Hardt, M. (2007). What affects are good for. In P. T. Clough & J. Halley (Eds.), *The affective turn: Theorizing the social* (pp. ix–xiii). Duke University Press.

Hlatshwayo, M. N., Shawa, L. B., & Nxumalo, S. A. (2020). Ubuntu currere in the academy: A case study from the South African experience. *Third World Thematics: A TWQ Journal, 5*(1/2), 120–136.

Hofstadter, D. R. (1985). *Metamagical themas: Questing for the essence of mind and pattern*. Basic Books.

Jones, P., & Evans, J. (2012). Rescue geography: Place making, affect and regeneration. *Urban Studies, 49*(11), 2315–2330.

Kerr, J. (2020). Spinoza: From art to philosophy. *Philosophy Today, 64*(1), 239–253. https://doi.org/10.5840/philtoday2020413330

Khampepe, S. (2022, October 25). Commission of Inquiry into allegations of racism at Stellenbosch University: Final report. *Politicsweb*. https://www.politicsweb.co.za/documents/sisi-khampepes-report-on-racism-at-stellenbosch-un

Klaasen, J. S. (2018). Khoisan identity: A contribution towards reconciliation in post-apartheid South Africa. *Studia Historiae Ecclesiasticae, 44*(2), 1–14.

Kolb, D. (2015). *Experiential learning: Experience as the source of learning and development* (2nd ed.). Prentice-Hall.

Kontra, C., Goldin-Meadow, S., & Beilock, S. L. (2012). Embodied learning across the life span. *Topics in Cognitive Science, 4*(4), 731–739.

Lave, J. (1977). Cognitive consequences of traditional apprenticeship training in West Africa. *Anthropology & Education Quarterly, 8*(3), 177–180.

Lefebvre, H. (1991). *The production of space*. Blackwell.

Macrine, S. L., & Fugate, J. M. B. (2022). *Movement matters: How embodied cognition informs teaching and learning*. The MIT Press.

Massey, D. (2013). *Space, place and gender*. Polity Press.

Manning, E. (2015). Against method. In *Non-representational methodologies* (pp. 52–71). Routledge.

Massumi, B. (2015). *Politics of affect*. Polity Press.

Mbembe, A. (2015). *Decolonizing knowledge and the question of the archive*. WISER. https://wiser.wits.ac.za/system/files/Achille%20Mbembe%20-%20Decolonizing%20Knowledge%20and%20the%20Question%20of%20the%20Archive.pdf

Mbembe, A. (2016). Decolonizing the university: New directions. *Arts and Humanities in Higher Education, 15*(1), 29–45.

McLaughlin, L. M. (2000). *Flexibility and mobility in apprenticeship training* [Unpublished MA thesis]. University of Manitoba.
Merleau-Ponty, B. M. (1962). *Phenomenology of perception* (C. Smith, Trans.). Routledge & Kegan Paul.
Merrifield, A. (2002). Henri Lefebvre: A socialist in space. In M. Crang & N. Thrift (Eds.), *Thinking space* (pp. 167–182). Routledge.
Middleton, J. (2011). Walking in the city: The geographies of everyday pedestrian practices. *Geography Compass, 5*(2), 90–105.
Ndlovu-Gatsheni, S. J. (2018). Rhodes must fall. In S. J. Ndlovu-Gatsheni (Ed.), *Epistemic freedom in Africa: Deprovincialization and decolonization* (pp. 215–237). Taylor & Francis.
Noble, T. F. X. (2012). *Images, iconoclasm, and the Carolingians*. The University of Pennsylvania Press.
Norman, A. (2022). *Alison Norman*. https://trentu.academia.edu/alisonnorman
O'Rourke, K. (2013). *Walking and mapping: Artists as cartographers*. The MIT Press.
Rosiek, J., Snyder, J., & Pratt, S. (2019). The new materialisms and Indigenous theories of non-human agency: The promise and necessity of respectful anti-colonial engagement. *Qualitative Inquiry, 26*(3/4), 331–346.
Rousell, D. (2019). Inhuman forms of life: On art as a problem for post-qualitative research. *International Journal of Qualitative Studies in Education, 32*(7), 887–908.
Sibiya, A. T., & Ndaba, M. (2023). Moving from discourse to praxis: Situating academics at the centre of decolonisation struggle. *South African Journal of Higher Education, 37*(3), 214–228.
Somerville, C., Somerville, K., & Wyld, F. (2010). Martu storytellers: Aboriginal narratives within the academy. *The Australian Journal of Indigenous Education, 39*(S1), 96–102.
Sousa, L. P. D. Q., & Pessoa, R. R. (2019). Humans, nonhuman others, matter and language: A discussion from post humanist and decolonial perspectives. *Trabalhos em Linguística Aplicada, 58*(2), 520–543.
Spinoza, B. (1992). *Ethics: Treatise on the emendation of the intellect and selected letters* (S. Shirley, Trans.). Hacket.
Springgay, S., & Truman, S. E. (2017). A transmaterial approach to walking methodologies: Embodiment, affect, and a sonic art performance. *Body & Society, 23*(4), 27–58.
Springgay, S., & Zaliwska, Z. (2015). Diagrams and cuts: A materialist approach to research-creation. *Cultural Studies, Critical Methodologies, 15*(2), 136–144.
Stellenbosch University. (2021). *Visual redress policy*. https://www.sun.ac.za/english/transformation/Documents/Visual_Redress_Policy_2021.pdf
St. Pierre, E. A. (2015). Practices for the "new" in the new empiricisms, the new materialisms, and post qualitative inquiry. In N. K. Denzin & M. D. Giardina (Eds.), *Qualitative inquiry and the politics of research* (pp. 75–95). Left Coast Press.
Tuck, E., & Yang, K. W. (2012). Decolonization is not a metaphor. *Decolonization: Indigeneity, Education & Society, 1*(1), 9–28.
Wa Thiong'o, N. (1986). *Decolonizing the mind: The politics of language in African literature*. James Currey.

Watts, V. (2013). Indigenous place-thought and agency amongst humans and nonhumans (First Woman and Sky Woman go on a European world tour!). *Decolonization: Indigeneity, Education & Society, 2*(1), 20–34.

Zavala, M. (2016). Decolonial methodologies in education. In M. A. Peters (Ed.), *Encyclopaedia of education theory* (pp. 1–6). Springer Science+Business.

· 10 ·

SOME CONCLUDING THOUGHTS: POSSIBILITIES FOR IMAGINING NEW DECOLONIAL EDUCATIONAL FUTURITIES

George Jerry Sefa Dei, Wambui Karanja, Ephraim Avea Nsoh, and Daniel Yelkpieri

This Anthology has offered de/anti-colonial perspectives and insights on possibilities for envisioning subversive forms of education that reject colonial education and narratives of knowledge production into what counts as legitimate knowledge and education. In this anthology, colonial education is defined as an institutional framework through which colonial policies of teaching and learning colonially accumulated knowledge, creativity, techniques of colonial thinking, problem-solving skills to advance colonial exploitation, colonial cultural values, accepted mode of colonized behavior, habits, colonial linguistic skills and communication skills (Amin, 1989). Colonial education defines and applies colonial philosophies, knowledges and ways of reasoning to entrench colonial knowledge system and ways of life (Dompere, 2018a) and negates Indigenous knowledge systems, epistemologies, spiritualities and pedagogies (Fanon, 1967). The goal of colonial education is ultimately, to exert mental power and control over the colonized (Sicherman, 2014; Wa Thiong'o, 1986), consistent with colonial needs for hegemony, domination and subservience of the colonized.

Upon reading this anthology, we invite the reader to consider the potentialities of African Indigeneity as a salient entry point counter colonial education and its epistemic violence and to produce counter-hegemonic ways of knowing (Wilson, 2008) and as a bedrock for centering Indigenous African knowledges and perspectives in the decolonization of education, curriculum and pedagogy. The anthology further offers insights into new educational futurities and acknowledges the many sites of knowledge and knowledge production including embodied spiritual, sensory and relational knowledges as sites of knowing and knowledge production and how these embodied knowledges and ontologies can be engaged in foregrounding decolonial and anticolonial educational futurities that draw from local contexts to decolonize the body, mind and spirit interface as critical pathways toward the decolonization of education (Dei, 2012).

The anthology invites the reader to think how embodied knowledge production and education are enacted and manifested in the daily lives of people and how endogenous science in Africa, for example, can be applied to advance the decolonial project for multi-centric knowledge systems and ways of knowing that challenge global modernity and coloniality theories of education, knowledge production and ways of knowing (Dei, 1996; Dei & Asgharzadeh, 2001). The call to acknowledge the richness of Indigenous knowledges and the learner as a knowing body and co-knowledge producer challenges is a decolonial stand and therefore, oppositional to prevailing dominant Eurocentric paradigms of knowledge production and meaning making. It requires a critical examination of how colonial education and its pervasive theories of what constitutes knowledge has systemically served to silence and negate African Indigenous knowledges, voices, agency and spiritual ontologies. Decolonization of African education therefore requires a deep foregrounding and centering of African Indigenous knowledges, ways of knowing, pedagogies, spiritual ontologies and the agency of Indigenous knowledge holders, learners and their communities (Dei et al., 2022).

Decolonial education critically interrogates and rejects the coloniality and hegemony embedded in the use of English Language in schools and calls for the reclamation and re-centering of local African Indigenous languages and cultures in educational curricula and pedagogical practices to foster a decolonized African-centered education that engages Indigenous philosophies, spiritual ontologies and embodied knowledges, skills and values of learners and their communities to foreground the needs and aspirations of the people, to enable them to realize their true and full potential, agency, identity and sense of community. As a multifaceted and subversive endeavor, rethinking new educational futurities counters enables the disentanglement of education and learning from its colonial heritage and structures by foregrounding Indigenous Land-based epistemologies, spiritualities, ways of knowing and being.

As spelled out in this collection, an Indigenized education involves embodied connections with Spirit and acknowledges African Spirituality as a way of knowing and being to offer critical and meaningful educational possibilities for Indigenous learners despite their diasporic locations. More critically, a Indigenized decolonial education considers and privileges the local realities, needs and aspirations of learners in all areas of educational administration and delivery and acknowledges the sacredness of Land as the source of knowledge, Land-based epistemologies and relationships with the Land as inseparable from knowledge, where Land as manifestation of Spirit (Wane, 2019) and relationships with the Land evoke Spiritual, psychic, and emotional connections and attachments to the Land beyond colonial conceptions of Land (Karanja, 1991, 2018). This is a critical message conveyed by the various articles in this anthology.

Indigenous epistemology sees learning and education as lifelong processes that take place in every aspect of life and in multiple sites including family, home, community, nature and society through everyday living and social activities (Semali, 1999). Elders and family members are engaged in imparting knowledge of personal, social and community responsibility to the young with learning taking place in every aspect of living on the Land and in the community with teaching taking place through ancestral epistemologies of proverbs, sayings, songs, dreams, divinations, stories and other forms of cultural expression inherited from the ancestors. In Indigenous epistemology, the learner is embodied and imbued with psychic knowledge, agency and an Indigenous identity and is not an empty to be filled with schooled knowledge (Freire, 1970; see also Pratt & Danyluk 2017). The contributors therefore, reject and challenge current education systems that use narrow conceptualizations of what counts as education, science and intellectuality, and call for liberatory Indigenized alternatives to learning that are more relevant to learners and their lived experiences and that offer opportunities for the mental/physical and spiritual health, safety and well-being of learners as knowing subjects.

Calling for anti-colonial education, the contributors reject colonizing educational universalist practices, policies, sites of education and discourses based on the deficit model of conceptualizations of African learners and their selves as underdeveloped and unknowing (Fanon, 1952, Freire, 1968) that are in essence, alien to Indigenous African ways of knowing, knowledge production, meaning making and being. Decolonial education requires the rejection of colonial education's erasures of Indigenous identities, histories, relationships with and conceptions of and presence on Indigenous Lands. Indigenist and anti-colonial theorists have argued that one of the goals of colonial education was to inculcate feelings of inferiority, deculturalization and negation of the sense of self, agency and feelings of self-worth with a depreciation of the African imagination among Indigenous learners (Enaifoghe, 2019; wa Thion'go, 1986) the effect of which was the cultural estrangement and alienation of the learner (Sanderson, 2019). Decolonial education then is about disentangling education from European/Euro-American dominance and cultural imperialism (Abdi, 2012; Dei, 1998; Shizha, 2007) to re-inscribe Indigenous epistemologies into education and learning. This endeavor is not about creating binaries in knowledge hierarchies but is rather, it is about acknowledging the existence of multiple ways of knowing, knowledge production, learning and pedagogies that acknowledges multiple sites of and ways of knowledge production and sees Indigenous knowledges as valid knowledge systems with their own philosophical, ontological, spiritual and epistemological underpinning.

Decolonial education is about acknowledging the Indigenous as a site of embodied and inherent power (Dei & Asgharzadeh, 2001) and speaks power to Indigenous ways of knowing and knowledge production. Dei (2016) argues that the Indigene is imbued with power to resist colonial structures of education and its coloniality to resurge Indigenous epistemologies and Indigenous worldviews and to imagine possibilities for new educational futures and pedagogical possibilities and frameworks rooted in Indigenous knowledges (Alfred,1999; Dei, 2019). Harnessing and unleashing this power requires us to ask questions as to the kind of educational futures we seek (Nyamnjoh, 2012), resists, disrupt and subverts the power, domination and privilege of colonial education and knowledge systems, ways of thinking and education and entrenches decolonial Indigenous knowledges, education and ways of being to enable learners to reconnect with their Land, cultures, histories, identities, and communities in relational ways that amplify and foreground Indigenous epistemes, identities, cultures and viewpoints and values of respect, humility, reciprocity, sharing, and mutual interdependence (Semali & Kincheloe, 2002). Critically, decolonial education affirms Indigenous identities, cultures and histories and challenges the inferiorization of African ways knowing and epistemes (Ndlovu-Gathsheni, 2015).

Decolonizing education challenges the epistemic privilege and universality accorded to the English language and colonialism's failure to acknowledge the interconnected of language, identity and culture as intertwined. Denying the language of an Indigene is a denial of one's culture and identity and a form of cultural and epistemic violence on learners. Omolewa (2007) and Wa Thiong'o (1986) remind us that language and orality are the mediums through which culture is transmitted and experienced and cultural activities such as dance and music are central to African ways of life, equipping the learner with skills to work effectively in learning, including language learning, speech, literacy and numeracy, etc., and furthermore, it is central to identity and how people see themselves.

Oral tradition, for example, is the wealth of knowledge from which Africans learn about their origins, history, culture and religion, and the meaning and reality of life, morality, norms and survival techniques (see also, Ngara, 2007) and is enacted through idioms, legends, folklore, stories, proverbs and myths which are rich sources of African orality, wisdom and philosophy (Abdi, 2009; Adeyemi, M. B., & Adeyinka, A. A. (2003); Dei et al., 2022). According to Wa Thiong'o (1986), learning though colonial languages lead to the distortion of one's identity and history and the loss and diminution of sense of self. Indigenous languages are the vehicles for preserving, transmitting, and implementing Indigenous knowledges in schools and therefore, emphasizing the teaching of local languages and cultures, is critical to building and developing a strong identity and appreciation for culture among learners and enhancing cultural re-engagement, enfranchisement and values in learners (Asante, 1990). Recognition of and integration of Indigenous languages in education is a decolonizing endeavor that challenges the superiorization and privileging of English and elevates Indigenous knowledges, cultures and ways of being, and further, enables students to see themselves as knowledge holders and as powerful agents and actors in the co-creation of knowledge and dissemination. Decolonization of education also requires that we wrestle with the uncomfortable question of our own complicities and implications. How do we decolonize while still steeped in the colonial structures we resist and seek to subvert? Engaging these questions will call for deep conscious and critical thinking into what kind of education we envision for the future.

Wresting with Uncomfortable Question of our own Implication and Complicity in Education

Scholars have argued that decolonization of education requires that we become aware of our own complicities in maintaining contemporary colonial narratives and practices of education (Dei, 2000, 2002, 2019; Dei & McDermott, 2014; Dei et al., 2000). Similarly, Mazrui (1978) has noted that very few educated Africans are even aware of their own implication in advancing colonial education and its attendant cultural bondage and are still prisoners of Western culture, and further, that the curriculum remains a powerful tool of colonialism and imperialism that has led to a colonial mindset and the entrapment of African minds and ways of thinking (Sicherman (1995), Wa Thiong'o 1986). The question is, how do we bring and inculcate authenticity in decolonizing our scholarship and education systems? How do we decolonize our own minds (Wa Thiong'o, 1986) and those of our learners? Yankah calls for us to pioneer new analytical systems for understanding our own communities "steeped in our home-grown cultural perspectives" (Yankah, 2004, p. 25).

Dei (2016) calls upon us to critically embrace sustainable global partnerships in African education from the shared orientations of Indigenous African philosophy, cosmology, aesthetics, axiology and epistemology. Speaking to the subversion of the African University, he opines that we do not have "African Universities" but rather, that we have Universities in Africa which are colonial satellites of the western academy. He argues that African scholars and learners fail to assert our authentic, true selves, souls, voices and their African humanhood and continually seek validation, legitimation and acceptance from the west. Consequently, they suffer spiritual, emotional, and psychological wounding and become intellectual impostors (Nyamnjoh, 2012).

This anthology is an attempt to write back to the imperial narrative (Dei, 1998) and the colonial educational project to advance new speculative educational imaginaries with a call to offer and envision alternative systems of education and learning grounded in our Indigenous knowledge systems and epistemes, spiritualities and cultural perspectives. It requires asking critical, often uncomfortable questions: how do we challenge colonial narratives of education and knowledge production when we are deeply implicated as theorists and scholars schooled in western education? How do we educate and call upon learners to choose decolonial pathways to education when they are still subjected to, steeped in and caught up in neo-liberal neocolonial globalized and internationalized capitalist education systems that offers material gains; in short, how do we wrestle from the seduction of western education with all its material affordances? In answering these critical questions, we must not look for answers within the same oppressive structures that are the root causes of the issues in education we seek to decolonize. Harney and Moten (2013) invite us to explore the potentialities of fleeing from without leaving; the practice of fleeing from carceral logics without leaving the possibilities of creating critical spaces for decolonization.

Challenging our complicity in education requires among others, that we invoke our Indigeneity as a pathway to resist colonial ways of thinking and educational structures by asserting Indigenous African epistemologies in education to challenge, replace and reimagine alternatives to colonial thinking and practice (Odora Hoppers, 2001). It requires us to engage with the politics of refusal to engage in colonial logics of educational epistemicide and the amputation of our Indigenous ways of knowing, being and learning, a refusal to engage in the extermination of our spiritual ontologies and cultural heritage and a refusal to engage in a system of education that defines and contains us within its own paradigm of destruction and distraction of our ways of knowing and being. Educational futures require the intentional consciousness to engage with and think through the politics of refusal as a decolonial politics that allows us to challenge education curricula, pedagogy and spaces that deny the validity and humanity of Indigenous knowledges and bodies. Such politics reclaim Indigenous curricula, pedagogies, schools and schooling and imbue them with the potential to become cultural spaces and sites for the reclamation and revitalization of African knowledges and identities (Mazrui & Mazrui, 1993).

The politics of refusal compel us to a quest for mental decolonization and a deep desire to refuse to engage in colonial logics of educational epistemicide and the amputation of our Selves and our Indigenous ways of knowing, being and learning. It is a refusal to engage in the extermination of our epistemes, spiritual ontologies and cultural heritage and a refusal to engage in a system of education that defines and contains us within its own paradigm of destruction and distraction, insisting on our mental extinction, spiritual dismemberment and fragmented humanity (Anzaldúa, 1987; Dei, 2012). It calls for a futurity that enables us to work toward seeing, freeing and emancipating our bodies, psyches and pedagogical practices from the colonial systems we seek to subvert.

Ultimately, a de/anticolonized educational system must interrogate, subvert and abolish colonial education and its conventional school systems including the sites of education, policies, curriculum and pedagogical practices in all areas of education theory, administration and delivery that continue to colonize African Indigenous knowledge systems and pedagogies. It is about drawing from Indigenous philosophies, knowledges, epistemes, spiritual ontologies and ways of being that pre-date the colonial encounter. To this extent, for decolonization of education to be achieved, Indigenization offers a critical and perhaps the only starting point for such an endeavor; not as a superimposition of one knowledge system of education over another as in colonial hierarchies and binaries, but rather, as a rejection if colonial hegemony and the privileging of some knowledge systems over others, to acknowledge and create equal space for the existence of multiple knowledge systems and ways of knowing in education. Dei and Adhami (2021) remind us that decolonizing education is about creating and thinking through possibilities of multicentricity of epistemes that acknowledge the validity of different knowledge systems and knowledge production, multiple ways of knowing and being. Embedded in these knowledge systems are epistemological, ontological and pedagogical logics, values and implications that characterize, define and undergird each knowledge system (Dei et al., 2022).

Re-inscribing Pedagogies of the Land in Education

The quest for a decolonial education would not be complete without re-inscribing Indigenous African spirituality into the curriculum. African Indigenous education is about teachings rooted in African spirituality and connections to the Land as source of knowledge and as manifestation of Spirit. It is about teachings from the Land, beyond the narrow western conceptualizations of Land as space, to conceptualize Land as a living thing that is not only the source of Life, but also as incorporating the universe, all living and non-living things and as intertwined with Spirit (Craft, 2013; Dei, 2008; Howes, 1996; Karanja, 2018). Indigenous epistemology recognizes the self, Land and the natural world as interconnected and inseparable from each other (Craft, 2013) in an epistemological link that sees Land as the Source of Indigenous knowledge, understanding and knowledge production (Dei, 2008; Howes, 1996; Simpson 2014; Wildcat et al., 2014; Zinga & Styres, 2011). It is a relationship of inseparability and guardianship of the Land (Robbins, 2011) and the pedagogy of Land includes not just its materiality but also its spiritual, emotional, and intellectual aspects (Cajete, 2008) as pedagogy and as first teacher of truths that have been proven over time (Styres et al., 2013).

For Indigenous scholars, the epistemic implications of Land as both source, pedagogy and teacher emanate from and arise from the ontological rootedness in the Land and Land relationships (Simpson, 2014). Land then becomes not just the source of knowledge but is also, teacher, pedagogy and the source of the community's collective and personal knowledge (Zinga & Styres, 2011). Land and education are constitutive of each other and colonial dispossession of Indigenous people of their Lands and the disruption of this intricate relational interconnectedness with the Land resulted in deculturation, alienation and separation of Indigenous people from the sources of their knowledge systems, ways of knowing, Land-based pedagogies and being (Wildcat et.al., 2014) as a form oof epistemic genocide Grosfoguel (2015). It is critical then, that decolonizing education must have at its objective, the concerted effort to re-engage people with the social relations, knowledges and languages that arise from the Land (Simpson, 2014; Wildcat et.al 2014) through pathways that center Indigenous epistemological, ontological, language and indigenous understandings of Land (Tuck et al., 2014). Inscribing Land-based pedagogy in education calls for learning through interaction with the Land and with the learner's embodied epistemes, lived experience culture, language, and spirituality, to center the learner as a knowing subject imbued with the capacity for knowledge production and co-creation of a valid body of knowledge. Engaging learners with Land-based pedagogies extends the boundaries of the sites of knowledge beyond the classroom to learning in and from the Land at home, in the community (Semali, 1999). More critically, it imbues the learner with confidence, empowerment and agency as a knowledge producer and co-creator and not just as a depository of knowledge (Freire, 1970).

Re-inscribing pedagogies of the Land in education must wrestle with the risk of conflating Land/place-based education with community education. Styres (2018) argues that literacies of the Land are decolonizing frameworks that center the criticality of understanding and acknowledging Land and place as sites imbued with cultural meanings, histories, text, stories, oral traditions and literacies that are living and emergent (p. 14), and the importance therefore, of understanding, acknowledging and engaging with the politics of place in literacy education. Contrary, space as in community space/education must be emplaced with these cultural meanings, histories and languages to become sites of meaningful decolonizing Indigenous education. Literacies of the Land then are therefore complex and involve deep historical and ancestral Land relationships that speak to how the Land speaks and communicates to and with Indigenous people, historical long-term Land/self experiences with and on the Land.

Land-based education interrogates the politics of the intersectionality of place, colonialism and settler colonialism. Unlike community education which takes place in socially constructed spaces devoid of politics and devoid of an analysis of the intersectionality of Land and colonialism (Lefebvre, 1991) places are permeated with politics and Land-based education must therefore, center Indigenous realities and place Indigenous people at the center of learning (Calderon, 2014). Centering Indigenous pedagogies of the Land in education must also place Elders at the center of learning. In Indigenous epistemology, community Elders are endowed with wisdom and knowledge and are generally looked upon with respect and reverence not only as guardians of culture and tradition but also as teachers of traditional social and community values and teachings that help socialize and guide youth into responsible citizenship (Dei et al., 2022; Dei & McDermott, 2014). This knowledge comes from Elders' long-term occupancy of the place/Land, and by their experience of the daily intricate interactions or nexus of society, culture, and Nature (Abdi, 2020; Dei, 2012).

As custodians and teachers of Indigenous knowledges, Indigenous Elders' cultural knowledges are critical frameworks for disrupting colonial narratives of education and are best placed to re-engage learners with Land-based education through Indigenous Land-based pedagogies (Alfred, 2009). As well, they allow for the reclamation and recovery of Indigenous ways of knowing, thinking, and problem-solving and speak to Indigenous histories, cultures, identities, spiritual ontologies to center the politics of the Indigenous identity and culture (Cajete, 1994; Dei & Jajj, 2018; Smith, 2012; Wane et al., 2013). As custodians of Indigenous knowledges, Elders play a key role as facilitators of lifelong learning through knowledge transfer and encourage learners to resurge and utilize their embodied knowledges as sites of knowing (Boateng, 1990).

As holistic knowledges, Elders' cultural knowledges serve to foreground individual consciousness as well as the emotional, spiritual, intellectual, and physical well-being of the learner in a spirit of interconnectedness and mutuality of all living and non-living things, to center and locate Indigenous bodies within their own cultural specificities (Faris, 2012). The integration of Elders and their cultural knowledges in schooling is, therefore, not only subversive of colonial narratives of education but also is also implicated in encouraging new educational futurities that promote ideals of multicentricity of knowledge systems, self and the community relationships (Battiste & Henderson 2009). The overarching goal of incorporating Elders' cultural knowledges in schools enables the teaching of social, personal responsibility and community building and is subversive of colonial theories of knowledge production and their attendant hierarchies, binaries and legacies (Dabashi, 2013). Ultimately incorporating Elders' cultural knowledges in education challenges the epistemic privilege of colonial education, colonial epistemicide imperialism, marginalization of Indigenous bodies and epistemes, the dehumanization and disenfranchisement of Indigenous learners and the Eurocentric worldview and dislocate these colonial logics from their dominant self ascribed positions in all areas if education delivery and pedagogy to center multicentricity and multi-logicality in learning (Dei, 1996, 2012).

As mentioned in the introduction to this anthology, Spirituality is a critical element of Indigenous education, and the decolonization of education cannot be complete without the integration and infusion of spirituality in education as a valid knowledge system., pedagogy and way of knowing and being. In decolonizing education, Spirituality forms the basis from which dominant forms of knowing and education that decenter the learner's spiritual selves are challenged and resisted and to this extent, asserting one's spirituality and incorporating spiritual values, beliefs and practices in education becomes a political act that is crucial to asserting one's individual sense of purpose, meaning and being, enabling the learner to experience wholeness and connection with the self and the universe. Re-envisioning and decolonizing African education must therefore place spirituality and spiritual ontologies as foundational to any decolonization efforts to counter colonial narratives of education and imperial worldviews Smith (2012). The integration of these spiritual ontologies is counter-hegemonic and resistive of cultural decolonization. It challenges Eurocentrism (Mazama, 1998) and enables the healing of colonial spiritual wounds and spirit injury to allow for the wholeness of Indigenous bodies, beings and ways of life that have been fragmented and dismembered by western hegemony and colonial education.

The key question to ask then is, how do we engage spirituality as a healing pedagogy to dream and imagine new educational futures that reclaim and re-center Indigenous epistemes, pedagogies and spiritual ontologies in education? How do we center spirituality in education to subvert and transform our education systems premised on new epistemological, ontological and spiritual educational imaginaries? These are critical questions that call for inflection as we seek to decolonize and reclaim education from its colonial and neocolonial stranglehold.

Dreaming new Educational Imaginaries and Futures

Many scholars have maintained that before colonization, Africans had their own forms of Indigenous education and learning system that were informed by African philosophies and knowledge systems and that shaped the development of people and their social and cultural responsibilities to each other and to the community (Abdi, 2011). These knowledge systems acquired and practiced through long-term occupancy of the Land and collective and community-oriented processes (Dei, 2000; Owusu-Ansah & Mji, 2013) were experiential and rooted in a relational worldview and culture that emphasized wholeness, community harmony, interdependence, interconnectedness and the role of Elders as holders, teachers and guardians of community knowledge (Dei et al., 2022; Mkabela, 2005; Shizha, 2008).

Colonialism and colonial education's disruption of these knowledge systems and Indigenous pedagogies has called for the decolonization of education by dreaming and imagining new educational futures that center and re-inscribe Indigenous knowledges and spiritual ontologies in education.

Colonialism and its legacies continue to inform all forms of education and continues to cause epistemic damage to the learner's psyche and being (Adzahlie-Mensah & Dunne, 2018) as learners continue to be schooled in education systems that are firmly anchored in Eurocentric theories, ideologies and practices that continue to dismiss and demean the richness of African knowledges, bodies, psyches and spiritualities. It is imperative then that we dream new educational futurities as a pathway to the decolonization of education and that these imaginaries are informed by and re-center Indigenous epistemes and spiritualities. This requires us to critically and deeply reflect on and dream possibilities for new subversive decolonized education systems premised on Indigenous philosophical knowledges and spiritualities that center the Land and relationships with the Land.

Decolonized educational futurities serve the physical, spiritual and emotional needs of the learner and the community in a process that engages the humility of knowing (Dei, 2012) and the possibilities of decolonization in the context of a tangible unknown (Sium et.al., 2012), where despite centering Indigenous philosophies, people and Land, the future remains a "tangible unknown," a space where power, place, identity and sovereignty are constantly being contested, re/negotiated with Indigeneity being the springboard and standpoint for enacting decolonization as a challenge to colonial power and colonial ways of thinking. Dreaming new educational futures requires our conscious awareness of our own complicity in maintaining contemporary colonial narratives and philosophies of education by decolonizing our minds (wa Thiong'o, 1986) to enable our crucial and urgent engagement with subversive pedagogies of resistance, reclamation and resurgence of our Indigenous identities, epistemes and spiritual ways of coming to know. It means disentangling our thinking from colonial ways of thinking and doing, to engage African Indigeneity and Indigenous knowledges and philosophies in education (Dei, 2000). Decolonization of the mind requires a conscious and intentional determination to move from theorizing and imagining new educational futurities to positive action.

Dei and Asgharzadeh (2001) have argued that for social theory to be of value, it must have a social and political corrective, an intentional practice to wrestle with and resist dominant ideologies, practices and mind-sets that benefit from the status quo; to imagine new imaginative and speculative imaginaries of education that place Land at the center of learning and allow students to engage with and explore their own histories, cultures and relevant ways of knowing (Battiste, 2013; Dei & McDermott, 2014). Indigenous epistemologies are grounded in a deep appreciation of the relational attributes of Land, the Self, the Spiritual, and the known and unknown worlds as interconnected and grounded in a people, a place and a history, where Land is imbued with both material and spiritual realms and the Self is integral to nature and the other (Dei, 2000, p. 115). In this sense, educational futures must foreground and acknowledge the criticality of Land as source of Indigenous knowledge and epistemology as co-created and place the cultural teachings of Elders as teachers and knowledge keepers at the center of learning (Dei, 2000). Dreaming new educational imaginaries challenges and interrogates critics of Indigenous knowledges who argue that Indigenous knowledges are simplistic, unscientific, lack rationality and cannot be subjected to proof testing. Such theories, however, fail to acknowledge that Indigenous knowledges are valid knowledge systems in their own right whose validity cannot be contained within or measured through Eurocentric frameworks (Emeagwali 2020).

Decolonized educational futurities embed Indigenous African values of responsibility, respect, excellence, caring, compassion, understanding, tolerance, honesty, trustworthiness, spirituality and ethical behavior (Mugumbate

& Chereni, 2019) in education. These values flow from ontological Indigenous African ways of knowing, philosophies, pedagogies, spiritualities and relationships with the Land and are passed on to the younger generation through pedagogies of storytelling, music, healing practices, song, dance, etc. (Zavala, 2016). The call then, is for engendering epistemological equity through the reclamation and legitimation of Indigenous identities, knowledges and the politics of embodiment, and the legitimation of the process and practice of "knowing" as a legitimate process for knowledge production that contests and challenges and contests the dominance of colonial theories of knowledge production (Dei, 1996).

Dei further argues that the broader politics of educational futurity must engage critical questions and ideas informed by the teaching of African Indigeneity and Indigenous knowledges in schools and, involves repositioning African people as holders and custodians of territorial and cultural rights and not subjects of Euro-colonial knowledges (Dei, 2020). As well, for decolonial African futurities in education to be sustained, the process must be conceptualized and implemented from an early age to allow learners to be reared and educated with strong anchorage in their own cultural, linguistic and ancestral value systems (Boukary, 2018). Critically, educational futurities must reposition African people as holders and custodians of their own territorial and cultural knowledges and rights and not subjects of Euro-colonial theories of knowledge production and Land relationships.

Educational futures must challenge the colonial matrix of power (Mignolo, 1995) and must engage in imaginaries of learning and education outside of colonial and Eurocentric ideologies, institutions and arrangements and must also engender hope in the struggles against colonialism and its logics. Educational imaginaries enable a decolonized and transformative education that rejects the entrapment of colonial education (Rodney, 1972). These pathways insist on challenging, rejecting and resisting colonial theories of dehumanization of the African (Abdi, 2011) and contests colonial legacies and logics. Todd (2019) maintains that decolonial futures will require engaging spirituality and spiritual visions of futures that call attention to the inherent power and spiritual capability of Indigenous people to offer possibilities and glimpses of worlds where species work harmoniously with Spirit, the Lifeforce, to offer counter-visions to colonial hegemony.

Colonialism's disruption, dismemberment and fragmentation of Indigenous conceptions of and relationships with the Land, Indigenous cultures, pedagogies and knowledge production (Karanja, 2018; Dei et al.,

2022) calls for the imagination of new educational futurities that underscore and center the epistemic, pedagogical and spiritual saliency and attributes of Land and relationships with the Land. It must involve engaging pathways that reclaim and engender Indigenous relationships with the Land, culture and spiritual ontologies in education to reconnect people with their Indigenous selves, knowledges and cultural roots (Abdi, 2020; Wane, 2003).

Magesa (1998) warns us against committing what he terms as communal suicide by failing to acknowledge that no society chooses to build its future on foreign cultures, values and systems and that every society is obliged to search deep into its own history, culture, religion and morality in order to discover the values upon which its development and liberation, its civilization and identity should be based (p. 9). He warns that failing to do so is an act of self-inflicted communal suicide against us. Decolonizing education and dreaming new educational imaginaries and futures is one of the critical pathways to resisting colonial structures and refusing to engage in communal epistemic suicide emanating from colonial education. It is about reclaiming Indigenous knowledges, cultural identities and cultures, language, healing and spiritual ontologies (Zavala, 2016) and placing them at the center of learning through the prism of an Indigenous African philosophical thought and African-centered epistemological and pedagogical frameworks that foreground African spiritual ontologies, identities and the Land as sites of knowing and Knowledge production (Dei et al., 2022). It is as much about incorporating experiential learning and relationships with and on the Land as site of Indigenous knowledges and pedagogies in education as it is about rejecting this incorporation as an integrationist "add-on" that has no transformative value (Yakubu, 2000), but rather, it is about valuing and utilizing the wealth of knowledge embedded in African cultures and traditions, in all areas of education and learning Mbiti, J. (1990).

Ndlovu-Gatsheni (2015) maintains that decolonial approaches should move from a mere reversal of institutions of colonialism to challenging the history and configuration of the modern world which places coloniality at the center. It is therefore a process, a mindset coupled with social action of which the decolonization of education is just one integral part. The impact of colonial education in the undermining the histories, identities, cultures, Land relationships and spirituality reach beyond colonial education to include the totality of human relationships and endeavors and call for wrestling with and resisting coloniality; the long-standing patterns of power that emerged as a result of colonialism that define culture, labor, intersubjectivity relations, and knowledge production well beyond the strict limits of colonial administrations (Maldonado-Torres, 2007. p. 243). Consequently, new educational imaginaries must refuse to confine themselves to the education delivery alone, to ask further pertinent questions such as, How do we make education more relevant and meaningful to the learner and to society? What social and community goals do we want education to achieve? What is the role of education in society? Decolonizing education is not about academic success; rather, it is about questioning colonial and unequal power relations and coloniality that continues to permeate and to inform contemporary societies" (Ndlovu-Gatsheni, 2013).

Due to the pervasiveness and complexity of colonialism and coloniality, new educational futures must be obliged to engage deep critical thinking and practical and social possibilities for deconstructing colonial thinking and detaching African epistemologies and educational practices from colonial dependency and structures (Abdi 2012; Dei, 2000; Dei et al., 2022; Ndlovu-Gatsheni (2015); wa Thiong'o, 1986). New educational imaginaries must also think through and engage pathways for the reclamation and resurgence of the recreative power of our embodied epistemologies (Macedonia, 2019) and a reclamation and centering of Land-based epistemologies and spiritual knowledges (Purcell,1998; Karanja, 2018; Dei et al., 2022) in and beyond education.

In conclusion, this anthology has offered anti/decolonial options, possibilities and opportunities for transforming education in Africa. These possibilities are offered in the context of the ongoing resurgence of Indigenous knowledges and the call by Indigenist scholars for the decolonization of education in local and diasporic settings. While not exhaustive, the anthology provides possible practical and philosophical options that can be engaged in the journey toward decolonization of education and offers possibilities from different sites of education in Africa. The overarching consensus among the contributors is the acknowledgment of the negative consequences of colonialism and its logics in negating, dehumanizing and demonizing Indigenous bodies, knowledges, psyches, cultures, languages and spiritualities but more importantly, the acknowledgment of the power of the colonized to think through and offer subversive decolonial and anti-colonial perspectives and alternatives for reclaiming Indigenous education from its colonial legacies and heritage and to dare to imagine new resistive decolonial educational futures grounded in Indigenous philosophical thought.

These subversive approaches resist and challenge colonial power in education and beyond, reclaim Indigenous knowledges and pedagogies and more critically, position the Land, the learner and Indigenous epistemologies at the center of learning. Dei and Emeagwali (2014) maintain that the revival and reclamation of Indigenous knowledges is not a return to a mythic past but a pragmatic and political realization that such knowledges had their relevance and utility within local cultural ecologies and cosmologies (see also Shizha 2014, (Wane, 2013)) and further, that a push toward the revitalization of African Indigenous knowledges is to reclaim and re-center these knowledges as valid epistemes and to challenge and resist the prevailing coloniality and neo-liberal theories and policies in education (Dei, 2012). In this revitalization and dreaming of new educational futures, the disruptive African intellectual power is rebirthed, reclaimed and re-asserted. It is also hoped that this anthology will encourage further research and scholarship on decolonization of African education and educational imaginaries as the work of decolonizing education continues.

References

Abdi, A. (2009). Recentering the philosophical foundations of knowledge: The case of Africa with a special focus on the global role of teachers. *The Alberta Journal of Educational Research, 55*(3), 269–283.

Abdi, A. (2011). Chapter five: African philosophies of education: Deconstructing the colonial and reconstructing the indigenous. *Counterpoints, 379*, 80–91.

Abdi, A. A. (2012). Decolonizing philosophies of education: An introduction In *Decolonizing philosophies of education* (pp. 1–13). Brill.

Abdi, A. A. (2020). Decolonizing knowledge, education and social development: Africanist perspectives. *Beijing International Review of Education, 2*(4), 503–518.

Alfred, T. (1999). Peace. *Power, Righteousness*: An Indigenous Manifesto Anzaldúa, G. (1987). In *How to tame a wild tongue* (pp. 2947–2955).

Alfred, T. (2009). *Wasase: Indigenous pathways of action*. University of Toronto Press.

Asante, M. K. (1990). Afrocentricity and the critique of drama. *The Western Journal of Black Studies, 14*(2), 136.

Amin, S. (1989). *Eurocentrism*. NYU Press.

Boateng, F. (1990). African traditional education: A tool for inter- generational communication. In M. K. Asante & K. W. Asante (Eds.), *African culture: The rhythms of unity* (pp. 109–122). African World Press.

Battiste, M. A. (2009). *Reclaiming indigenous voice and vision*. Vancouver, UBC Press.

Battiste, M. (2013). *Decolonizing education: Nourishing the learning spirit*. Purich Publishing.

Boukary, H. (2018). Putting the cart before the horse? Early childhood care and education (ECCE) the quest for Ubuntu educational foundation in Africa. In E. J. Takyi-Amoako & N. T. Assié-Lumumba (Eds.), *Re-visioning education in Africa: Ubuntu-inspired education for humanity* (pp. 135–145). Palgrave Macmillan.

Craft, A. (2013). *Breathing lift into the Stone Fort Treaty: An Anishnabe understanding of Treaty One*. Purich Publishing Company UBC Press.

Calderon, D. (2014). Speaking back to Manifest Destinies: A land education-based approach to critical curriculum inquiry. *Environmental Education Research, 20*(1), 24–36. https://doi.org/10.1080/13504622.2013.865114

Cajete, G. (1994). *Seven orientations for the development of indigenous science education*. Sage Publications.

Cajete, G. (2008). Seven orientations for the development of indigenous science education. In *Handbook of Critical and Indigenous Methodologies* (pp. 487–496). SAGE Publications, Inc., https://doi.org/10.4135/9781483385686

Dabashi, H. (2013). But there is neither east nor west. In *Being a Muslim in the world* (pp. 7–18). Palgrave Macmillan US.

Dompere, K. K. (2018a). The theory of info-dynamics: An introduction to its conceptual frame. *The theory of info-dynamics: Rational foundations of information–Knowledge dynamics* (pp. 63–90).

Dei, G. (2016). Decolonizing the university: The challenges and possibilities of inclusive Éducation. *Socialist Studies/Études Socialistes, 11*(1), 23–23.

Dei, G. J. (1998). "Why Write Back?": The role of Afrocentric discourse in social change. *Canadian Journal of Education, 23*, 200.

Dei, G. J. (2012). "Suahunu," the Trialectic Space. *Journal of Black Studies, 43*(8), 823–846.

Dei, G. S. (2012). Indigenous anti-colonial knowledge as "heritage knowledge for promoting Black/African education in diasporic contexts." *Decolonization: Indigeneity, Education & Society, 1*(1).

Dei, G. J. S. (1998). Education for development: relevance and implications for the African content. *Canadian Journal of Développent Studies/Revue canadienne D'études du développement, 19*(3), 509–527.

Dei, G. J. S. (2000). Rethinking the role of indigenous knowledges in the academy. *International Journal of Inclusive Education, 4*(2), 111–132.

Dei, G. J. S. (2002). Spiritual knowing and transformative learning. In *Expanding the boundaries of transformative learning: Essays on theory and praxis* (pp. 121–133). Palgrave Macmillan US.

Dei, G. J. S. (2008). *Racists beware: Uncovering racial politics in the post- modern society* (Vol. 21). Brill.

Dei, G. J. S., & McDermott, M. (2014). *Introduction to the politics of anti-racism education: In search of strategies for transformative learning* (pp. 1–11). Springer Netherlands.

Dei (Nana Adusei Sefa Tweneboah), G.J., & Adhami, A. (2021). Coming to Know and Knowing Differently: Implications of Educational Leadership. *Educational Administration Quarterly, 58*, 780–809.

Dei, G. J. S., & Adhami, A. (2022). Educating for critical race and anti-colonial intersections. In *The Palgrave handbook on critical theories of education* (pp. 81–95). Springer International Publishing.

Dei, G. J. S., & Asgharzadeh, A. (2001). The power of social theory: The anti-colonial discursive framework. *The Journal of Educational Thought (JET)/Revue De La Pensée Éducative, 35*, 297–323.

Dei, G. J. S., & Jajj, M. (2018). *Knowledge and decolonial politics: A critical reader* (Vol. 6). Brill.

Dei, G. J. S., Karanja, W., Erger, G., Dei, G. J. S., Karanja, W., & Erger, G. (2022). Responding to the epistemic challenge—A decolonial project. In *Elders' Cultural Knowledges and the Question of Black/African Indigeneity in Education*, pp. 79–111.

Dei, G. J. S., & McDermott, M. (2014). *Introduction to the politics of anti-racism education: In search of strategies for transformative learning* (pp. 1–11). Springer.

Dei, G. J. S., & McDermott, M. (Eds.). (2019). *Centering African proverbs, Indigenous folktales, and cultural stories in curriculum: Units and lesson plans for inclusive education*. Canadian Scholars, an imprint of CSP Books.

Dei, S. (1996). The role of Afrocentricity in the inclusive curriculum in Canadian Schools. *Canadian Journal of Education/Revue canadienne de l'éducation, 21*(2), 170–186.

Dunne, M. (2018). Continuing in the shadows of colonialism: The educational experiences of the African Child in Ghana. *Perspectives in Education, 36*(2), 44–60.

Emeagwali, G. (2020). African indigenous knowledge systems and the legacy of Africa. In Oloruntoba, S., Afolayan, A., & Yacob-Haliso, O. (Eds.), *Indigenous knowledge systems and development in Africa*. Palgrave Macmillan. https://doi.org/10.1007/978-3-030-34304-0_3

Emeagwali, G., & Dei, G. J. S. (2014). *African indigenous knowledge and the disciplines*. Springer.

Enaifoghe, A. O. (2019). Gender based violence and the global gendered viewpoint approaches to building a peaceful South Africa. *Journal of Social and Development Sciences, 10*(2(S)), 15–25.

Fanon, F. (1952). *Black Skin, White Masks*. New York: Grove Press.

Faris, S. B. (2012). *Restoring local spiritual and cultural values in science education: The case of Ethiopia*. University of Toronto.

Freire, P. (1970). *Pedagogy of the oppressed*. Continuum.

Grosfoguel, R. (2015). Epistemic racism/sexism, Westernized universities and the four genocides/epistemicides of the long sixteenth century. In M. Araujo & S. R. Maeso (Eds.), *Eurocentrism, racism and knowledge*. Cham: Springer.

Harney, S., & Moten, F. (2013). Blackness and governance. In *The undercommons: Fugitive planning and Black study* (pp. 44–57). Minor Compositions.

Howes, D. (1996). Cultural appropriation and resistance in the American West: Decommodifying Indianness. In D. Howes (ed), *Cross-cultural consumption: Global markets local realities* (pp. 138–160). Routledge.

Karanja, P. W. (1991). Women's land ownership rights in Kenya. *Third World Legal Studies, 109*.

Karanja, W. (2018). An inconvenient truth: Centering land as the site of indigenous knowledge protection. In *Knowledge and decolonial politics, a critical reader*. Brill.

Lefebvre, H. (1991). *The production of space*. Blackwell.

Macedonia, M. (2019). Embodied learning: Why at school the mind needs the body. *Frontiers in Psychology, 10*, 2098.

Magesa, Laurenti (1998). *African religion: the moral traditions of abundant life*. Nairobi, Kenya: Paulines Publications Africa.

Maldonado-Torres, N. (2007). On the coloniality of being—Contributions to the development of a concept. *Cultural studies, 21*(2–3), 240–270. Master's thesis, University of British Columbia, Vancouver, BC.

Mazama, A. (1998). The Eurocentric discourse on writing: An exercise in self-glorification. *Journal of Black Studies, 29*(1), 3–16. https://doi.org/10.1177/002193479802900101

Mazrui, A. A. (1978). *Political values and the educated class in Africa*. Univ of California Press.

Mazrui, A. M., & Mazrui, A. A. (1993). Dominant languages in a plural society: English and Kiswahili in post-colonial East Africa. *International Political Science Review, 14*(3), 275–292.

Mbiti, J. (1990). *African religions and philosophy* (2nd ed.). Heinemann.

Mkabela, Q. (2005). Using the Afrocentric method in researching indigenous African culture. *The Qualitative Report, 10*(1), 178–189.

Mignolo, W. D. (1995). *The darker side of the renaissance: Literacy, territoriality, and colonization*. University of Michigan Press.

Mugumbate, J., & Chereni, A. (2019). Now- the theory of Ubuntu has its space in social work. *African Journal of Social Work, 10*(1), v–xvii.

Ndlovu-Gatsheni, S. J. (2015). Decoloniality as the future of Africa. *History Compass, 13*(10), 485–496.

Ngara, C. (2007). African ways of knowing and pedagogy revisited. *Journal of Contemporary Issues in Education, 2*, 7–20. https://doi.org/10.20355/C5301M

Omolewa, M. (2007). Traditional African modes of education: Their relevance in the modern world. *International Review of Education, 53*, 593–612.

Owusu-Ansah, F. E., & Mji, G. (2013). African indigenous knowledge and research. *African Journal of Disability, 2*(1), 1–5.

Robbins, J. A. (2011). Traditional indigenous approaches to healing and the modern welfare of traditional knowledge, spirituality and lands: A critical reflection on practices and policies taken from the Canadian indigenous example. *The International Indigenous Policy Journal, 2*(4), 1–20.

Ritskes, E. J. (Eds.). *Spirituality, education & society*. Sense Publishers.

Rodney, W. (1972). How Europe Underdeveloped Africa Verso Books.

Sanderson, S. K. (2019). The evolution of societies and world-systems. In *Core/periphery relations in precapitalist worlds* (pp. 167–192). Routledge.

Semali, L. (1999). Community as classroom: Dilemmas of valuing African indigenous literacy in education. *International Review of Education, 45*, 305–319. https://doi.org/10.1023/A:1003859023590

Semali, L. M., & Kincheloe, J. L. (2002). *What is indigenous knowledge? Voices from the academy*. Routledge.

Shizha, E. (2007). Critical analysis of problems encountered in incorporating indigenous knowledge in science teaching by primary school teachers in Zimbabwe. *Alberta Journal of Educational Research, 53*(3).

Shizha, E. (2008). Indigenous? What indigenous knowledge? Beliefs and attitudes of rural primary school teachers towards indigenous knowledge in the science curriculum in Zimbabwe. *The Australian Journal of Indigenous Education, 37*(1), 80–90.

Shizha, E. (2014). The indigenous knowledge systems and the curriculum. In *African indigenous knowledge and the disciplines* (pp. 113–129). Brill.

Sicherman C. Ngugi's Colonial Education (1995): "The Subversion... of the African Mind." *African Studies Review.* 38(3):11–41. doi:10.2307/524791.

Sium, A., Desai, C., & Ritskes, E. (2012). Towards the "tangible unknown": Decolonization and the Indigenous future. *Decolonization: Indigeneity, Education & Society, 1.*

Smith, L. T. (2012). *Decolonizing methodologies: Research and indigenous peoples* (2nd ed., 256 pp). Zed Books.

Styres, S., Haig-Brown, C., & Blimkie, M. (2013). Toward a pedagogy of land: The urban context. *Canadian Journal of Education/Revue canadienne de l'éducation, 36*(2), 188–221.

Styres, S. (2018). Literacies of land: decolonizing narratives, storying, and literature. In L. T. Smith, E. Tuck & K. W. Yang (Eds.), *Indigenous and decolonizing studies in education: Mapping the long view* (pp. 24-37). Routledge.

Todd, K. L. (2019). Shedding of the colonial skin: The decolonial potentialities of dreaming. *Decolonizing the Spirit in Education and Beyond: Resistance and Solidarity, 153–175.*

Tuck, E., McKenzie, M., & McCoy, K. (2014). Editorial: Land education: Indigenous, post colonial, and decolonizing perspectives. *Environmental Education Research, 20*(1), 1–23.

wa Thiong'o, N. (1986). Decolonising the mind: The politics of language in African literature (James Currey, London, and Heinemann, Kenya). Peter Worsley in EP Thompson (ed.).

Wane, N. (2003). Embu women: Food production and traditional knowledge. *Resources for Feminist Research, 30*(1–2), 137–149.

Wane, N. N. (2013). [Re]claiming indigenous knowledge: Challenges, resistance, and opportunities. *Decolonization: Indigeneity, Education & Society, 2*(1).

Wane, N. N. (2019). Is decolonizing the spirit possible? In N. Wane, M. Todorova, & K. Todd (Eds.), *Decolonizing the spirit in education and beyond. Spirituality, religion, and education.* Palgrave Macmillan. https://doi.org/10.1007/978-3-030-25320-2_2

Wildcat, M., McDonald, M., Irlbacher-Fox, S., & Coulthard, G. (2014). Learning from the Land: Indigenous Land-based pedagogy and decolonization. *Decolonization: Indigeneity, Education & Society, 3*(3).

Wilson, M. D. (2008). *Writing home: Indigenous narratives of resistance.* American Indian Studies.

Yakubu, J. A. (2000). Trends in constitution-making in Nigeria. *Transnational Law & Contemporary Problems, 10,* 423.

Yankah, K. (2004). Narrative in times of crisis: AIDS stories in Ghana. *Journal of Folklore Research, 41,* 181–198.

Zavala, M. (2016). Decolonial methodologies in education. In M. Peters (Ed.), *Encyclopedia of educational philosophy and theory* (pp. 1–6). Springer.

Zinga, D., & Styres, S. (2011). Pedagogy of the land: Tensions, challenges, and contradictions. *First Nations Perspectives, 4*(1), 59–83.

NOTES ON CONTRIBUTORS

About the Editors

WAMBUI KARANJA is a PhD A.B.D. in the Department of Social Justice Education at the Ontario Institute for Studies in Education, University of Toronto (OISE/UT). She has a master's degree in law from the University of Toronto, Canada and a Bachelor of Laws Degree from the University of Nairobi, Kenya. Her research interests lie in the fields of anti-colonial theorizing, Indigenous philosophies and epistemologies, decolonization, Indigenous Land Rights, Research methodologies, gender issues, Law and development theories. Wambui has published widely on Land, Indigeneity and knowledge production, colonial education, Decolonization, Indigenous healing, research and African Women's Land Ownership Rights. She is the author of "Women's Land Ownership Rights in Kenya," *Third World Legal Studies*, Vol. 10, Article 6. Available at: http://scholar.valpo.edu/twls/vol10/iss1/6 (1991) and is co-author of the critically acclaimed anthology, "Elders' Cultural Knowledges and the Question of Black African Indigeneity in Education" (Springer, 2022) and "Decoloniality and African Education: Contested Issues and Challenges" (Upcoming, 2025), among others.

AVEA E. NSOH is an Associate Professor of Linguistics, Literacy, Language, and culture at the University of Education Winneba, Ghana. He has a PhD from the University of Ghana. Prof. Nsoh was formerly the Director of the Institute for Educational Research and Innovation Studies and Principal of a College of the University. He has 30 years of experience in research, teaching, and community work. He was the Principal Investigator in the Farefari (Gurenɛ) literacy project. The project produced a dictionary, glossary, and facilitated the creation of departments of the Farefari language at some universities and colleges. He is currently involved in two language documentation projects on two Mabia (Gur) languages. He has published several books and articles in refereed journals and attended many international conferences. Professor Nsoh is a member of the Linguistic Association of Ghana (LAG) and the West African Languages Society (WALS). He also runs an NGO focusing on local governance, disability, and women empowerment. As a politician, Professor Nsoh became a Minister of State in Ghana.

GEORGE J. SEFA DEI is a Ghanaian-born, Canadian anti-racist educator who has been working on inclusive, decolonial schooling and education from the Standpoint of African Indigeneity for the last couple of decades. In my work on African Indigeneity, I have been highlighting the need to simultaneously investigate the nature of colonialist and anti-colonialist philosophy and practice as developed to advance scholarship and politics. I center African Indigeneity in my work asking questions such as: How do we re-envision schooling and education to subvert the incorporation of the logic of Western science that fails to fully engage with a more global consideration of Indigenous knowledges/sciences and political practice, and the interface between multiple worldviews/world senses/world sensations? I utilize the conceptual grammar of the Empire as subversive language and practice to articulate the power of embodied Indigenous knowledge highlighting the urgency for mainstream knowledge to begin to authentically reconcile with Indigenous cultural knowledges and Indigenous peoples.

DANIEL YELKPIERI is a Senior Research Fellow, Centre for Educational Policy Studies at the Institute for Educational Research, and Innovative Studies (IERIS) in the University of Education, Winneba. He holds a Doctorate in Social Sciences (DSocSci) from the University of Leicester in the UK. He also has M.Phil. degree in Educational Administration, B.Ed. (Psychology) and a Diploma in History which ran concurrently from the University of Cape Coast and a Postgraduate Diploma in Teaching and Learning in Higher Education

(PGDTLHE) from the University of Education, Winneba. He has taught courses in Educational Administration, Human Resource Development, and Human Resource Management. Currently, he is the Deputy Director of the Institute for Educational Research and Innovation Studies (IERIS) and immediate past Head of the Department of the Centre for School and Community Science and Technology Studies (SACOST). His research interests are in youth education, learning, and training and Professional staff development and training issues.

About the Contributors

ALI A. ABDI is a professor of social development education at the University of British Columbia (Vancouver campus), Canada. His areas of research and teaching include education and social development, critical foundations of education, human rights education and anti-colonial studies in education. He was the Founding Editor of the *Journal of Contemporary Issues in Education* and Co-founding Editor of *Cultural and Pedagogical Inquiry*. His books include *Educating for Human Rights and Global Citizenship* (with Lynette Shultz); *Decolonizing Philosophies of Education*; and *Palgrave Handbook on Critical Theories of Education* (with Greg Misiaszek).

ATIPOKA HELEN ADONGO is a senior lecturer at the University of Education, Winneba. She has a PhD in Linguistics from the University of Ghana, Legon, a Master of Philosophy (M.Phil.) in Applied Linguistics and a Bachelor of Education (B.Ed.) in Ghanaian Language Education from the University of Education, Winneba. Her research interest includes studies in Mabia Languages with a special interest in Phonetics and Phonology, Indigenous Language Documentation and Education, and Research Methods.

ELMARIE COSTANDIUS (in Memoriam)[1] was an associate professor in Visual Arts and coordinates the Master of Arts in Visual Arts (Art Education) at Stellenbosch University, South Africa. She studied Information Design at the University of Pretoria and continued her studies at the Gerrit Rietveld Academy, Amsterdam. She completed a master's in Globalization and Higher Education at the University of the Western Cape. Her PhD in Curriculum Studies (Stellenbosch University) focused on social responsibility and critical citizenship in art education. She published her first book with Professor Eli Bitzer, titled *Engaging Higher Education Curricula: A Critical Citizenship*

Education Perspective in 2015 and in 2016 edited the book, *The Relevance of Critical Citizenship in Africa* with Professor Freeborn Odiboh from the University of Benin, Nigeria. In 2019, she edited a book on *Citizen's Designers in South Africa* and in 2022 edited a book with Professor Aslam Fataar, *Evoking Transformation: Visual Redress in Stellenbosch University*. In 2023 she edited the book, *Visual Redress in Africa from an Indigenous and New Materialist Perspective* published by Routledge. Elmarie was a member of various task teams at Stellenbosch University, namely the task team on Decolonizing the Curriculum (2019); the team responsible for revisioning the Stellenbosch University Learning and Teaching Policy (2020); the Transformation Task Team for the Renaming of Buildings, Sites and Facilities; and Visual Redress at Stellenbosch University (2020–currently).

WANJA GITARI is an associate professor of science education at the University of Toronto Mississauga (UTM) Institute for the Study of University Pedagogy and the Department of Curriculum, Teaching and Learning at OISE/UT. Professor Gitari's research investigates the relationship between aspects of school science and everyday life, including appropriation and application of school science in low-income contexts.

RACHAEL KALABA is a PhD candidate (ABD) at the Ontario Institute for Studies in Education (OISE), University of Toronto, specializing in Adult Education and Community Development, Specializing in Women and Gender studies, and Comparative International Development Education. She is the founder of ZAMWILL, a women-led organization in Africa dedicated to empowering women through Ubuntu Leadership and Mentorship Ethos. Her research centers on Indigenous Knowledge, women's leadership, education policy, Afro-feminism, and decolonization, all guided by the Ubuntu philosophy. Her doctoral research focuses on "African Women Leadership in Zambia: Using Ubuntu Lenses and African Indigenous Leadership Frameworks." Rachael is a recognized voice in academic circles, frequently presenting at global conferences and contributing scholarly work on topics ranging from Women and sports development to African women's leadership using African Indigenous Frameworks. She actively volunteers with the University of Toronto. Her academic credentials include a master's in development Practice, A master's in management, a Postgraduate Diploma in Responsible Leadership from SIMP Sweden, and a BA in International Development. Rachael's leadership and vision have earned her prestigious recognitions, including the Emerging African Leader of the Year 2023, a place among Canada's Top 100 Black

Women to Watch in 2023, and the 2024 African Scholars Distinguished Volunteer Award by the University of Toronto, African Alumni Association.

MAUREEN K. KANCHEBELE-SINYANGWE is the Deputy Director in the Directorate of Research Postgraduate Studies and Innovation at Kwame Nkrumah University in Kabwe, Zambia. She is also a lecturer and researcher in Pre-Mathematics, Mathematics and Mathematics Education in the School of Natural Sciences with a history of working in primary, secondary and higher education in Zambia. Dr. Kanchebele-Sinyangwe is passionate about contributing toward improving the quality of education especially in areas of Mathematics and researching into the various aspects of Mathematics and Mathematics Education with a special interest in supporting and empowering both learners, student/trainee teachers and serving teachers in their continuing learning and development in the field. Other areas of research interest include, but not limited to: Stem/Steam/Stream; Health Education including HIV/AIDS and mental well-being; Special and Inclusive Education; Education and Development and ICT.

SEIN KIPUSI received her doctorate in Social Justice Education from the Ontario Institute for Studies in Education (OISE) at the University of Toronto. Her doctoral work investigated financial literacy education among racialized business owners in Toronto. Her research and advocacy centers on anti-colonial and African and Indigenous knowledge frameworks. Sein completed a two-year postdoctoral fellowship at the University of Toronto, Scarborough Campus at the pilot Transitional Year Program focusing on the challenges and successes of curriculum development, equity in recruitment and inclusive diversity in access programs. In her leisure time she loves to garden, write poetry, and paint.

DR. ANN LOPEZ is a Jamaican-born professor of educational leadership and policy at the Ontario Institute for Studies in Education (OISE), University of Toronto, Canada. A former public-school teacher and administrator she is a leading voice and scholar on anti-racist, decolonizing and equity education in K-12 schooling. She is the Director of the Center for Leadership and Diversity, Co-Director Centre for Black Studies in Education, and Provostial Advisor, Access Programs. Dr. Lopez has recently been appointed as Professor Extraordinarius at UNISA, South Africa and Visiting Professor Kwame Nkrumah University, Zambia. She is a teacher educator and held the position of Academic Director, Initial Teacher Education at OISE/UT. Her recent research projects have focused on school leadership in Canada,

Jamaica, Kenya, Ghana and Zambia where she collaborates with local scholars. Dr. Lopez is the author of several journal articles and books including her most recent book entitled, *Decolonizing Educational Leadership: Alternative Approach to Leading Schools*. Professor Lopez is co-Editor-In-Chief of the *Journal of School Leadership* and Co-Series Editor, *Studies in Educational Administration*. Professor Lopez has been honored for her work and is the recipient of the of the OISE 2020 Award for Distinguished Contributions to Teaching, and the 2022 University of Toronto Award of Excellence and Jus Memorial Human Rights Prize—Influential Leader.

PROF. NJOKI NATHANI WANE is a distinguished scholar and educator in the areas of Black Feminisms, African Indigenous knowledges and spirituality, African and African Canadian women's teaching and learning, anti-racism education and Anti-Black Racism. She has published 4 books, 18 edited volumes, and dozens of book chapters, and refereed journal articles. She has presented her work at over 300 conferences locally and internationally, often as a keynote speaker. Prof. Wane is the Chair of the Department of Social Justice Education, Ontario Institute for Studies in Education, University of Toronto. From 2011 to 2014, Professor Wane served as the University of Toronto's Special Advisor on Status of Women Issues; 2018–2021 she also served as Special Advisor to Vice-President; Human Resources and Equity, contributing to research and policy development concerning the intersectionality of gender with race, disability, sexual orientation, and aboriginal status, and the impact of these issues on the lived experiences of women faculty, staff and students. She also served as Director of the Center for Integrative Anti-Racism Studies (CIARS) at OISE from 2006 to 2014. She is currently serving as Co-Director for the Center for Black Studies in Education.

BATHSEBA OPINI is an associate professor at the Department of Educational Studies, Faculty of Education, University of British Columbia. Her research and teaching interests are in the areas of teaching practices, decolonizing education and curriculum, critical race perspectives, critical disability studies, global Indigenous knowledges with a focus on Africa, and teacher education.

SHERRY PRYDE (she/they) is an educator, researcher and multimodal creative currently based in Cape Town, South Africa. She has a master's in visual arts education from Stellenbosch University. Her research interests lie at the intersections of queer theory, global south perspectives, visual culture and decolonization.

NOTES ON CONTRIBUTORS

KOFI QUAN-BAFFOUR is Professor Extraordinary in the Department of Adult Education and Continuing Education at the University of South Africa (UNISA). His research interests focus on TVET/Community Colleges, & IKS.

AVEA E. NSOH is an Associate Professor of Linguistics, Literacy, Language, and culture at the University of Education Winneba, Ghana. He has a PhD from the University of Ghana. Prof. Nsoh was formerly the Director of the Institute for Educational Research and Innovation Studies and Principal of a College of the University. He has 30 years of experience in research, teaching, and community work. He was the Principal Investigator in the Farefari (Gurenɛ) literacy project. The project produced a dictionary, glossary, and facilitated the creation of departments of the Farefari language at some universities and colleges. He is currently involved in two language documentation projects on two Mabia (Gur) languages. He has several books and articles in refereed journals and attended many international conferences. Prof Nsoh is a member of the Linguistic Association of Ghana (LAG) and the West African Languages Society (WALS). He also runs an NGO focusing on local governance, disability, and women empowerment. As a politician, Professor Nsoh became a Minister of State in Ghana.

DANIEL YELKPIERI is a Senior Research Fellow, Centre for Educational Policy Studies at the Institute for Educational Research, and Innovative Studies (IERIS) in the University of Education, Winneba. He holds a Doctorate in Social Sciences (DSocSci) from the University of Leicester in the UK. He also has M.Phil. degree in Educational Administration, B.Ed. (Psychology) and a Diploma in History which ran concurrently from the University of Cape Coast and a Post-graduate Diploma in Teaching and Learning in Higher Education (PGDTLHE) from the University of Education, Winneba. He has taught courses in Educational Administration, Human Resource Development, and Human Resource Management. Currently, he is the Deputy Director of the Institute for Educational Research and Innovation Studies (IERIS) and immediate past Head of the Department of the Centre for School and Community Science and Technology Studies (SACOST). His research interests in youth education, learning, and training and Professional staff development and training issues.

Note

1 Professor Constandius unfortunately passed away during the publication of this Anthology.

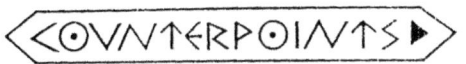

Studies in Criticality

Series Editor
Shirley R. Steinberg

Counterpoints publishes the most compelling and imaginative books being written in Education and Cultural Studies today. Grounded on the theoretical advances in critical theory, feminism, and postcolonialism in the last two decades of the twentieth century, Counterpoints engages the meaning of these innovations in various forms of educational expression. Committed to the proposition that theoretical literature should be accessible to a variety of audiences, the series insists that its authors avoid esoteric and jargonistic languages that transform educational scholarship into an elite discourse for the initiated. Scholarly work matters only to the degree it affects consciousness and practice at multiple sites. The editorial policy of *Counterpoints* is based on these principles and the ability of scholars to break new ground, to open new conversations, to go where educators have never gone before.

For additional information about this series or for the submission of manuscripts, please contact:

>Shirley R. Steinberg, Series Editor
>msgramsci@gmail.com

To order other books in this series, please contact our Customer Service Department:

>peterlang@presswarehouse.com (within the U.S.)
>orders@peterlang.com (outside the U.S.)

Or browse online by series:

>www.peterlang.com

www.ingramcontent.com/pod-product-compliance
Lightning Source LLC
Chambersburg PA
CBHW061710300426
44115CB00014B/2633